LACE

Sons Of The Profits

SONS OF THE PROFITS

or,

There's No Business Like Grow Business!

The Seattle Story, 1851-1901

by William C. Speidel

Seattle, Washington

Nettle Creek Publishing Company 1967

FIRST EDITION

Library of Congress Catalog Card Number 67-31657
ALSO BY WILLIAM C. SPEIDEL
You Can't Eat Mt. Rainier
Be My Guest in the Pacific Northwest
You Still Can't Eat Mt. Rainier!

Published by The Seattle Guide, Inc.
d/b/a Nettle Creek Publishing Company, Seattle, Washington

International Standard Book Number—0-914890-00-X

Second Printing, April, 1968
Third Printing, November, 1969
Fourth Printing, November, 1970
Fifth Printing, November, 1972
Sixth Printing, February, 1974
Seventh Printing, June, 1974
Printed in the United States of America
by George Banta Company, Inc., Menasha, Wisconsin

In the spirit of Seattle's founding fathers, this book is dedicated with warmest appreciation to the most important people in the world—the men, women and children who buy it.

TABLE OF CONTENTS

LIST OF ILLUSTRATIONS

I

Our Father

I'm sure there must have been *somebody* who participated in the construction of Seattle without first determining whether there was a buck in it for himself, but this book isn't about him.

This is the story of how the fellas who built Seattle made their money.

That they built a city in the process was purely coincidental. If they could have made more money by *not* building a city, then that is what they would have done. If the same laws had been on the books that exist today, they would have turned to some other line of work.

It would never have occurred to them that it was the things *they* did which created some of the laws of today.

They regarded the Indians, the Legislature, the federal government, the competing towns on the Sound, their fellow businessmen down the street, the mud, trees, hills, the Northern Pacific Railroad and the hop louse of the 1890's as necessary evils that must be coped with.

Their brand of coping presumed that the end justified the means.

They fought bitterly among themselves so that they were in fighting trim when an outsider stuck his nose in their business and found himself in the position of a boy who has poked a stick in a hornet's nest. Only once did they forget to present a united front to outsiders. And that time they lost control of King County's coal, their greatest natural economic resource.

It was a lesson they never forgot.

Seattle lucked out on a lot of things, the most important of which was her geographic location on the center of the Sound. She also has had an uncanny faculty for attracting the right man in the right spot

1

at the right time. But even the right man has never enjoyed complete control. There was always somebody up the street tough enough to knock his block off if he got too much out of line.

Which really has been quite a good thing.

Never on Sunday

Arthur Denny, the father of Seattle, had his first encounter with those Indians on July 6, 1851 at American Falls on the Snake River. It was Sunday, a beautiful day, and the scenery in what we now know as Idaho was inspirational.

That is, until Arthur noted a large encampment of Indians on the north side of the river and an armed party of eight or ten crossing the river just at the foot of the falls. The Indians paused in front of his train, which consisted of four wagons and seven men plus an assortment of women and children. The Indians announced that they wished to do a little trading.

But Arthur didn't like their looks and shouted to the other drivers to take the wagon train on through. They whipped up their horses and plunged on through, scattering Indians like a bunch of chickens . . . a process which annoyed the Indians no end and resulted in what is known as a "hail of bullets," being fired in the general direction of the on-rushing wagon train.

The episode was still vivid in Arthur's memory thirty-seven years later when he wrote a small book called *Pioneer Days on Puget Sound:*

> . . . on looking to the rear we could only see the puffs of smoke when they fired from behind the rocks, and at the same time we could hear the bullets whistle and see the dust fly where they struck, but fortunately they did not hit any of us.

About that time, Arthur saw more Indians crossing the river in an effort to halt the wagon train in a ravine, but they weren't fast enough. The wagons reached the top of the ravine. He decided it might be fairly intelligent to take advantage of some big rocks up there.

While he never did business on Sunday under normal circumstances, it looked as if they might be doing a little trading of bullets with his red brethren . . . and he always made it a practice to do his trading from an advantageous position. The latter was a lifetime habit and he was not about to relinquish it just because of the Sabbath. He could make his peace with the Lord later on. But he had to stay alive in order to make those future negotiations.

This was the only time when the Denny Party, which made up the nucleus of people who founded Seattle, encountered hostile Indians, and it came out of the encounter with all scalps intact . . . which was more than the occupants of a lot of wagon trains headed west could say.

The Indians took what the whites considered an entirely unreasonable position—that the land belonged to them, and that while the United States was a pretty powerful outfit, it had failed to negotiate any treaties by which the Indians could be recompensed for the theft of their lands. They figured that the white men were invaders and should be subjected to the hardships that resulted from their invasion.

An unbiased person might well agree they had a point there.

But Denny, and a good many others like him, felt the Lord was on his side and that whatever he did was honorable, righteous and Christian. He always attended church. He never smoked or drank. He never cheated at cards . . .

Which would have been difficult, because he never played cards.

Arthur was twenty-nine years old at the time he met the hostile Indians. He was a God-fearing man, but not the kind who turned the other cheek. He was positive, stubborn, unbending and generally strong-minded. He was an out-spoken prohibitionist and until later in life when the ladies got the vote and deeply wounded his pride, he was an advocate of women's suffrage.

He had shrewd common sense and a ruthless sense of land acquisition that made him wealthy, but didn't necessarily endear him to those around him. He was notably lacking in imagination, compassion and brilliance. But he was a real hard worker who seldom sub-

mitted to the thought that he might have made a mistake. If he believed in one thing and the other guy believed in something else—
then the other guy was wrong.

He was six feet tall, a compact one hundred and seventy pounds of
muscle and he steadfastly refused to believe that he ever could suffer
from a physical ailment.

For instance, Arthur was laid low with the Mountain Fever when
the wagons encountered that party of Indians . . . and remained sick
much of the time for the first year he was here, but never once mentioned it. Those Indians were in his way . . . and if anything got in
his way, he just plowed through.

He didn't go around.

It was typical of Arthur that he brought the town its first church
(which nobody attended), introduced to the Territorial Legislature
its first bill against liquor (which everybody drank), and clung to his
land like a hoarding miser when others played free and loose with
theirs.

This sort of undeviating stubbornness built a city, provided Arthur
with a fortune and respect . . . but not necessarily affection. Nevertheless he was a Son of the Profits who made good at what he set
out to do.

The supporting cast

The Dennys have a family tree as long as your arm, and if you'd
really like to go into it, there are books on it in the Seattle Public
Library.

But I'll just stick with the ones that affect our story.

Arthur's father, John, was an admirable man with leadership qualities and a superb sense of humor which failed to materialize in Arthur. I especially like the story about him regarding an incident that
took place when he and Abraham Lincoln were the only two Whigs
in the Illinois Legislature. Although totally out-voted on a piece of
legislation which they opposed, they successfully defeated it by leap-

ing out the second story of the legislative building . . . leaving their Democrat colleagues without a quorum.

When John's wife died in 1841, he was left with four sons: Arthur, two older brothers who never made it to Puget Sound . . . and a younger brother, David, who did.

David was a good example of the old saying that "nice guys don't win ball games." Docile, easy-going and pleasant, David, unlike Arthur, loved the beauty of the land to which he emigrated more than the money that could be extracted from the place.

He was not the type to become one of Seattle's Sons of the Profits.

Now you get into a part of the family relationships where you need a score-card.

Father John re-married, to the widow of a Baptist minister named Boren. Mrs. Boren brought two daughters and a son into the Denny family. So there were two step-sisters, name of Mary Ann and Louisa Boren, and a step-brother named Carson D. Boren.

The kids called Carson Boren "Uncle Dobbins."

They were right.

He was henpecked by his mother . . . his sisters . . . his wife and by his leader, "Our Father" Arthur. I suspect he was henpecked by his daughters, too. He came along on the trip west because it was easier than staying home. Talk about a reluctant empire builder . . . and you're talking about old Uncle Dobbins. I think he rather enjoyed life, which horrified the rest of the clan. On the other hand, he outlived the whole bunch.

Well, on November 23, 1843—eight years before starting west—Arthur married his new step-sister Mary Ann.

That was tying the families pretty tight.

David was eleven years old at the time. Mary Ann's younger sister, Louisa, was sixteen, and a very strong-minded young lady. She got over being sixteen, but she never got over being strong-minded. Some ten years later she became the first young lady to marry in Seattle.

Her bridegroom turned out to be none other than her step-brother, David, which proved one thing . . .

Denny men sure went for Boren women.

They were lawed and in-lawed all over the place. Anyway, these were the folks that started out from Cherry Grove, Illinois on April 10, 1851 headed for what they believed would be fame and fortune in the Willamette Valley at the end of the Oregon Trail.

The day after their encounter with the Indians, they fell in with a fellow by the name of John Low, kind of a relaxed character from Ohio who was not bent on setting the world on fire. He was crazy about pure-bred cattle and thought he'd find some better pasture for his herd out in the Oregon Territory. Low was thirty-one years old, had a few bucks to invest in a new location and by a freak of fate found himself one of the founders of Seattle . . . an honor which would have been a matter of supreme indifference to him had he been around at the time it was accorded to him.

A couple of weeks later the Denny Party, now augmented by the Low Party, encountered a fellow named Brock at Burnt River in Eastern Oregon. In his memoirs, Denny couldn't remember Brock's first name—but he must have been a whale of a salesman. He talked about a place called Puget Sound. Denny never had heard of Puget Sound before . . . and he never had anticipated settling anywhere but the Willamette Valley.

But after Brock it was Puget Sound all the way for Arthur. He never saw Brock again after that brief encounter, but Brock was a human signpost at a crossroads in Denny's life—and in the beginnings of Seattle.

The new recruit

From that point on, Denny stubbornly set his sights on Puget Sound, but in Portland, he was laid low with what they called "the ague" in those days. They got to Portland on August 22—a hundred and eight days out of Cherry Grove.

But that was it for Arthur, brother . . .

For nearly three months.

Arthur would have travelled, but his body just couldn't take it. On September 2, Mary Ann complicated matters by not only having the ague herself, but by giving birth to Rolland H. Denny.

While Arthur was rendered more or less hors de combat in Portland, he still managed to enlist a couple more recruits to the cause of a city on Puget Sound. The first was William N. Bell, a thirty-four-year-old peace-loving farmer from Illinois who really had no business getting into the city-building business. But, much to the annoyance of Bell's wife, Arthur won him over to the idea of moving on to Puget Sound . . . and to eventual official recognition as one of the founders of our city.

Arthur's final recruit was a bright young man by the name of Charles C. Terry. Terry was born in Waterville, Oneida County, New York. Much to the disappointment of his parents, Terry had left the old farm in 1849 and headed around the Horn for the California gold rush where he had ambitions to become a wealthy man in the shortest possible time.

Terry was bright-eyed and bushy-tailed, but found that the only real killings in San Francisco were those made in the by-ways and back alleys, not the gold fields. We think of Chicago as being a tough town in the 1930's when as many as three hundred people were murdered in one year. In San Francisco between 1847 and 1854, 4,200 persons were murdered, six hundred murders a year for seven years. Charlie Terry felt uncomfortable in that atmosphere. A born trader, Terry heard about the Willamette Valley and headed north with notions of opening a general store some place. He was twenty-one years old at the time he and his brother Leander, who had come west to the gold fields with him, left San Francisco.

"Lee" Terry was a restless soul. I doubt that he had ever met Mr. Brock, but he had heard of Puget Sound somewhere, and decided to head on up there to see what he could see.

Charlie, on the other hand, stuck around Portland and heard the feverish Arthur Denny's spiel on the wonders of a country he knew only through Brock. I'll bet there were times later on when Arthur wished he'd kept his big mouth shut when he talked Terry into taking the journey to Puget Sound with him. On the other hand, I wonder if Arthur would have died a millionaire if he hadn't made Charlie Terry a member of the cast.

I've been mentioning the ages of everybody as we go along because subconsciously all of us think of our pioneer forefathers as old ducks with long gray beards. The reason we think of them as old ducks with long gray beards is because that's what they look like in our history books. They look terribly stern, like their heads were in a vise when their pictures were taken.

And they were. Their necks were choked with collars they were unaccustomed to wearing. The stern expression comes from the fact they didn't want to have their pictures taken but their wives insisted on it. And the pictures were costing them money.

They were the patriarchs . . . but not at the time they founded Seattle. The average age of the men who arrived on Puget Sound on November 13, 1851 to found a city some place was twenty-six years. A pretty stupid bunch, too, the men listed in our records as the founders of Seattle—they didn't know a city couldn't be built where they built it, or, putting it more accurately, where *some* of them built it.

Big Mike Simmons

While Arthur was flat on his back in Portland, he finally persuaded his brother David to head north for a look-see at the Puget Sound area before winter set in and the whole venture might be delayed for another year.

David was the only one in the family Arthur could influence. Father John and his other brothers were not sold on the deal. They liked it just fine in the Willamette Valley. John Low was willing to go along with the gag because he had heard there was excellent pasturage for his cattle in the Chehalis Valley, south of Puget Sound.

Once he got his cattle settled down for the winter in a good location, he obliged Arthur and satisfied his own curiosity by setting out to take a longer look at the Puget Sound country before deciding on a place to homestead.

Meanwhile, up in Olympia, a big fellow by the name of Michael T.

Simmons who never was either a founder or resident of Seattle, was putting himself in the position of being an enormous factor in the location, naming and growth of Seattle.

Hubert H. Bancroft, the great historian of the West, presents Mike in his volume on Washington, Idaho and Montana:

> Simmons was a fine specimen of a man and a good representative of the class that went into Washington about this time (1844) determined to remain there, particularly if England's majesty ordered them out . . . possessing the grand physique of the early man of Kentucky, unlettered but not unenlightened, he possessed the qualities which in feudal times made men chiefs and founders of families. His courage was equalled only by his independence . . .

Mike was to the town of Tumwater, Washington what Arthur Denny was to be to Seattle. He headed a group of seven men and their families (including George W. Bush, the first Negro to settle in the territory and after whom Bush Prairie is named) to Budd Inlet in 1845. Mike might have settled on Puget Sound anyway, but the British ordered him not to . . . and quite naturally that was all Mike needed to finalize his decision to do it. He and his group became the first Americans to settle north of the Columbia River. Mike built a flour mill and a sawmill, although the latter was hydraulically operated and produced boards that looked like big shingles—thicker at one end than the other. Nevertheless, Mike was able to sell off his two mills and his land in 1849 for $35,000 . . . which was about $34,999 more than Mike had ever had in one chunk in his life.

In 1850, the fellows who were platting Olympia gave Mike two choice lots on which to open a mercantile establishment . . . and by the following September when Lee Terry, en route to investigate Puget Sound, showed up at Olympia, Mike was living mighty high on the hog, a circumstance that was duly noted by Lee.

Over-looking the fact that Mike had worked hard for his money, Terry figured that if he could just get a town started he could duplicate Mike's good fortune.

Lee's talent in the world—if he had one—lay in his remarkable capacity for avoiding work.

A town is born

Lee was mulling over the more reasonable possibilities for getting his own town going—somewhere a little bit north and more toward the geographic center of Puget Sound—when who should come trudging out of the underbrush from Portland than a fellow by the name of John Low. He was followed by this kid by the name of Denny.

They announced that hey were looking for a townsite. They were Lee Terry's kind of people!

The three of them took passage on a boat headed north. Sixty miles up the Sound, they came across the prominent projection of level land that today is known as Alki Point. It was by far and away the best location they had seen on their trip on the Sound so they had the captain unload them and their gear and continue on his way. They explored the Duwamish River Valley, conversed with a couple of characters who had preceded them to homestead that area and concluded in a matter of twenty-four hours that the Point was the spot they wanted.

They promptly built a lean-to out of fir boughs to serve as temporary housing while they constructed the first cabin in their new world.

On September 28, 1851, a lovely Indian Summer day with the sun shining and the leaves turning and the smoke from the campfire drifting comfortably straight up through the windless trees—they laid the foundation for the first cabin at Alki Point. A day or so later, Low bummed a ride on a boat headed for Olympia to report back to the main Denny Party.

Before he left, he employed David and Lee to finish the construction of the cabin so that the Denny party would have a warm, comfortable little home when they arrived. It was an easy job and he was secure in the knowledge that the work would be done upon his return.

But Lee Terry found any physical labor irksome. He and David sublet some of the job to Indians who didn't mind lifting those heavy logs if there were a few chews of snoose in it. What with David doing the cooking and other housework around the camp, Terry found life somewhat tolerable.

Then Lee made a delightful discovery: they had forgotten to bring a frow.

Now, a frow is a device for making cedar shakes. Without a frow, they couldn't have a roof on their cabin.

Lee promptly used this problem as a device for getting out of work Shortly after Low left, Lee found some people going up Sound in a scow and joined with them to go somewhere and find a frow.

This left David alone with the Indians and the job . . . and when the rains came he got the flu and a case of rheumatism and practically whacked off his foot with a slippery ax. So, for a couple of weeks prior to the arrival of the enterprising party, he lay around in the lean-to raising a temperature instead of the cabin.

The sound of music

John Low returned to Portland in about mid-October, bubbling over with the great news that the end of the rainbow with its pot of gold had been found on Puget Sound . . . which was quite a switch for John who, prior to that time, had been a lot more interested in finding feed for his cattle than a site for a city.

It must have been a fair bit of startlement to Charlie Terry—and most certainly the biggest coincidence in the history of early Seattle —that the advance party for Denny's expedition had fallen in with his brother, Lee, while completely without Lee's knowledge, Charlie joined with the main body of the Denny group.

Low brought with him a letter from David to his older brother. The letter read in toto: "We have examined the valley of the Duwamish river and find it a fine country. There is plenty of room for one thousand settlers. Come at once."

Low proceeded to describe the Promised Land.

While the entire east shore of the area was made up of about two thousand acres of tideflats there was this projection of land to the west with a sandy beach and level shore that had a bold outlook on the water and a commanding view of the Olympic Mountains.

It was located in the geographic center of Puget Sound . . . and all ships sailing either north or south on the Sound would pass it and find an easy anchorage on the north shore, which was completely protected from the prevailing southwest winds. Vessels would find it easy to tack into this location. While there was nothing but mudflats east of this spot, there was the great valley of the Duwamish River to the southwest which David had mentioned in his letter . . . and the point of land would serve as their outlet to the sea.

The point was made up of about 130 acres some ten feet or so above the high water mark. Behind it at a slight elevation was a plateau loaded with timber. The point itself had been partially burned, making it easy to construct cabins.

The Hudson's Bay Company had once thought of establishing a fort at this spot because it was so centrally located . . . and the Indians from all around the Sound had used it for their conclaves for the same reason. It was, indeed the hub of the Sound.

The Indian name for the area which we now call West Seattle was Sgwudux, the point we call Alki Point was called Smoquamox, but Low reported that Lee Terry had thought the location at the point looked so much like Manhattan Island that he had re-named it after his favorite city—New York.

Everybody had heard of New York.

The magic of that name set visions of glory blooming in the minds of everyone, even Arthur Denny—in spite of the fact that he still was a pretty sick fellow.

Opportunist Charlie Terry immediately went out to buy the necessary merchandise for the general store he would stock on Puget Sound.

The whole idea was music to all ears.

Ho, ho, ho . . . and away we go!

Arthur Denny was a determined man . . . and sick or not he was busting to get out of Portland and settle in the new land before another winter had set in.

At the time, the Schooner "Exact" was outfitting in Portland for a voyage to Queen Charlotte Island with gold prospectors, and for a reasonable price the captain was willing to touch at Puget Sound en route. She started from Portland on November 5, 1851, and headed out over the Columbia River Bar after touching at Astoria two days later.

Now the Columbia River Bar at best is no mill pond.

While these midwesterners had become accustomed to the motion of a prairie schooner, it also had been the largest conveyance in their experience. And there is no place between Cherry Grove and Portland where the motion of a tiny schooner going over the bar is exactly duplicated. And to make the trip memorable, there was this bargain that Mrs. Denny had struck with an Indian fisherman in Astoria, at the mouth of the Columbia.

For one thin dime, she had bought one thick salmon.

On the way to the turbulence of the bar, she had started frying this beast in the only cabin which the little schooner possessed. The cabin was below decks and uncomfortably warm, and because of the waves ahead, the cabin was thoroughly battened down. It promised to be a disaster area.

They all got, like, you know—sick.

Arthur had been afraid from time to time for several weeks that he was going to die, but this time he was afraid he wasn't going to die. And, speaking of fear, even the captain got a full dish of it at one point.

The boat hit bottom!

The captain realized that one more bounce would be the last one for any of them in this world. He sent an emissary to the paying customers in the cabin to suggest they make peace with their maker, and the Father of Seattle, whose face at that moment bore a strong resemblance to a piece of mouldy cheese, came up with one of his famous historical remarks. He said, "I don't much care whether she sinks or not!" As usual, Arthur was telling the truth.

It was a great start to the Promised Land.

They had rain and rough weather all the way and the hardy little band remained seasick for the next six days. The tide was out and it still was raining when they arrived at what we now know as Alki Point.

They had to unload their gear in the mud so the schooner could be on its way north, and then take it piecemeal up the beach above high water. I don't know how many Indians had gathered from around the Sound to witness this unusual event at their favorite camp ground. The estimates run as high as a thousand.

Let it suffice there were enough to add essence to the occasion.

I used to wonder how those Indians could run around in the rain without any clothes on—and now I know. They anointed themselves with repeated applications of dogfish oil. I don't know whether the average reader has ever whiffed dogfish oil, but I suggest it is not on the list of ten best fragrances.

When it's new and fresh, dogfish oil is a runner up to castor oil to the olfactory nerve. When it's rancid, castor oil isn't even in the ball park. When it's rancid and heated by human bodies, it's the grand "champeen" in all classes.

So the physical dispositions of our hardy little band were affected by six seasick days . . . the particular odor of a low tide . . . and by the evil-looking and pungently anointed Indians who crowded around them on that dismal, rainy afternoon.

Ho, ho, ho.

Adding to the general hilarity of the occasion, David limped out of the woods with a bandage around his head and a busted open foot. Through chattering lips he made a quote famous in Seattle's history.

He said: "I wish you hadn't come!"

Just great!

I suppose they shook hands . . . and they might just as well have . . . their ill bodies already were shaking like a couple of jack-hammers anyway.

Lee Terry wasn't back from his junket, naturally. But Arthur had a frow; naturally, Arthur would. Arthur always had everything. He also had a big shadow. Typically, on this occasion, he out-performed and overshadowed his younger brother. He got out the necessary tools and by nightfall only half of the cabin was dripping wet. The other half was roofed with shakes.

Arthur, who never once mentioned in his memoirs that he ever had been ill, did give some indication in his memoirs that he was distressed on that particular Thursday afternoon:

> When the goods were secured, I went to look after the women and found on my approach their faces were concealed. On closer inspection I discovered they were in tears, having discovered the gravity of the situation, but I did not discover for some time that I had gone a step too far. In fact it was not until I discovered my wife and helpless children were exposed to the murderous attacks of hostile savages that it dawned upon me that I had made a desperate venture . . .

Arthur was quite capable of handling those hostile Indians. The first time they got out of line, about forty members of opposing tribes were standing in front of the new cabin with loaded guns, pawing the ground and breathing fire at one another.

Denny was about twice as high and twice as hefty as any of the Indians in the group. He collared Pat Kanim, one of the chiefs who was a party to the belligerence. He took Pat around behind the house and told him he'd knock his block off if he didn't behave.

"Can't I just sneak around the cabin and sink my knife in the back of the other chief?" Pat Kanim is reputed to have pleaded. "You can pretend you didn't know anything about it."

"No, you can't!" Arthur retorted.

From then on the Indians were afraid of Arthur. Pat Kanim became his friend. Some years later. Arthur revoked an idiot decision made by the Army to kill Kanim off . . . and Kanim in return helped save the town from disaster during the Indian War.

But neither the Indians nor the women were Arthur's big trouble on that abysmal afternoon. As far as he was concerned, sick or well, pessimistic or optimistic, he had reached the Promised Land . . . and **here he would build his city.**

He agreed that this was the best site for a town on all of Puget Sound.

And so it was . . . so fine a place that before he left for the south, Low had joined with Lee Terry in driving their stakes, laying claim to the entire area for a jointly-owned townsite. They had thoughtfully partitioned their property off in town lots just like the fellows in Olympia did the year before.

And how would Arthur like a couple of free lots in *their* town?

Needless to say, Arthur simply was not the type to sit down on a big rock and cry. Neither was he going to accept the deal. He hadn't come across the continent to be satisfied with a couple of lots in somebody else's town. But he was a sick man (and would continue to be a sick man for nearly another year). Winter was on them and he and his family—for that matter everybody in the party—had to have warm and safe quarters in which to live.

He turned to with a will and finished the cabin that had been started. Then went about building an even bigger cabin for himself and finally helped build a split-cedar cabin for the Bell family.

During his spare time—what little he had—he went about exploring the possibilities elsewhere in the neighborhood that might be suitable as a site for his city.

He would find his own city at his own location in his own time . . . and thank you very much for absolutely nothing!

The bonds of friendship—cold cash

Half a century after the fact—on the occasion of David Denny's death—the *Seattle Post-Intelligencer* carried a nostalgic item that read in part: "A. A. Denny, Low, Boren, Bell and C. C. Terry arrived at Alki Point, joining D. T. Denny. *That made a happy little family . . .*" (Ed. note: Italics mine.)

Some family!

Arthur and Charlie Terry headed two warring camps. I suppose the Dennys and the Borens were speaking to each other. David Denny and Louisa Boren must have exchanged a word or two—they were in love. And I would imagine that the Terry brothers and John Low

had a cheerful outlook on the world. Charlie had brought the merchandise for a store and was trading with everyone. Of the six men
on the premises, three were on Arthur's side and three on the Terry
side. Bell was the only neutral and both sides were wooing him.

Fortunately—for us—they were having a hot time in San Francisco.

In the two-year period preceding the November 13 arrival of our
settlers, San Francisco was wiped out by fire six times. There was no
rail transportation to the Bay City at that point. Everything was carried on ships . . . but those fires kept burning down the piers. The
last burnout took place five months before our team landed at Alki
and the San Franciscans had boats out pointing their noses around
anywhere for the long pilings and the big timbers necessary to replace their life-lines on the water front.

And on December 10, 1851, the brig "Leonesa" noted the lights at
the Point and hollered out to see if anybody had pilings for sale.

That was the first whiff of money ever wafted our way.

You bet we had pilings!

What *were* pilings?

Well, I'll tell you, our boys may have been from the midwest, but
they found out what pilings were in a hurry . . . and they produced
them in a hurry. A sudden heart-warming harmony found its way
into the breasts of the hardy little band. Suddenly they were all part-
ners again . . . and in twenty-one days they produced a shipload of
piling and rough-hewn timbers of the desired twelve by twelve inches
and thirty feet long.

They got a thousand bucks—hard cash.

The piling sold in San Francisco a couple weeks later for $6,800, but
they didn't care. They had learned from the captain of the "Leonesa" that there were buyers in San Francisco for all the sticks of piling they could haul out of the woods for an indefinite period. Nobody had laid claim to any of the land within miles and all they
needed was hard work along the shoreline to haul in the money.

It's interesting to note who did what to establish that early economy on Puget Sound. Low was the man with some money, so he was the one with whom the captain of the brig signed the contract. Charlie Terry, who was the fast man with the figures, served as timekeeper and checker.

Lee Terry, who was just as fast at avoiding work, went up the Duwamish Valley looking for a yoke of oxen to haul the logs.

Boren and Bell had nice strong backs.

And Arthur . . .

Of course, he did his share of the work . . . but he also made a deal with the captain. In those days any thrifty captain carried a stock of merchandise to sell to the pioneers. The captain of the "Leonesa" was no exception. But, after he had sold everything he could sell he still had a large stock remaining. Arthur pointed out that since the brig was fully loaded, there wouldn't be any stops between the Point and San Francisco . . . and he couldn't sell his merchandise on the high seas.

On the other hand, Arthur had plenty of room in his big cabin. He would handle the merchandise for a percentage of the gross and pay off when the captain returned for more pilings.

The opportunist, Charlie Terry, had bought a stock of merchandise to set up his store.

The canny Arthur got a store going without putting up a cent.

He bet on the right horse shoes

The morning after the "Leonesa" had been loaded, our hardy little band of pioneers had a horrible fright.

They had worked late the night before loading the ship, and then had tumbled into bed without collecting their money. And when they awoke the next morning, the "Leonesa" was gone!

The settlers really thought they'd been had.

But the "Leonesa" had slipped anchor during the night and had drifted north to a more or less comfortable repository in the mudflats of Smith Cove and had been forced to remain there until the next high tide re-floated it. Our team was delighted when the captain returned and paid them for their labors.

They were more than delighted at the knowledge that San Francisco would buy all the future pilings and timbers they could cut for years to come. They had arrived here not knowing what they would use to establish their economy. Now they knew they needn't depend on farming for a living. They had a paying industry.

From the time of his arrival, Arthur had been contemplating methods of finding some place—any place—other than the Point at which to locate his own town.

He'd gone to Commencement Bay—where Tacoma is today—and Port Orchard and turned them down. He'd gone up the Duwamish River to where Puyallup now is located and over to Smith Cove and turned both of them down. He had not explored the area between Smith Cove and the Duwamish River because it looked as though the delta of the Duwamish covered the entire area.

This is hard for us to visualize today because the delta of the Duwamish—some fifteen hundred acres—has been filled and dredged so that we have either deep water or dry land. It was totally different in Arthur's time. From either Smith Cove or the west side of the Duwamish, it looked as though everything was tideflats at low water.

It was a real shocker to Arthur twenty years later when the Northern Pacific Railroad selected his rejected Commencement Bay area as the site for its terminus. Arthur was not the kind of a guy who would philosophically accept any situation where he had been proved wrong.

I'm sure the railroad must have been influenced in its selection of its terminus by the report of the Charles Wilkes expedition . . . but it wasn't published and widely distributed until ten years after Arthur went to work.

Wilkes, an officer in the United States Navy, had taken off in 1838 with a complete complement of naturalists, botanists, mineralogists, taxidermists, philologists and chartmakers to find out what the Pacific Ocean was all about.

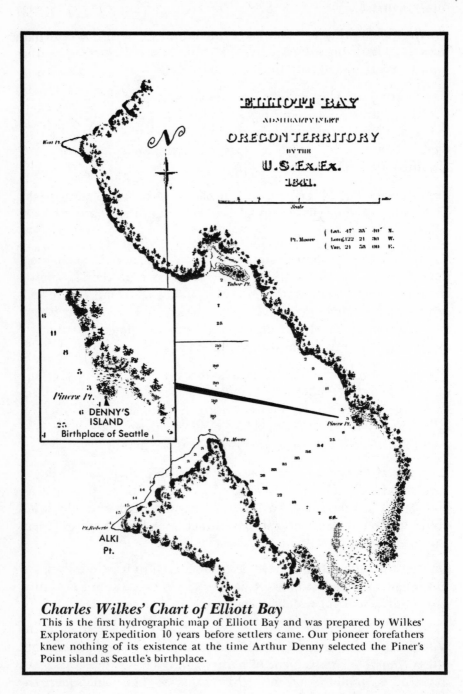

ELLIOTT BAY
ADMIRALTY INLET
OREGON TERRITORY
BY THE
U.S. Ex. Ex.
1841.

Scale

Pt. Moore
{ Lat. 47° 35' 40" N.
{ Long 122° 21' 30" W.
{ Var. 21° 58' 00" E.

DENNY'S
ISLAND
Birthplace of Seattle

ALKI
Pt.

Charles Wilkes' Chart of Elliott Bay

This is the first hydrographic map of Elliott Bay and was prepared by Wilkes' Exploratory Expedition 10 years before settlers came. Our pioneer forefathers knew nothing of its existence at the time Arthur Denny selected the Piner's Point island as Seattle's birthplace.

At the time, we were having a little argument with Great Britain over the north boundary of the Oregon Territory . . . and we were muttering things like "Fifty-four forty or fight!" and Wilkes was ordered to include the Pacific Northwest coast in his studies. He did little things like measuring the height of Mount Rainier and charting Puget Sound. He started with Commencement Bay, which was how it got its name . . . because he commenced there.

He also charted Elliott Bay.

Now, ten years later, Arthur was looking for a location that would satisfy his economic needs. They ran out of timber early in the game at Alki and had to go scrounging for it across the Sound or any place else they could lay their hand on. And what Arthur wanted was a good sheltered harbor close to a lot of timber that could easily be skidded into saltwater.

One look at Wilkes' chart would have given him the answer. But he didn't have either the Wilkes Chart . . . or a helicopter . . . or a fathometer. He only had a clothesline and a couple of horse shoes. No, that's not quite correct.

He had Boren and Bell. He had persuaded Bell that he was going to win out over Charlie Terry & Co. So Bell and old Uncle Dobbins paddled canoes all over the coastline for a couple of months while Arthur stood up like George Washington and heaved the lead (speaking nautically).

David didn't participate. He had cut himself again.

Finally, as sort of a last resort, they figured they'd better check out the southeast area of Elliott Bay—which had been named Piner's Point by Wilkes, but they didn't know it.

(It is interesting but puzzling that they knew the name Elliott Bay and West Point, which Wilkes had named, but none of the other handles he'd hung on places.)

Anyway, early in February, they took a run at this unprepossessing place and ran smack into a little island of about eight acres—right where they had figured there was nothing but tideflats. And just south of that little island they found a sand bar at about where the railroad depots are today.

By a strange quirk of nature, the current of the Duwamish at this location swept strongly out to sea, and right off the little island where they had anticipated finding about a foot of water at high tide, they found about thirty or forty feet of water. That was as much depth at the same distance from the shore as that they were so proud of at Lee Terry's Point. Most of the island was only a few feet above high tide and there was a huge saltwater lagoon behind it as large as the island itself: And the whole place was pretty muddy. But it was the "least worst" spot they'd found in over a month.

I call it Denny's tight little island.

Arthur got pretty enthusiastic.

"Fellas," he should have said, "This is a site for sore eyes."

If he had been Archimedes, he would have hollered, "Eureka, Eureka," and run home without his clothes on. But being Arthur Denny, who wouldn't have taken his clothes off in the first place, he simply realized this was the spot for the city.

But, just to be sure, they then paddled up to the head of the bay which turned out to be nothing but mudflats as they had expected, and then back along the east side of West Seattle and out to Lee Terry's Point, finding nothing better.

After studying the idea from every angle for the next two weeks, Arthur still figured "Eureka." Denny, Boren and Bell went back across the bay and staked their claims of 320 acres each, running for a couple of miles along the waterfront.

On that day, Sunday, February 15, 1852, the town of Seattle was born.

And from that day there started a battle for survival between Terry's town and the town of Seattle that would last for the next five years.

Thank God I'm a civilian!

One of the most refreshing glimpses provided for us into the character of the Father of Seattle comes from his brush with the Army.

The Army, I am pleased to note, lost its ever-loving shirt!

In this one, Arthur really let freedom ring.

The whole thing started on December 10, 1854 when Arthur introduced a joint resolution into the house of the Territorial Legislature. It requested Congress to authorize the Governor of the Territory to accept the services of two companies of mounted volunteers for the quelling of Indian troubles, which were mounting in astronomic proportions.

Out of this the Territorial Militia was formed. Arthur became a first lieutenant in Company "A," the first company formed in Seattle. One General James Tilton, who was the Territory's Surveyor-General in normal life was made Adjutant General, a position which he fully enjoyed. It gave him an opportunity to vent the frustrations he had built up as a civil servant forced to deal with such independent spirits as "Our Father."

Tilton was a Democrat. Arthur was a Whig.

That added just the right touch of spice to the contretemps.

Some six months after the January 26, 1856 Battle of Seattle, the town's one-day fight with the Indians, General Tilton ordered Arthur to lead his company into a battle with the underbrush by constructing a military road across Snoqualmie Pass.

Arthur informed the General in no uncertain terms he only got in this act to protect his town and he was not about to disrupt his and his Company's lives to build some fool road some place.

He told Tilton to go fly a kite.

Tilton relieved him of command and promoted Second Lieutenant D. A. Neely to succeed him. Neely and the rest of the company then signed a resolution which read:

We do not approve of the course of the Commander-in-Chief in suspending Lieutenant Denny from his command, but on the contrary, consider it an act of injustice, and an insult to the Company, wholly unjustifiable and uncalled for.

The company then told Tilton to go fly *two* kites.

Instead, Tilton blew his cork.

He dispatched a lieutenant colonel, wearing his full dress uniform including cocked hat and epaulets, from the War Department in Olympia to explain to the members of Company "A" that if they had been in the Regular Army, they would have been court-martialed and shot . . . and wouldn't they *please* repudiate at least the part about telling Tilton to go fly a couple of kites?

He reported to the General that he talked to everybody in "A" Company individually and in small groups. His visit reached its quixotic climax when he mustered the entire company in the heart of town.

With the usual collection of drunks standing idly around, the man in the epaulets and cocked hat had his lounging "grenadiers" brought to stiff attention and then smartly cried out, "All those who wish to rescind those petitions step forward!" If he had taken off his cocked hat, he would have been knocked into it.

Nobody moved.

The General retaliated by refusing to receive the final muster roll, which meant they were dishonorably discharged . . . and what was even worse—they wouldn't get their pay.

Hah!

Arthur was still a member of the Legislature and on December 24, 1856, that body just happened to pass a resolution that ordered General Tilton to put Company "A" back on the muster roll and requisition their pay for them. The Legislature also sent a resolution to Congress stating that despite rumors to the contrary, Company "A" was made up of good guys and should be in the same position as other companies of the same regiment.

They got the money.

A few years later, in what was otherwise a Democratic landslide, Tilton ran against Denny for Congress.

Denny beat the socks off him.

Birth of "The Seattle Spirit"

Ever since the 1890's, when the original founding fathers of the city had either died off or were approaching an euphoric and genial senility, we have been attempting to stomach something referred to in chauvinistic terms as "The Seattle Spirit." It has acquired a saccharin quality which attributes to our pioneers a degree of saintliness they neither wanted nor deserved.

Frederic Grant, one of the early historians, put it this way: "Nothing seems to the historian more kindly and good tempered than the disposition of the pioneers, who had a city already in view and knew something of the value of their land, to give to new arrivals an equal advantage with themselves . . ." He hedged his bet by adding, "It was, it is true, good policy to favor active men with business interests, and to offer inducements to locate here; but such a liberal line of action is seen and appreciated only by the liberal." Referring to a later era in the city's history, newsman J. Willis Sayre defined the Seattle Spirit as a "determination to subordinate personal interests to those of the city, to stick together and to overcome all obstacles."

Actually, as I see it, the kindest connotation of "The Seattle Spirit" is that of enlightened self-interest. The Pollyanna version is alleged to have been initiated when Dr. David S. Maynard arrived on the scene a month after Denny, Boren and Bell staked their claims. The "pie" along the waterfront bounded by today's King Street on one side and Denny Way on the other, had been split three ways. Boren had the south claim, Denny had the middle and Bell had the north claim.

According to legend, when Maynard, Seattle's first bona-fide drunk, arrived with a proposal to set up a salmon-salting business those who already had land "gladly" moved their stakes to make room for Maynard, and he ended up with a claim running from King Street north three blocks to Yesler Way.

That's the legend I had always accepted—until recently when I checked out the facts.

It is true that the south boundary of Boren's claim was moved from

King Street north three blocks to Yesler Way, and it is true that this included almost all the level land in the city.

However, Boren had left Seattle a week before Maynard's arrival to pick up his cattle in the Willamette Valley. Just walking the distance between Seattle and Portland would take two weeks, let alone driving a herd of cattle. So Boren was out of town when that great phenomenon of this city came into being. He was en route to the Willamette Valley.

The "Seattle Spirit" was born . . .

When Denny gave *Boren's* land to Maynard!

II

The Saga of Charlie Terry

Charlie Terry's life so admirably illustrates the theme of this book it's a pity it's a short story and he had to die at the age of 37. He was the representative of the less stuffy side of what even today is Seattle's split personality. And for the first fifty years, Charlie's side of our town was by all odds the more persuasive.

He was twenty-two at the time he arrived from Portland with the Denny party. From what I know of him, I'm as sure that everybody called him "Charlie" as I am that nobody called Arthur Armstrong Denny, "Art." The two men were certainly the chief protagonists of the early days and presented a complete contrast in personalities. Terry was a personable, free-booting, sharp-trading opportunist and Denny we already know was something of a stern-faced, church-going prohibitionist. Without him as a counterpoise, Denny would have built a deadly little puritanical town. Between them, they made her the top town from the very beginning.

I could admire Denny.

I could *like* Charlie Terry.

Arthur placed his fate in the hands of the Lord, but not Charlie Terry. When he stepped ashore that rainy November 13, he had a more definitive approach to the problem. Having noted what kind of supplies California settlers needed, he came prepared to open a general store and his first goods had travelled up to Puget Sound with him on the "Exact."

Being meticulous about the care and feeding of money, he kept a little black notebook which is still preserved, neatly listing all the items. He had thoughtfully provided the pioneer settlers with one keg of whiskey, one keg of brandy, neither of which he would ever be able to sell to Arthur Denny, one box of tobacco, one box of raisins, one box of tinware and one box of axes. He quickly put together a cabin in order to display his goods and was in business as "The New York Cash Store," with John Low as a partner, in a matter of days. By this time he had also acquired from the captain of a trading schooner: more whiskey, some pork, flour, molasses, hard bread, boots, brogan shoes, prints, hickory shirts, window sashes, a glass, grindstones, crosscut saws, files, mustard, pepper-sauce and sugar.

He was never one to dilly-dally—if there was a buck to be made.

Alki—the metropolis of Elliott Bay

Naturally, most of the people listed as Seattle's founders and builders had little or nothing to do either with the founding or the building of the city . . .

For instance, Charlie is listed as a founder although he spent his first three years trying to wipe Seattle off the map.

Six months after his arrival, the footloose Lee Terry, another "founder," had bid his brother goodbye and set off for his old home in New York, never to return. About a year later John Low sold his interest in the Point to Charlie and moved to Olympia. Charlie was now the sole owner, the others in the original party having gone across the Bay to help Arthur start his town.

To all practical purposes, Charlie Terry *was* Alki.

We also have another kindly little Seattle legend that goes along with the "one-big-happy-family" bit. The legend is that all of the settlers got together and named the town on the Point "New York." Visitors from elsewhere on the Sound saw the struggling little settlement which called itself New York, smiled a little and said, "Yeah, by-and-by . . . maybe . . ." or "in a pig's eye!" The Indian word for "by and by" is "Alki," so it became New York-Alki, then just plain "Alki." The truth is that the name New York wasn't selling worth a hang in the Pacific Northwest. We didn't like big cities in the first place or we wouldn't have come clear out here. And we didn't like people who pretended they were big citizens.

Charlie, who was as gregarious a guy as you can get, noted the name New York was going over like a lead balloon and was bad for business. The name Seattle, on the other hand, was a popular item in the public mind, so he figured he'd better get an Indian name as quick as he could. If Japanese names had been better on the market at the time he would have called the place Takahashi, or something like that.

So he hung the name Alki on his location and got a big plug out of the editor of the *Columbian* in Olympia, the only paper north of the Columbia River:

> Our enterprising friend (Ed. note . . . And a big advertiser), C. C. Terry, has made an excellent change of name for his flourishing town at the entrance to Duwamish Bay, hitherto called New York. It is henceforth to be known by the name "Alki." We never fancied the name of New York on account of its appropriateness: but Alki we subscribe to instanter . . . it is not borrowed or stolen from any other town or city, and is in its meaning expressive unto prophecy, (Ed. note: You can say that again, brother!) the interpretation of the word Alki being "by-and-by," "in a little while" or "hereafter." We must approve its application to a growing and hopeful place. Well done, friend Terry to thee and thy Alki.

For the first year, before Yesler got his mill under way, Charlie really hauled the money in. For one thing, he had the Indian trade. And in this he played both ends against the middle. He bought his merchandise wholesale in San Francisco and sold it at exorbitant prices to the Indians. They didn't have money, so they brought in logs and timbers which he bought cheap and sold dear. He was aware that the captain on the "Leonesa" had made nearly seven hundred per cent on the logs he'd bought from the settlers. Before Charlie was through there were thirty-eight ships in the Puget Sound-San Francisco trade . . . and Charlie used the competition to lower the profit margin of the ships' captains and increase his. He soon ran out of lumber at Alki and moved his Indian crews across the Sound to Port Orchard.

Meanwhile, Denny was sick for most of that first year. Maynard, Charlie's only other real competitor, was incapacitating himself with liquor and pursuing the wild goose chase of salting salmon for the San Francisco trade. The salmon spoiled in transit and the doctor lost his shirt. But Alki had a cooper's shop and collected for the barrel staves that Maynard ordered from there.

Charlie had about six stores and fifty houses on the Point and was rapidly out-distancing Seattle when Henry Yesler came along from Ohio and started his sawmill in Seattle. Ezra Meeker, the great publicist for the Oregon Trail, visited both places shortly after Henry started sawing lumber and had this to write about them:

> Here (Alki) we met the irrepressible Charlie Terry, proprietor of the new townsite, who was keenly alive to the importance of adding population to his town . . . We did not stay too long in Seattle, not being favorably impressed with the place. There was not much of a town, probably twenty cabins in all . . . The lagoon presented an uninviting appearance and scent, where the process of filling with slabs and sawdust already has begun . . .

The "scent" referred to by Ezra Meeker was to remain a part of Seattle's personality for a whole generation.

We are inclined to think Seattle had the edge from the start. Nothing was farther from the truth as long as Charlie Terry was the moving force at Alki. He outmatched Seattle project for project. For instance, when Seattle got a post office, Charlie got a better post office *and* a place for people to leave messages for their friends around the Sound.

A subtle but important difference between Arthur and Charlie shows up in the matter of platting the two towns. Arthur was what you could call a pretty good "hater." If you were on the other side, he had no use for you at all. If the situation had been reversed and Charlie had been a surveyor rather than Arthur, Seattle wouldn't have been platted until some surveyor other than Charlie came along.

Charlie cheerfully hired Denny to plat Alki.

And Denny, by the same token, cheerfully platted Alki—for the money.

It was platted into six blocks of eight lots . . . and most of them had buildings on them that were in use. There weren't eight level, usable blocks in all of Seattle.

Alki was clearly the metropolis of Elliott Bay for the first couple of years.

On the whole Sound, only Olympia exceeded it in population—and even there not by much.

The Lord and David Blaine

Charlie Terry was not what you could call an irreligious man. He was more of a non-religious man. In this respect he was clearly representative of the majority of the men on Puget Sound. I think his attitude on the matter is aptly expressed in the story that came out of his first meeting with David E. Blaine. The latter was en route from Olympia to Seattle with his bride at the behest of Arthur Denny to initiate formal religion in our town.

David and his wife, Catherine, were missionaries for the Methodist-Episcopal church. They had never been outside of a big eastern city and were totally unprepared either by training or experience to cope with conditions here. The trip from Olympia as far as Alki wore them out, and they were glad to stay the night at Charlie's house.

Blaine had spent the trip around the Horn writing a batch of sermons that may have gone over splendidly in the East, but sure didn't sell in Seattle at that time. When he told the Indians that God had died to save them, it was their wish that God would do something about the white people who were rapidly killing them off. He didn't make much more of a dent on the white people, who were too busy killing off the Indians to pause for philosophic repartee.

Even though he thought that this religion business was a little premature, Charlie took the attitude that missionaries did mean more money in the long run and should be encouraged. After that first sermon, Charlie got up saying, "I don't know about Methodism, but I do know about this" . . . and passed the hat. He collected $12.50 which he handed over to young Blaine.

Arthur and his wife welcomed the Blaines with open arms the next day and let them live in their house until the Blaines could get settled.

To Arthur, providing the town with proper religious services was essential to its growth. But he drew the wrong pair of people for the job. There was pretty good attendance at the dedication of Seattle's first church, but the minister and his wife were disturbed by the fact that the women let their dripping umbrellas drip inside, not outside, the church . . . that the men put their muddy feet on the pews and spit tobacco juice on the floor . . .

It's simple to see the Blaines were totally unreasonable.

They didn't like sleeping in the dirty bed clothes they were given when they went visiting around the countryside . . . and they were absolutely horrified that the Indian children went swimming in the nude. They also were discouraged by the fact that they and the Arthur Dennys were usually the only ones at the prayer meetings . . . and there were usually only six people, including the Blaines, at the regular Sunday services.

Let's face it, Arthur Denny was counting on The Church as a major plus in the sound construction of his town. He was out of step with the times and it didn't work. The Blaines were also out of step. Maynard and Boren offered them land for a seminary, but they didn't stay around long enough to accept the offers. The Indian attack on Seattle scared them completely and the church remained empty until a few years later when another minister from another denomination came along and was required to use it.

Blaine didn't come out of it so bad financially: he invested two hundred bucks in Henry Yesler's mill out of the three hundred and fifty given to him in advance for his first year's salary . . . and realized a handsome profit on the deal.

But, whether he liked it or not, Arthur needed a Charlie Terry for the healthy development of Seattle a lot more than he needed a David Blaine.

And here's how he got him.

Good bye Alki . . .

When Yesler built the steam sawmill in Seattle, Charlie Terry went into partnership with William R. Renton and built a better mill at Alki. Charlie already dominated the piling and timber trade on Puget Sound. He prepared to also add the lumber business to that domination.

And that's where Mother Nature knocked him out.

Renton's mill was constructed on the north side of Alki Point and was sheltered from the prevailing southwest wind. In those days, people made the mistake of thinking that because it was an inland sea, any place on Puget Sound was a good harbor.

A sad mistake.

During the winter, the north wind, building up the tides in front of it, comes sweeping down the Sound out of Canada, piling mighty waves on Alki Point. Beginning with Terry and Renton and including a lot of smart men since, nobody has been able to build anything out in the water at Alki that will withstand those waves.

Henry Yesler, who was privy to previous information about those waves, passed up an opportunity to establish his mill at Alki, although Charlie Terry moved heaven and earth to get him there.

It was the north wind, not the powerful competition from Arthur Denny and the competitive spirit of Seattle, that made Terry lose out with Henry. And it made him lose out with Renton, who took his sawmill and left.

Charlie realized that he could never have a major port at Alki—not with that north wind. He had a healthy, growing town at the time he realized he was licked, but he was not a man to stick stubbornly to a losing proposition. Practicing a philosophy of *caveat emptor,* he sold out everything he owned at Alki Point at a handsome profit—except the land. Charlie believed in owning land. He bought a huge acreage in the Duwamish Valley, for instance . . . paid $1,500 for it . . . used it to raise barley, oats, hay and onions. He liked the onions the best; they made the most money. He constructed a summer home there and called it the Onion Farm.

He kept his Alki property, though. How did he know that a "Mr. Right" wouldn't come along . . . somebody who liked the view of the Olympics and wouldn't give a tinker's dam about the north wind?

Charlie had got the property for nothing in the first place.

With taxes being almost nil, he could keep it at the same price.

Charlie was planning a trip to New York, and he used this as his reason for selling out his business. He told the folks he had a considerable amount of business in New York, although his primary reason for going there was to raise more capital to enlarge his holdings on Puget Sound. He also was in pursuit of a business associate who had absconded with $2,000 of Charlie's money. He arranged to pay for the New York trip by accepting commissions as an agent for a number of people on the Sound who needed business done in New York.

On September 4, 1854, fate intervened.

Charlie was elected to the Territorial Legislature.

It wouldn't convene for three months, but the delay was worth it. Charlie's chances of raising money in New York would be enhanced by the fact that he was a member of the Upper Council of the Territorial Legislature. The delay proved doubly worthwhile in the long run, because when he finally got to New York the following spring the eastern visit caused him to miss the Indian uprisings in Seattle.

Good buy Seattle

While he was serving in the Legislature, Charlie learned that Carson Boren's attempt as an empire builder had broken down. He was suffering a bad case of being "Uncle Dobbins". He wanted to go some place and be alone.

Boren wasn't getting along with his wife, or his sisters or his big, strong-minded step-brother, brother-in-law Arthur Denny. I doubt if he was particularly anti-Arthur just because the latter gave away part of his claim to Maynard—after all, Boren turned around a few months later and gave away more of it to Yesler—but he certainly didn't feel it incumbent upon himself to sell any of his land to Arthur.

So Boren was ripe for a shrewd, personable buyer like Charlie Terry. He agreed to sell the west 160 acres of his claim. That was the portion of his claim from the waterfront to the top of First Hill. It was by far and away the choicest part of the land which he had left. Charlie didn't have the cash to consummate the deal alone, so he took Chief Justice Edward M. Lander with him on a fifty-fifty basis. Each put in $250 for the 160 acres.

When Terry bought Lander's half ten years later, it was already worth $30,000.

In 1965, the Seattle First National Bank bought one block of this claim for their new skyscraper, paid $1,600,000 for the block and was glad to get it at that price. On Terry's original purchase from Boren in 1855, that block cost him $4.47—the same price Charlie was getting for a bushel of his onions.

So appropriately enough, when Charlie decided to become a part of Seattle, he did it via the biggest land steal in our city's history.

Incidentally, the onion farm didn't prove to be such a bad buy either.

It is now the King County Airport.

The "In" justice of the times

The same year Charlie went into the Legislature, he was named the foreman of the first grand jury ever called together in Seattle. A short time before, a couple of Seattle's leading citizens—(they were all leading citizens in those days because otherwise there wouldn't be enough to go around)—had strung up an Indian by the name of Masachie Jim without the benefit of a trial.

Arthur Denny had been telling them and telling them not to string up Indians. Arthur believed that fellows who strung up Indians should be put on trial . . . and if found guilty, they should also be hung. On the other hand the Indians had a nasty habit of taking white peoples' scalps and not returning them.

The general consensus of the community was that killing an Indian was a matter of no graver consequence than shooting a cougar or a bear—and far more valuable to the community. So the fellows kept stringing up Indians. But they hung Jim at a rather awkward time . . . just prior to the arrival of Justice Lander who had just taken an oath that he would uphold the laws of the United States, and there was nothing in his book that made an exception about hanging Indians.

There was no jury in Seattle at that time who would hang a white man because he killed an Indian. Had there been, it would have ended up as a hung jury . . . and I don't mean by a division of opinion. I mean by the neck.

Maynard was the only white man in the area who had a deep sympathy for the Indians. Chief Seattle was his closest friend. He risked his life tending to the wants of those Indians who were not fighting during the Indian War . . . got himself dubbed an "Indian Lover" and ostracized by the rest of the community.

Judge Lander opened court in Henry Yesler's cook house and asked the grand jury for suggestions about the guilt or innocence of the alleged hangers. There was no doubt about whether they did it because most of the people in the town saw or were involved in the hanging.

Charlie's first embarrassment came when the prosecution charged that one William Heebner, a prominent man about town, had participated in the necktie party.

But Heebner, himself, was on the grand jury.

Charlie didn't think it was fair to force Heebner to indict himself. It just wasn't part of the Code of the West. So Heebner was excused from the room for a few minutes until they could get him indicted. Then he returned to hear the other cases before the jury.

An uneducated man by the name of David Maurer also was indicted.

Then the fellas, all except Heebner and Maurer, took off their grand jury hats and put on their just plain jury hats. Arthur was on the jury although Charlie was still running it. And that was a good thing too, because if Arthur acted on his principles—and I know of no time that Arthur didn't act on his principles—he would have voted "guilty" regardless of the consequences.

Judge Lander informed the jury in unequivocal terms that if the men were found guilty he would sentence them to hanging.

So if Arthur had represented the majority, we would have had a preview of the Civil War in Seattle some years before it happened. The relatives and friends of the white people who had been killed by Indians would have disposed of our first supreme court justice—and the jury.

The problem lay in the fact that everybody knew the men were guilty, but nobody could figure out some way of finding them not guilty ... that is, nobody but Charlie.

Heebner swore that not only was he not guilty but was not even in the county at the time of the incident ... and plenty of eyewitnesses corroborated his testimony. What was a little perjury if it helped a fellow citizen?

Maurer, on the other hand may have had a strong back, but he was a little thick in the bone on the top of his neck.

"How do you plead," he was asked. "Guilty or not guilty?" "Well, I guess I'm guilty, Judge," Maurer replied.

"Not guilty, you idiot!" Charlie hissed from the jury box, "Not guilty!"

The startled Maurer entered a plea of "Not guilty," but the prosecution proved cold turkey that by his own admission many times over, Maurer was guilty ... and the jury could put that in its pipe and smoke it.

For the next thirty hours, the jury debated the matter, which meant that for the first time Charlie met Arthur head-on in Arthur's home territory. And it was more than a matter of Maurer's fate. In a way, it was a decision of the course that the city of Seattle would take for the next half-century. Would it reflect Arthur Denny's puritanical principles and would the man be hung? Or did the jurors represent Charlie Terry's "win a few and lose a few" philosophy?

The jury held that the prosecution had mis-spelled Masachie Jim's name and therefore Maurer was innocent.

Lander decided to let it ride at that.

Law . . . and . . . orders

Another delightful insight into the life and times of Charlie Terry is illustrated by the battle between the Law, as represented by Justice Lander, and the Orders issued by peppery little Governor Isaac M. Stevens who was appointed by the President of the United States at the same time as Lander but was a little closer to the majority opinion of the people.

The Law emerged with a moral victory . . .

But Stevens won the fight.

Stevens was charged with the business of removing some 30,000 Indians from land they had come to believe was their own after several centuries of occupancy. He was to put them on some of the poorer pieces of land that the settlers had no use for and theoretically he was to give them a plow, some blankets and food and a teacher. In this process he could summon forth a bag full of promises, but no cash to back them up.

It occurred to some of the Indians they were getting a bad bargain.

The white people contributed to this notion by occupying nice chunks of land like Seattle years before the government made any treaties with our red brethren . . . and unceremoniously bustled the Indians out of some of their favorite camp grounds, fishing holes and clam beaches. They passed laws prohibiting Indians from entering their towns or taking short cuts across their fenced fields.

It also occurred to some of those Indians there were less than four thousand whites in the whole Territory . . . and if they were killed or otherwise frightened off, the Indians could either permanently solve their problem or at least make a better deal with the Great White Chief back in Washington, D.C.

Stevens would hold treaty-signing bees with batches of Indians and think he had a problem area taken care of only to find a little later the Indians had changed their minds and gone back to scalping whites. Endeavoring to fight fire with fire, Stevens adopted the interesting practice of scalping Indians.

He put a bounty on the scalps of the scalpers. Friendly Indians interested in picking up pocket money delivered the scalps to the front lawn of the Governor's mansion where they were counted and the payment made.

At one time some friendly Indians got a little eager and killed an Indian prisoner in Stevens' office. This annoyed our chief executive no end . . . not because of the murder, but because they got his office all messed up with blood in the process.

Stevens wasn't a stickler for the Marquis of Queensbury rules, or any other rules—up to and including those established by the Constitution of the United States.

Lander, the dignified, albeit genial jurist, took a dim view of people who took a dim view of the Constitution.

Well, there were some families living in Pierce County comprised of French Canadian men married to Indian women . . . and although scalps were being either neatly or not so neatly removed from Americans, these folks never got molested at all by their red brethren. There was a distinct suspicion among the rest of the folks that they were supplying the Indians with food, clothing, shelter—and ammunition.

So Stevens had a couple of the Pierce County men captured and lodged in the guardhouse at Fort Steilacoom. When he had them in the pokey, he told the officer of the day that some shyster lawyer might come along with a writ of habeas corpus. Stevens told the officer to disregard the writ. But the officer demurred.

He indicated he might get in trouble because he felt that the writ was considered important by the federal government. So Stevens eliminated the problem by declaring martial law in Pierce County. On May 7, 1856—three months after the Battle of Seattle—Lander disregarded the martial law and issued writs of habeas corpus.

Stevens responded to that one by throwing Lander in the clink.

After a couple of days, Stevens succumbed to public pressure and let Lander out of the guardhouse and on May 12, 1856, Lander moved court to Thurston County where there was no martial law. There was some suspicion on Stevens' part that the lawyers for the incarcerated men would once more apply for a writ. This suspicion was enhanced by the fact that Lander summoned a whole bunch of armed United States Marshals to stand around the courtroom while it was in session.

Stevens didn't want to be forced into any drastic action, so he just put an armed guard around the courthouse. Then he rolled up a cannon on the front lawn and aimed it at the spot where Lander's mouth would be if he opened it to grant that writ.

When the lawyers for the defense approached the court house, Stevens declared martial law again—this time in Thurston County.

Lander still proposed to open his mouth.

Stevens sent enough of a supply of soldiers into the courtroom to overcome the objections of the United States Marshals . . . and proceeded not only to remove Lander kicking and screaming from the courtroom, but to throw him in jail.

Lander stayed in jail for two weeks that time.

Some months later, Lander got a court going again and fined Stevens $50 for contempt of court . . . and Stevens paid the fine, which took care of the dignity of the Law.

Then Stevens, the Governor, pardoned Stevens, the Citizen . . .

And had the fifty bucks returned.

The pin-up girl

The pioneers crossing the plains to the Promised Land encountered a wide variety of problems. For example, fifty per cent of the people on one wagon train coming to Seattle died of cholera.

Samuel Russell, head of one of the families that first settled at Alki

Point, however, had one of the most unique problems in pioneer history. Sam's problem was his daughter, Jane . . . Jane Russell.

Not the pin-up movie actress of a century later . . . but a real sexy girl, nonetheless.

Jane was some problem.

Every Indian who caught sight of her on the wagon trail wanted her. It finally got so bad they couldn't let her out of the covered wagon except at night . . . and then only with a bushel basket over her head and a couple of armed guards walking her while she got a little exer-cise.

If they'd had cameras in those days, some enterprising pioneer would have shot pictures of Jane in the most provocative poses possible at the time—like, say, showing a little bit of her ankle—and she would have been the pin-up girl in every teepee from the Missouri River to Puget Sound.

Charlie Terry was a pretty good looking fellow—with a fine head of dark hair and a pair of whimsical, wide-set eyes. He was a smart dresser, had a delightful sense of humor, a lot of money and when Jane arrived at Alki, he developed a complete understanding of what it was about her that had attracted the Indians.

Had attracted them?

She still attracted them.

Charlie and Jane became enamored with one another and Charlie started sharing Sam's concern about the irresistible Jane. It might cool the Indians interest in her if the two of them got married, but Charlie doubted that alone would do it. And as usual, Charlie had the necessary imagination to solve the problem.

A year after his real estate *coup* with Boren, he arranged to have the wedding in an Indian war canoe off the Suquamish Indian Reserva-tion in full view of several thousand panting bucks.

He also arranged for Chief Seattle to be the honored guest.

Chief Justice Lander officiated at the most unusual wedding in Seat-tle's early history, but as far as Charlie was concerned, Chief Seattle was the most important guest on hand. Seattle was a real tough character when he wanted to be. We always picture him as sort of a benign old soul, but the Hudson's Bay records show that he was considered a bad Indian in his earlier days, and the piratical Haida Indians from Canada figured him a threat they wouldn't get within ten miles of.

Chief Seattle was the head man of six tribes on Puget Sound, and his presence at the wedding said in effect to the rest of the Indians on the Sound:

"Okay, you guys. From now on you lay off. This gal is married to a friend of mine!"

From that time on, Jane may have occasionally found Charlie annoying, but she was never bothered by Indians.

Life with the irrepressible Charlie must have held some unusual moments for Mary Jane . . . like the time she nagged him to bring home a chamber pot and he kept forgetting. To make his point when he finally remembered them he got an entire wagon load and had the whole lot dumped on the front porch.

What's in a name?

For well over a century now, the people of Seattle have abided with a deep sense of shame over the fact that our city is named after a man who really didn't want us to use his name at all . . . that while we fought the rest of the Indians fair and square and won, we "used" an old man in his dotage just because we didn't like some of the other names that had been hung on the location.

I can't say I blame our founders for wanting to change the only Indian names that were in use at the time to designate the general locality in which we are situated.

There was Tsehalalicht, for instance, a real tongue-twister which would seem a little provincial today for our home address. Or Mulckmukum, which bears a horrible resemblance to someone being sick. The Thurston County Commissioners who were in charge before King County came into existence selected the name

Duwumps, which was the name on early maps of a body of water we presently refer to as Lake Washington.

Denny couldn't have cared less what they called his town as long as it grew in population and increased his property values.

Doc Maynard, on the other hand, was sensitive to such things and wanted an interesting name for his town. He's the one generally credited with providing us with our name and I wouldn't be at all surprised if he got some aid from the last bit of juice in the bottom of a whiskey barrel.

Whatever the cause, Doc was eager to name the town after his favorite Indian chief, Seattle. The Chief demurred that it was against his religious principles, but the good doctor promised he'd make things right for the Chief. And the historians have taken it from there with varying degrees of humor that have really not assuaged the guilt complex that we have held deep in our hearts ever since.

Bagley pointed out that the Chief was "not moved to emotional depths that made any ripple on his usual dignified bearing when he became acquainted with the fact that the honor had been conferred upon him . . ." And Roberta Frye Watt in her *Four Wagons West* indicated that the Chief "was not favorably impressed." Mrs. Watts pointed out that according to Indian superstition every time his name was spoken after his death the Chief would roll over in his grave . . .

And if that's the case, he's sure spinning off into eternity.

But now everybody can put his mind to rest.

Maynard made things right for the Chief. There's no question about that. He agreed that the businessmen of the community would pay Chief Seattle for the privilege of using his name for our city. And it must have amused Charlie Terry no end to find when he joined up with the town of Seattle there was a quiet little tax levied that hadn't been necessary at Alki.

Henry Yesler, who got annoyed at anything that cost him money, was the one who peached on the chief's "tax", and he did his peaching to Historian Hubert H. Bancroft whose *Works* is the most comprehensive compilation of the events that built the west.

The Chief put it—and I think reasonably—to the fellows on these grounds: according to his religion a town named in his honor would be a disturbance to his ghost. He felt that it was only fair that he should take his pay beforehand for the inconvenience he expected to suffer after his death, and they agreed to pay the tax.

I'll say this for Denny, Terry, Maynard, Boren and the rest of them. They'd made a bargain and they stuck to it for the rest of the Chief's life . . . and he carried out his side of the bargain with admirable fidelity. He talked six tribes—comprising about 4,000 warriors—out of participating in the Battle of Seattle.

We estimate that some thousand warriors from all around the Pacific Northwest took part in that battle. At one point only a handful of marines stood between the Indians and the demolition of Seattle.

What would the story have been if Chief Seattle had led his warriors into action against us? As it was, there was enough ruckus to scare people away and depress the area for years to come. If his gang had joined the fray, the Puget Sound settlement would have been set back a generation.

I'd always felt kind of sorry for the old Chief, myself. But now it gives me a deep sense of relief and satisfaction to know that our city is named after a wily old bird who got his while he was still here to enjoy it. Today, with our complex society we complain there are "too many chiefs and not enough Indians." Well, in his day there were plenty of Indians but only one Chief. And he ran the show.

I don't know what the Indian word for Benedict Arnold is, but the descendants of the Puget Sound Indian tribes would use it referring to Chief Seattle. They consider him a traitor of the first water. Their legends say he sold the Indians out. Nobody said how much the tax was, but the Chief lived high on the hog for nearly twenty years at our expense. He obviously got a lot more out of the deal than the $24 the red men got for Manhattan Island.

So Arthur has to be the second, not the first, Son of the Profits here.

Chief Seattle was the first.

The Kamikaze real estate agent

Psychiatrists have a point when they say it's perfectly normal for a man to wash his hands . . . but when he starts washing them every two minutes, twenty-four hours a day, he's about ready for the booby hatch.

It didn't distress Charlie much when he saw Doc Maynard giving away Seattle land or selling it at a tenth of its value—as long as Charlie was at Alki and trying to put Seattle out of business. He even realized that when Maynard gave Yesler a choice piece of property for a steam sawmill it was a good stroke of business. He would have done that himself.

He laughed along with everybody else when Doc completely outfitted a blacksmith's shop and sold it for fifteen bucks. There wasn't a horse within fifty miles.

But when Charlie came over to the other side and saw Doc giving away land in competition with the land that Charlie could otherwise have sold, he took a different view of the situation.

Doc not only continued his give-away program, but when in his cups he further complicated the situation by either giving or selling, at ridiculously low prices, the same piece of property to several different people . . . a program that added distinctly to the complications of Seattle real estate sales for years to come.

Charlie Terry decided he had to fight firewater with fire.

He pointed out that Seattle was indeed a pretty crummy place in which to live under any circumstances and that the land which May-nard owned consisted largely of mud and cliffs . . . while out there in the sunset against the inspirational backdrop of the Olympic Mountains lay beautiful Alki Point where the doctor could live as a gentleman farmer in peace and glory for the rest of his days. Terry failed to point out that Alki by now was a dead duck and that his land over there was virtually worthless.

There were those who felt that Charlie took advantage of Doc. Among them was Mrs. Maynard who expressed her sentiments to Historian Thomas Prosch in 1900:

Terry was the keenest and shrewdest of the local pioneers, full of energy and action. In trading, Maynard was no match for him. It did not take Terry long to effect an exchange of his Alki Point claim of 319 acres for the 260 acres of Maynard's claim then un-platted. On the 11th day of July, 1857, they passed deeds to the other, Terry acquiring land by the transaction worth today an average of perhaps $100,000 an acre, while Maynard got land that possibly might sell for $3,000 an acre.

She may have been right about the relative values of the land in-volved in 1900, but when Maynard grew disenchanted with his Alki bargain a year or so later he sold out for $460.

Charlie made out a little better.

Two years after he arrived in Seattle, largely as a result of his deals with Maynard and Boren, he owned 40 per cent of the land inside the city limits—and 90 per cent of the land in the central business district. He was the biggest land-holder in King County.

There was a Son of the Profits for you!

The "fairy" tale

I don't know what would have happened to Seattle in the earlier days without that piece of yeast called Charlie Terry, but he was like a Chinese pursued by seventy thousand devils . . . or perhaps I could say with the beautiful hindsight of a historian, like a man who knew he didn't have long to live.

That's where historians have the edge over other people. We know what the end result is going to be before we lay hand to the first word, and we can offer wonderful prescience.

The people who wrote about him when he was alive wrote about his inexhaustible energy . . . and you might be tempted to say he worked himself to death if it wasn't for the fact that his brother Lee, who never did a day's work he could avoid, succumbed to tuberculo-sis about four years before Charlie died.

And the kinds of things Charlie tore into—whether or not he succeeded in them—turned out to be the key in the development of Seattle in the hands of those who followed him.

For instance, he was either owner or part owner of the first three little ships on the Sound that ultimately developed into the mighty Mosquito Fleet . . . the collection of tiny steamers that dumped the wealth of Puget Sound in Seattle's lap and established trade routes early in the game.

Earlier historians disagree, but there is evidence that Charlie at one time was the owner of the steamer "Fairy" which Bagley credits with being the first ship of the Mosquito Fleet. The "Fairy" was a cranky little ship that arrived at Olympia on the night of October 31, 1853. She was the steamer that replaced the canoe and sailboat as the means of transportation between Elliott Bay and Olympia. Fare for the trip was ten bucks each way, but that was a lot better from both a cost and time standpoint than hiring some Indians to haul you between the two areas.

Charlie ended up as her owner and she ended up by blowing up at her dock in Olympia. Her hulk was found later about fifteen miles away, but her engines were never recovered.

Charlie's next purchase was the "Major Tomkins", which not only charged the ten dollar fare but had a $36,000 mail contract along with it . . . this was a lovely enticement indeed to Mr. Terry's acquisitive instincts. The "Major Tomkins" was brought in by a couple of other fellows, but fell into the hands of Captain Terry—I think he liked the thought of being called "Captain". But the "Major" ended her career up against a rocky beach off Victoria—happily without loss of life.

Charlie also had an interest in the third little steamship on the Sound. The "Water Lily" was a forty-nine-footer used to haul coal scows from the Black River to Seattle, but got hung up on a snag and sunk almost immediately after going to work.

Those were the ships that arrived here in 1853, '54 and '55.

They all sank. No wonder Charlie got out of the shipping business! But before he did, he formed the Puget Sound Navigation Company

. . . which died, but became the name of the biggest company in the Mosquito Fleet forty years later.

The Fraser River mining "excitement"

I don't know why, but historians always refer to the gold rush on the Fraser river in 1858 as the "Fraser River mining excitement." I suppose it came out that way because that's all it was . . . excitement.

No gold.

But it was both excitement and gold to Charlie. After the Indian War, the majority of the population on Puget Sound departed for a more peaceable clime . . . and Charlie, who usually was able to lay his hands on a couple of dimes in the interest of a good cause, picked up Bettman Brothers Mercantile Store on First Avenue South when that San Francisco outfit retreated sixty miles south to Olympia.

They say that a hundred thousand miners left San Francisco for that gold rush and headed for it by one route or another through Puget Sound. And Charlie was the only man in Seattle adequately prepared to serve them. He didn't get all the trade by any means. The estimate is that only about ten thousand of them came through Seattle.

But Charlie was on the ground floor and loaded a lot of pack trains with his merchandise . . . and if you're looking for a bit of comparison, it was just about forty years later that the Klondike gold rush headed north. The folks in Seattle got together and nailed down that gold rush as their very own. They figured that every miner who came to Seattle for his outfit was worth five hundred dollars to the merchants.

Surprisingly, from the standpoint of people on the move, the two gold rushes were the same size—a hundred thousand miners in each. Charlie was the major merchant to clip in on the first one . . . and even if only 10 per cent of them moved through Seattle that represented a nice piece of change for Charlie . . . The Fraser River gold rush swelled the little sawmill town of Whatcom, (now known as Bellingham), into a city of 10,000 almost overnight, and it marked the beginning of the end of the Indian-inspired depression in our city.

The gold rush wasn't a boon to everyone, though. It ruined a nice monopoly that had been operated by the Hudson's Bay Company. For a quarter of a century they'd had a little swapping game going with the Indians ...

They had been giving one ounce of lead for one ounce of gold.

The President of the Board

Charlie's second political venture came ten years after he served in the Legislature. It arose out of the inspired idea that there might be a few bucks in it for him and some of the other men if they could put together a real town. They applied for a charter from a legislature that had no right to grant one, and one was granted. In January, 1865, five Town Trustees were named to hold office, with Terry as president of the group until an election could be held in April. These same people were elected although there were some hard feelings and charges that the election of Terry was illegal. David Denny also was a trustee, as was Henry Yesler. The trustees began by levying a tax which raised $620.65 and a swarm of objections from the taxpayers who hadn't been saddled with this kind of thing before. They built a jail for $698 on land leased from Yesler under circumstances that caused legal problems for the next eighteen years. The second year Terry was president again and the trustees were really getting the hang of the thing. Bear in mind that it was not uncommon in those days to use public office for private gain.

This old custom has been revived from time to time in the course of Seattle's history, but is frowned upon by the courts.

In their second year, the trustees established a system of grades for the streets. This enabled the public to help increase the value of the land the trustees held and gave the taxpayers the opportunity to pay for clearing stumps out of the trustees' streets and installing some boardwalks.

Then Terry and Yesler got themselves a splendid new idea. They figured out a use for the small trees that were then a drug on the market. These were the ones that were too thin to be pilings and wouldn't produce enough two-by-fours to be worthwhile. They cut the logs into eight foot sections, bored two inch holes lengthwise through the centers, hooked them together and *voila!* a water system for the people.

While they were in the midst of laying thousands of feet of pipe which would connect with the springs on First Hill, someone pointed out that this was an illegal operation. So Terry and Yesler just took a run down to see the Legislature and came back with exclusive rights to bring water into the city, to lay the pipe where needed and to charge for the water.

Some seventy of these original pipes, still in excellent condition, were uncovered in 1964 when the North-South Freeway was cut across the face of First Hill.

Another "exclusive" that Terry and a partner picked up was stocking Lake Washington and Lake Union with eastern shad and alewives and doing all the catching and curing of them for the next thirty years.

How anybody else would fish in the two lakes without running into the danger of catching Terry's shad and alewives was not determined so, in effect, they gave themselves the exclusive fishing rights in these two bodies of water. They never got around to taking advantage of this franchise, but it shows they were thinking profit every minute.

The more conservative elements in town like Arthur Denny were some distressed at what a few narrow-minded folks called outrageous procedures, so they attempted to oust Charlie from the board. They knew that Henry was too unimaginative to come up with all of these outlandish ideas, so they concentrated on Charlie.

But Charlie was far too popular with the populace to be removed. They realized they'd have to resort to more definitive measures to get rid of him and Yesler, so they went to Olympia and had the town disincorporated.

A little drastic, but it did the trick . . .

And they didn't reincorporate until after Charlie was dead.

It's not the gift . . . it's the sentiment

Charlie, however, really didn't spend all his time figuring out how he could "take" his city. In a spirit of vast magnanimity, Terry and his friend Ed Lander gave an acre and two-thirds of their land toward the ten-acre site for the first University of Washington campus. It is because of this contribution that we have a Terry Hall and a Lander Hall today at the University.

While the contributions of the two men is not to be discounted—today it provides the University with an annual income of some $3,000,000—the gift was still indicative of their general attitude that parting is such sweet sorrow, if it means separating a man from actual or potential money. The land had accrued in value two or three times in the half decade since they had made their purchase, but it is unlikely the gift caused them financial consternation.

They had paid $5 for it.

The saga closes

There's some pathos in the end of the saga of C. C. Terry. Not merely because the ambitious and lively man died at the early age of thirty-seven, but he knew well in advance that the end was coming. He made out his will two months before his death. He was suffering from tuberculosis, which they called "consumption" at the time, and two brothers before him had already died of the same disease . . . the adventurous Lee Terry, and Alfred, who later had come out to Seattle for a while.

It is not unlikely that all three contracted their illness here, for no effective inroads were made against this disease in Seattle until 1908 when the U.S. Public Health Service notified the town that Seattle had the worst record in the country for this disease.

The day after Charlie died a little girl was born to Mrs. Terry.

It is ironic that seventy-five years after Terry's death, the county created a tuberculosis sanatorium at what is now 10440 Marginal Way South.

The building was Charlie's home on the Onion Farm.

An epitaph for Charlie

I've been reading strange writing on the big pylon that allegedly marks Seattle's birthplace out there at Sixty-Third Avenue Southwest and Alki Avenue, which is obviously something nobody has done for years.

The kids have marked it with crayons and the seagulls have considered it an excellent target for some time, but outside of that it really hasn't had much attention. The pylon and its satellites, a lead capsule and a replica of the Statue of Liberty, designate the wrong time and the wrong place for the birth of Seattle, but I wouldn't want to hurt the feelings of the people in West Seattle who really feel they're left out of the city most of the time anyway. And I wouldn't want to interfere with economic affairs of the tour buses, which do provide splendid outlooks on the city both coming and going to our "birthplace."

On the other hand, the messages on and around the pylon have changed from time to time as the spirit moved the people to do so . . . and it seems like a good time to make another change, the year of this writing being the hundredth anniversary of Charlie Terry's death.

The city celebrates November 13, 1851, as its birth date . . . not February 15, 1852 which all history books, almanacs and encyclopedias state as the actual birth date. It's a matter of timing and also the fact that we got the pylon for nothing, which quite logically is the town fathers' favorite price for anything.

But how come all this?

Well, if the citizens of the day had paused long enough to think about it when the town was platted in 1853, *they* most certainly wouldn't have noted Alki as the birthplace of Seattle. At that time they were engaged in a life and death struggle for existence with the dominant town on Elliott Bay, which was Alki.

Alki got tagged as the birthplace of Seattle by sort of an alumni meeting of a half dozen surviving pioneers thirty years after the city got started. A vote was cast for the people who qualified as the original "founders" and for the proper location of the city's birthplace.

There were six members on the committee: Arthur and David Denny, William Bell, Carson Boren, Henry L. Yesler and Henry Van Asselt.

I don't know where Van Asselt got in the act. He never did have anything to do with the building of the city in the first place. For all I know, he may even have cast the deciding vote.

Well, the fellows were getting along in years. They had it made and didn't really have to worry about where their next piece of bread would come from. They took a look at that area down around First Avenue South and South Main Street where the town was really born . . .

And shuddered.

This was the living heart of the city of Seattle . . . the pulse beat that was building our place toward the top spot on Puget Sound . . . the economic center from whence came the money that bought their ties, and suits and groceries. The essence of their city. Down here was the biggest garbage dump in town . . . an enormous sawmill . . . railroad trestles . . . houses of ill fame . . . gambling joints . . . saloons . . . dance halls and above all towered the coal bunkers about seven stories high.

This is what they had done to the landscape.

Alki Point, on the other hand, had proved a financial flop. By this time it may have had a population of one. Fire and the north wind had swept away all of man's efforts at civilization. It had a lovely, clean beach with an inspiring view of the Olympic Mountains.

And suddenly the disagreeable moments of the original landing disappeared. The day they arrived seemed the most important of their lives. Wasn't it jolly about David's busted open foot . . . and the smelly Indians . . . and the gentle rain from heaven.

Alki Point got the nod.

That was twenty-seven years before Alki Point was even admitted to the city limits.

In 1905, when further nostalgia had set in, Arthur Denny's daughter, Lenora, gave the city a free pylon and the services of a guy to chisel on the words that a committee determined were apropos. You know that kind of chiseling comes to a lot of money so they cut down on letters as much as possible and came up with the following cryptic message:

> Birthplace of Seattle—New York—Alki
> at this place
> on 13 November 1851
> there landed from
> the schooner Exact,
> Captain Folger,
> the little colony which
> developed into the
> City of Seattle

They were pretty cagey about hedging their bets on that pylon by referring to Seattle—New York—Alki, although common usage since has caused it to be known as the birthplace of Seattle and all the signs leading to it read this way.

In 1926, the Automobile Club of Washington got in the act by bringing a hunk of Plymouth Rock across the country in the first motorized transcontinental caravan of antique cars (vintage, 1926). They stuck another base under the pylon and inserted their publicity pitch on that.

Then, in 1951 when all possible resemblance to the facts had mouldered away, the location was additionally dedicated to the "men and women whose vision and efforts made this city . . ."

Well now, that's carrying things too far.

How many of the men with their names chiselled in that granite really qualify for that "vision and efforts" quotation?

Here's their score as proved out by subsequent events:

Lee Terry—Left the area permanently after 6 months

John Low—Left the area permanently after 17 months

W. N. Bell—Left the area after 4 years becouse of the Indian War, but kept land and returned 14 years later when the threat to Seattle's existence was long gone

C. D. Boren—Sold out his entire claim for $1,100 a few years later, and contributed little to the development of the city

C. C. Terry—Very effective but only lived for 16 years

D. T. Denny—Stayed and worked, but went bankrupt in 1893

A. A. Denny—"Father of Seattle." Stayed and died wealthy and respected in 1899.

I'd say it's time for another change.

Let's include David Maynard and Henry Yesler who really made contributions, and Charlie Terry should qualify for top billing.

He's the only one of the bunch that served as the head man of Seattle . . . New York . . . and Alki.

III

The Bastard

Henry Yesler was a bastard . . . but I hasten to add, not merely because of the accidental circumstance of his birth. Basing it on that alone would be manifestly unfair to a lot of perfectly nice men whose conception had not previously been blessed by either Church or State. Nor was he the kind of adjective that crops up in the casual conversation of, say, a seafaring man or a logger.

Unlike the others, Henry not only was born to the title, he worked at earning it day after day and year after year with a greater degree of success over a longer period of time than anybody else.

By the time he departed from our mortal premises, he was the undisputed holder of the crown.

This may seem like an unkind approach to a fellow after whom we've named one of our streets and a branch library. It also contradicts the historical concept of Henry as an old gentleman who used to stand around whittling a stick . . . or as the so-called benign "economic father" of the city. My view of Henry—the one I learned as a kid in Seattle—has done a complete about-face since I started the research for this book.

Henry came west in 1850 from Massillon, Ohio. He began his career in Seattle by skinning Carson Boren and David S. Maynard out of their eye-teeth. He never willingly paid his just debts. He cheated his friends until he ended with none. He utilized public office for private gain. He drove more wealth out of King County than he ever brought in. The City of Seattle made him a millionaire, yet he sued it . . . fought it . . . plundered it . . . and on two occasions he brought it to the brink of bankruptcy.

Outside of that I suppose he was a real nice fella.

What made Henry run?

Henry was born out of wedlock in Hagerstown, Maryland, on December 2, 1810. His parents probably didn't contribute much to his sense of security by attempting marriage after his birth and finding that the fact of his existence was insufficient cement to hold them together. They re-married other people, started other families and left Henry to pretty much shift for himself.

In addition to their contribution to his illegitimacy, his parents gave him a heritage of ignorance. He had no appreciation of the arts. He was tone-deaf. He had no comprehension of literature, was almost totally lacking in self-expression through the written word and murdered the King's English when he spoke. Religion was too abstract for him and he never became a member of any church. The "here" was everything to him. The "hereafter" meant nothing. He was an ignorant, amoral man and he had an overabundance of cupidity and acquisitiveness without any tempering judgment to go with them.

Had he been living today the law would have caught up with him early in the game, but in his time and his place the rules were just right for a tough little nut with no social conscience.

The King County Court records show that Henry was a phenomenon even in those days. For example, the file on Arthur Denny, who might be considered an above average litigant, is less than six inches thick.

The lawsuits instituted on behalf of or against Henry Yesler—and many of them were no more than one page—occupy three full packing boxes.

The sums named in the lawsuits against Henry ranged from fifteen dollars by a widow who desperately needed the money to thousands of dollars sought by the city, county, state or some of his business contemporaries. He never paid judgments found against him until the sheriff moved in and started carting away furniture. On the other hand, at the drop of a legal technicality, Henry rushed into court with lawsuits up to and including $156,000.

He was a bastard above and beyond the call of duty.

Why?

I think that in addition to his poor beginnings something happened to him in Massillon that not only caused him to come west in the first place but resulted in a life-long philosophy of not respecting himself or anybody else—only money.

Unlike most of the men in his day who married at an early age, Henry was not married until he was twenty-nine years old. There is every reason to assume he had reached a comfortable financial position in 1839 before he married Sarah Burgert, who was seventeen. A clue to his financial capabilities came recently from the curator of the Massillon Museum who pointed out that in 1842, the contracting firm of Yesler and Scherer was the low bidder on constructing the main building of a farm for training orphan boys and girls, a major building contract. He also had sufficient credit so that later on he was able to borrow $30,000 to build his mill in Seattle. That easily would amount to a line of credit in six figures in today's dollars.

In the historic westward movement in the United States, it is rare that you find men of Henry's age with such a sound financial position taking on the arduous efforts of the frontier. Henry was forty-two years old when he arrived in Seattle. And while Maynard was two years older, he had ample reason from both a marital and financial standpoint to try something new. The average age of the other founders of Seattle, as had been pointed out, was twenty six years.

So what motivated Henry to leave Massillon?

The same thing that motivated Henry throughout his life—a desire to make money. That, and a little-known fact about Henry's private life that was hard for a man of his ignorant and insensitive nature to cope with.

A son, Henry Leiter Yesler, Jr., was born to the Yeslers in 1846, seven years after their marriage. He was their first-born. He was only six years old when Henry went west.

I find no record which would indicate he ever saw that child again.

Mrs. Yesler stayed in Massillon for seven years after Henry had left. Yet when she departed for Seattle in 1857 the boy did not accompany her. It is inconceivable to me that both parents would have aban-

doned that child without a compelling reason—the rumor in Seattle
that the Yeslers had a boy who was not "quite right" may have been
that compelling reason. He was left in the care of an Edith B. Wilson.

The record shows further that the boy died at the age of thirteen in
June of 1859 and was buried in a family plot purchased by Henry as
one of his last acts in Massillon. In 1889 Yesler transferred the cemetery plot to an E. B. Wilson.

Henry Yesler & the Good Humor Men

Henry wandered the west for a bitter and frustrating two years looking for a place that would stop the itching in his feet. He had the
necessary financial backing from a Massillon capitalist, John E.
McLain, to start a steam sawmill once he had isolated the perfect location for such a structure. Steam sawmills were scarce as top hats in
a land where lumber was king, but Henry rejected locations right
and left until a sea captain painted a beautiful verbal portrait of
Puget Sound which brought Henry to the area sometime in October,
1852.

In his memoirs, Yesler said he met the captain in California shortly
after the latter had brought in a ship load of piling from Seattle. We
owe Henry's arrival here to the fact that the captain—whose name
does not appear anywhere—was an inquisitive man. It took about
three weeks to cut and load a cargo of piling and the captain spent
this time exploring the area in and around Elliott Bay.

His conclusions were the same general ones that have built Seattle as
the metropolis ever since. The location was in the center of the
Sound on the north-south axis. There was plenty of timber immediately adjacent to an excellent, well-protected deep harbor. There
was a hinterland of a thousand acres or more to feed a future city.
The captain even went into such details as the fact that there were
two warring communities in an area too small to permit two towns.
It was the captain's correct diagnosis that the north wind—which no
pier could withstand—would destroy Alki's hopes of survival as a
town. It is reasonable to assume that the captain also provided
Henry with a rundown on the personalities involved in the two

communities, including Doc Maynard, at that time the leading pro-
motor of Seattle. But even if he didn't, Maynard's open, free-handed
personality would be a quick reading for Henry's beady little eyes.

And Maynard clearly was the key to the door.

Henry approached the little settlement called Seattle with all of the
warm-hearted enthusiasm of an adding machine.

When he arrived on the beach of Elliott Bay, he looked unprepossessing enough—a dumpy little man with stooped shoulders and a
big beard. According to the legend he was whittling a piece of driftwood when Maynard descended on him like a friendly spaniel.
Henry said in his memoirs, written a quarter of a century later, that
"New York was a bad place for a mill, the place being exposed to the
wind blowing vessels ashore . . ."

He also said he had never even stopped at Alki, but led the Seattle
people to believe he had. As a further club in his negotiations he
had gone to the trouble of staking a claim south of their community
on the Duwamish River. He knew long before he even arrived on
Puget Sound that Seattle was the location he wanted. The business
about locating the mill at Alki or on the Duwamish was window-
dressing. Yesler was angling for as much prime land as he could get
thrown in with the deal for the mill.

Maynard had spent as much time covering the coast as Yesler. He
was acutely aware of what the existence of a steam sawmill would do
for the community. Boren, who was the second element involved in
Henry's decision to locate here, simply couldn't care less one way or
the other. He wasn't interested in building a city. He wasn't concerned with getting rich. According to the standards of the day, he
was a real nut.

Maynard took charge of selling Seattle to a "reluctant" Yesler. He
repeated the arguments Yesler had already heard from the ship captain and added that the people were honest, kind, thrifty, reverent,
hard-working—and generous.

Generous . . . that was the word!

How generous?

Well, what land would Mr. Yesler like?

Mr. Yesler would like the point of land at what is now First Avenue at Yesler Way. He would like a swath out of Maynard's and Boren's donation claims 450 feet wide leading up the hill to a box of land about ten blocks square and loaded with lovely timber. It was located between what are now 20th and 30th Avenues. He also would like to have the townfolk build a structure to house his mill machinery. The land he sought represented an ideal location for a mill. Outside of Denny's Little Island—at that time occupied by Maynard —it was the only level spot on the landscape. Behind it were bluffs which readily lent themselves to skidding logs. A nearby stream and springs in the hill provided fresh water. Just a few yards off shore the water was deep enough for ocean-going vessels.

New Year's Eve, 1852, was a big night for Doc Maynard. He had given Yesler the north 125 feet of the land that Denny had given him from Boren's claim. Boren had given Yesler the south 325 feet of his claim.

Yesler had been talked into the deal.

In Maynard's mind he had out-foxed Yesler . . . and for the exchange of a tiny bit of ground he had obtained a steam sawmill for Seattle.

Maynard died broke . . . but that little piece of land turned out to be worth over a million dollars to Yesler.

Seattle's economic father

Henry derived his title as the city's economic father because of his mill. It was a vital adjunct to the community because it gave Seattle its first leg up on the rest of the communities on the Sound. Because he happened to be helpful at that particular moment his subsequent activities which were contrary to the best interests of Seattle either were ignored by historians or twisted to indicate they were helpful to the town.

For the next three years or so, the rest of the communities on the Sound were in approximately the same position as our pioneers had been the year before the mill was established. It took them three weeks or a month to load a ship with about a thousand dollars worth of piles and timber.

Beginning in March, 1853, Henry's mill brought that much money into the community about three times a week. He got $35 a thousand feet for lumber.

He increased the economic value of timber to Seattle more than 900 per cent over that of timber to surrounding communities.

And what was more important, a ship could get loaded in a matter of a few days instead of a few weeks. Overnight, ships calling on Puget Sound ports preferred Seattle . . . they could make money faster.

It was a natural and accepted fact that Henry made more profit out of those cargoes than anybody else. So at the right time, he had a little extra cash and one of the brightest ideas of his entire career. He built the town's first public building. It brought him more profit and prestige than anything else he ever did in his life.

We know it as Yesler's cook house, the most famous building in early Seattle history. It did more to "set" the heart of the city in the middle of Yesler's property holdings than anything else Henry did. Henry never did make a lot of money out of his mill. It was the stretegic location of his land that made him a millionaire. Everything else in the city grew from around the cook house—and that made his land valuable.

If it had been Doc Maynard or one of the other fellows who built the cook house I would have accepted the idea that he had done it for the public good and let it go at that. But with my new-found concept of Henry, I checked into his motive for building the cook house in the first place and of course found it was economic rather than altruistic.

In his memoirs he points out he did it because hunger would get men to the cook house and food could be served soon enough to get them to work on time. "All must be prompt at the mill," he wrote, "at the tap of the bell. This is why all were required to eat at the cook house . . ."

Naturally, Henry made a tidy profit on each meal sold. He also made a profit leasing the building for public meetings and as a courthouse.

An obituary to an old cook house

It has occurred to me what a valuable piece of memorabilia the existence of Yesler's cook house would be in Seattle today . . . what a money-making tourist attraction, like some of those historic old structures that have been preserved in other cities around the nation.

It also seems to me that the overtones about historic old buildings which appeared in the *Puget Sound Dispatch* on July 30, 1866 when the cook house was torn down have equal application to some of the buildings which are facing destruction in the name of "progress" today.

So here's the verbatim "obituary" to Henry Yesler's cook house:

> It was with feelings akin to these that its proprietor and some of our oldest settlers last week witnessed the demolition of the old cook house of H. L .Yesler, in this town. There was nothing about this old cook house very peculiar, except the interest with which old memories had invested it. It was simply a dingy-looking hewed-log building, about twenty five feet square, a little more than one story high, with a shed addition in the rear, and to strangers and new-comers was rather an eye-sore and nuisance in the place—standing as it did in the business part of the town, among the more pretentious buildings of modern construction, like a quaint octogenarian, among a band of dandyish sprigs of young America. To the old settlers, however, its weather-worn roof and smoke-blackened walls, inside and out, were vastly interesting from long familiarity, and many pleasant and perhaps a few unpleasant recollections were connected with its early history, which we might make subjects of a small volume of great interest had we time to indite it. Suffice it to say, however, that this old cook house was one among the first buildings erected in Seattle; was built for the use of the sawmill many years since, and though designed especially for a cook house, has been used

for almost every conceivable purpose for which a log cabin, in a new and wild country, may be employed.

For many years the only place 100 miles or more along the eastern shores of Puget sound, where the pioneer settlers could be hospitably entertained by white men and get a square meal, was Yesler's cook house in Seattle, and whether he had money or not, no man ever found the latchstring of the cook house drawn in or went away hungry from the little cabin door; and many an old Puget Sounder remembers the happy hours, jolly nights, strange encounters and wild scenes he has enjoyed around the fireplace and hospitable board of Yesler's cook house.

During the Indian War this building was the general rendezvous of the volunteers engaged in defending the thinly populated country against the depredations of the savages, and was also the resort of the navy officers on the same duty on the Sound. Judge Lander's office was held in one corner of the dining room; the auditor's office, for some time, was kept under the same roof, and indeed it may be said to have been used for more purposes than any other building on the Pacific Coast. It was the general depository from which law and justice were dispensed throughout a large scope of surrounding country.

It has, at different times, served for town hall, court house, jail, military headquarters, storehouse, hotel and church; and in the early years of its history served all these purposes at once It was the place of holding elections, and political parties of all sorts held their meetings in it, and quarrelled and made friends again, and ate, drank, laughed, sung, wept, and slept under the same hospitable roof. If there was to be a public gathering of the settlers of any kind and for any purpose, no one ever asked where the place of meeting was to be, for all knew it was to be at the cook house.

The first sermon ever preached in King County was preached by the Rev. Mr. Close in the old cook house. The first lawsuit—which was the trial of the mate of "The Franklin Adams," for selling ship's stores and appropriating the proceeds—came off, of course, in the old cook house. Justice Maynard presided at this trial, and the accused was discharged from the old cook house with the wholesome advice that in the future he should be careful to make a correct return of all his private sales of other people's property.

Who, then, knowing the full history of this famous old relic of early times, can wonder that it has so long been suffered to stand and moulder, unused, in the midst of the more gaudy surroundings of a later civilization? And who can think it strange, when, at last, its old smokey walls were compelled to yield to the pressure of progression, and be tumbled heedlessly into the street, that the old settler looked sorrowfully upon the vandalish destruction, and silently dropped a tear over its levelled ruins. Peace to the ashes of the old cook house.

The cook house was thirteen years old at the time the story of its demise was written . . . an indication of the rapidity with which the town had grown in that period.

Yesler had such noteworthy success with the cook house that when he tore it down, he built the city's second public building, Yesler's Hall, at the southwest corner of First Avenue South and Yesler Way . . . and the city's third public building—Yesler's Pavilion—on the southeast corner of First Avenue and Cherry Street, which was used for public purposes until 1887.

That stupid Indian War

When it came to the Indian War, Yesler viewed it as pointless, an unnecessary interruption, an added cost of doing business and believed it was the result of sheer stupidity on the part of the white people. "I had no trouble with them (Indians)," he pointed out in his memoirs, "but was able to influence them easily. They will quarrel among themselves and if they kill one another, they settle the difficulty by paying blankets. An Indian killed his wife—then instead of leaving the Indians to settle the matter in their own way, the white men hung the Indian, and then the Indians killed two or three white men in revenge . . ."

Henry was immensely practical about the whole affair. He employed Indians in his mill and as an adjunct to his normal business operation he had Chief Seattle as a stool pigeon among the Indian tribes. When he was satisfied the town was going to be attacked, he off-loaded some San Francisco-bound timbers from a ship and gave them to the folks so they could build a blockhouse and a barricade to the mud flats a quarter of a mile away. Thus his mill wouldn't be damaged while the Indians and the townsfolk settled their differences.

When the attack was over the white people were yowling for hanging some of the Indians as criminals and murderers. Henry couldn't afford to lose any good mill workers, so he agreed to round them all up for the whites and was able to do so through Chief Seattle and by promising them nobody would get hung.

It was the first time in Seattle that justice was tempered in the interests of economics.

Yesler reported in his memoirs the Indians told him who the guilty ones were but he didn't mention this at the trials. A little perjury didn't bother Henry if it was good for business. "I was always their friend," Henry reports. "They thought I would do what I could for them. At the trial all were cleared ..."

Having the confidence of both the whites and the Indians, Henry went back to normal mill operation after a one-day interruption for the hostilities. So Henry was out one day's operation and a shipload of lumber.

For this he has been named one of the great heroes of Seattle's Indian War.

Yesler's mill?

My last brain-washed belief in the cotton candy version of Seattle's history got blasted while browsing around the back room of the county clerk's office. Among the yellowing, musty files on Seattle's so-called economic father there were clues that led to information that finally smashed the rose-colored glasses through which I had been taught to view Henry. We native school children are taught that Yesler and his operations were as pure as the water in Cedar River.

It's part of the code.

The code reveres the mill as the critical major industry of the city's beginning. It reveres Henry as the kindly, selfless old man that generously provided us with that mill. It was Henry who put the bread and butter in the lunch buckets of the little children who tromped off to school . . . after milking the cow at 4 a.m. and filling the wood boxes and doing the other chores that made our hardy forefathers hard—and not soft like today's children with their wheels and motors and regular weekly allowances.

"My" Henry does not pass the code . . . but he sure qualifies as one of the Sons of the Profits. Here's the real story on the birth of Yesler's mill and the man who put up the money.

Albert E. Hise, the curator of the Massillon Museum, talked with the grand-daughter of one John E. McLain at our request during the research for this book and we learned for the first time that Henry had a silent partner in the mill.

At least he was silent for a while.

It was McLain that put up the $30,000 that built the mill in the first place, and the folks in Massillon would like it to be known that the interest rate was only 8 per cent, contrary to Henry, who evidently hinted it was about twice that. We turn to the courthouse records here and find that although Henry was making money hand over fist in Seattle, he neglected the little detail of repaying his loan to McLain. The latter had to make several trips to Seattle to collect that dough . . . and evidently with sufficient pressure was able to pick up some of it.

Finally, McLain got tired of Henry's stalling. In the early 1860's, he hauled Henry before a King County Superior Court judge for a discussion of their mutual financial agreements—and collected the $18,000 balance that Henry owed him on the mill. As far as the record reveals, that was the first of the many friendships Henry had that broke up on the rocks of a courtroom lawsuit.

So, *you* can continue to call it Henry Yesler's mill if you like.

But to me from here on out, it's going to be John McLain's mill.

The man and the monkey business

It's little bits of information like that cited above which lead me to view Henry's life with a cold reportorial eye, and I find myself including material about Henry I might otherwise exclude. But when every other rock you overturn reveals black bugs you feel you might as well make the complete case.

We've noted that the first widespread and clearcut disenchantment with Henry on the part of his fellow citizens came in 1867. That was when they had the town dis-incorporated to force Yesler and Terry to quit their free-wheeling financial dealings as Town Trustees.

The dis-incorporation lasted for a couple of years and Seattle was operated by the County Commissioners until 1869 when the local folk petitioned the Legislature for and were granted an incorporation again.

But Henry'd had a taste of honey and he got himself a job as County Commissioner, an office in which he served from January 4, 1875 until December 20, 1876. Yesler's mill was under lease to J. M. Colman at the time, so Yesler had plenty of time for monkey business. And he went about utilizing his public office for private gain on such a grand scale they finally called in a grand jury to figure out what he was doing.

What he was "doing" was the public . . .

First through a lottery that initiated a crime wave that was to result in Seattle's only lynching and then through a couple of real estate transactions that have resounded through the halls of history ever since.

The grand lottery

On November 12, 1875, five weeks before Henry became a County Commissioner, the Legislature authorized the County Commissioners to issue licenses to responsible persons for the purpose of conducting lotteries that would raise money to construct a road across Snoqualmie Pass. The road was to be part of a wagon road between Seattle and Walla Walla.

It was after the first of the year before they got around to issuing any licenses and it is not surprising to find out that the first license was issued by the County Commissioners to County Commissioner Henry L. Yesler. After all, he'd been the one who lobbied the bill through the Legislature.

Yesler proceeded to put together "The First Grand Lottery of Washington Territory." Thousands of circulars describing the event were printed and sent all over the territory with tickets costing five dollars each. Huge advertisements were placed in the newspapers for months. The top prize was Henry's own mill, valued at $100,000 . . . and his wharf, with income from rentals totalling seven hundred dollars a month.

The drawing was to take place July 4, 1876.

There were those who thought that Henry had gone out of his cotton-pickin' mind. But he dropped everything to push his project because some other interlopers had taken advantage of the law and were conducting their own lotteries, although theirs didn't amount to much with the top prize of the whole bunch being a mere $20,000.

The theory was that 10 per cent of all the money taken in would be turned over to a group of trustees appointed by the County Commissioners. These trustees, in turn, were to hand the dough to the County Treasurer. Henry's advertising said, "No scheme of this kind ever offered to the public presents such inducements to try for a fortune. The general public can invest with the greatest confidence, the distribution being authorized by law and guarded in every particular. Nothing of the kind can be fairer for all concerned."

Some suspicion began to attach itself to the project after several months of enthusiastic notices that tickets were selling like hotcakes —because no money was being turned in for building the Snoqualmie road.

The parties conducting the lotteries were haled into court by a

group of low-minded people who figured something was fishy. The
court held that the lotteries were illegal and the men conducting
them should be prosecuted.

Attorney W. H. White was employed to present the cases before Supreme Court Justice J. R. Lewis who fined six out of the eight men
brought before him $25 apiece . . . handed the seventh a fine of $150
and the eighth a sentence of fifty-three days in jail. Nobody knows
how many thousands of dollars were milked out of the public with
the lotteries . . . although it was obvious that Henry got the lion's
share. No money ever was turned over to the county for the construction of the Snoqualmie Pass Road.

And what happened to Henry? I find no record that shows Henry
was in any way punished, and he didn't lose his mill.

The Osborne Legacy

For nearly half a century, the Osborne Legacy was one of the great
mysteries of Seattle history, and until this date the whole story had
never been put together in one neat package showing how back in
1878 Henry Yesler made it possible for a minor mite on the sands of
time to become a major contributor to one of our city's finest buildings today.

One of the criticisms voiced by the grand jury that was called in
1876 to study the efforts of the County Commissioners concerned a
small matter involving the granting of licenses to sell liquors and
conduct lotteries, which the jury scathingly opined were granted in
a "loose, wholesale and indiscriminate manner . . . it being possible
for any individual or corporation to obtain any kind of a license at
any time for any place . . ."

Henry felt the jury was woefully lacking in an understanding of the
impact that the granting of such licenses had on the real estate of the
community. For example, whether it was legal or not, Henry issued
one particular liquor license (to his own great benefit) that this city
certainly cannot complain about even today. It was to a James Osborne, who wished to operate a saloon on a piece of the property
Maynard had so eagerly given Henry for his mill.

The lot was twenty four feet wide on the street and at Henry's price of four hundred and fifty dollars per square foot, it represented the stiffest asking price for property in Seattle to that date. It also represented a Yesler kind of leverage.

It wasn't until Osborne agreed to cough up the steep amount to property-owner Yesler that he would get the all-important liquor license from County Commissioner Yesler.

This little transaction completed, Mr. Osborne erected on this location an establishment known as the Gem Saloon. From his obituary we learn that "He maintained a reputable saloon patronized by the best citizens of the type that patronized saloons." But that wasn't the total impact of James Osborne on Seattle's history by any means.

To begin with, Osborne had the strongest will in King County history to that time.

The will specified, for one thing, that his brother-in-law—who had thrown him out of the house once—was not to get "one thin dime." It also stated flatly that he forbade anyone to take his body into—or even *near*—any church and there were to be *no* religious ceremonies conducted at the funeral.

Instead he asked that the funeral be held at Yesler's Pavilion, that a competent brass band be employed to liven up the occasion, and that a good free-thinker like Judge I. R. W. Hall be paid one hundred dollars for the oration . . . and failing Judge Hall, that "either Thomas Burke or W. H. White will do." The services were to end with burial in Lakeview Cemetery by the Ancient Order of United Workmen.

The will then proceeded to give instructions about disposing of some city lots here and there, after which the executors of the estate were to offer the balance of his estate to the city—with the condition that the city would match the sum and construct a public building with the money. That must have made the eyeballs of the administrators bulge.

The balance of the estate totalled $22,380.88; the total income of the city that year—about $18,000.

Seattle couldn't possibly match the bequest.

The long and short of it was that just about every Osborne in the
United States tried to lay claim to that money along with the federal, state and county governments. But the city was able to hang onto
it against all comers until 1927 when the estate had reached an accumulated total of over $120,000.

At that time the voters passed a bond issue that matched the Osborne Legacy and the total sum was used to build the Civic Audi-
torium . . . which as we all know has since been transformed into
Seattle's luxurious Opera House.

So that we can truthfully tell you that the "father" of our Opera
House was an atheistic saloon keeper from the Skid Road.

Lead us not into temptation

Across the street from the Frye Hotel at Third Avenue and Yesler
Way there is a pleasant little triangular park where the weary way-
farer may rest his bones while he's waiting for a bus. The little triangle, which runs about thirty feet to the side, is dedicated to Father F.
X. Prefontaine, the first Roman Catholic priest to minister to the
needs of his people. In the fall of 1867, it was the location of his
home and his chapel. The land was a piece of the corridor that
Boren had "gladly" given Henry Yesler when the latter first arrived.

We think it is fitting and proper that this piece of land be dedicated
to a man who did much for the spiritual needs of our city during an
early and trying period of our existence. On the other hand we believe that situated as it is—in full view of our elected representatives in the county courthouse—that this hallowed ground should be
viewed with an even deeper spiritual significance.

Our elected officials will want to remember it together with the
phrase, "Lead us not into temptation . . . but deliver us from evil—
or the law will clobber you." For it was with that very same piece of
property that Henry Yesler taught the people of the County of King
a well-remembered lesson.

For Henry demonstrated what may occur if you have a crooked politician in office and no law to punish him if he happens to walk a
crooked mile. Although he annoyed the members of that rather

stuffy grand jury to pieces, he did provide the county government with the motivation to create a law or two. . .like it no longer is legal for an elected country official to do business with the county as a private citizen.

It came to pass in 1872 that the Legislature agreed that King County was in need of a stout jail. So that body authorized the county to set aside certain sums from license fees and hold them until the amount reached $12,000.

To the best of my knowledge, it was the first lay-away program ever instituted in the area.

The Legislature also specified that no more than $12,000 could be spent on the entire project.

By the time Arthur Denny and other appointees had dutifully accumulated the money for the new jail it was 1876. Henry was chairman of the King County Board of Commissioners and Father Prefontaine had moved on to the greater financial rewards of a fine new location.

This left Henry with a piece of real estate on his hands, and it took him no time at all to decide that this was the very jail site that he and his fellow commissioners should buy.

He graciously made it easy for the county to purchase this excellent $500 piece of property for $3,500.

Henry and the commissioners then proceeded to spend an additional $12,500 to construct the desired jail, airily exceeding the Legislature's budget specification by $4,000 . . . an expenditure that upset the Legislature and caused the call of the grand jury in 1876.

The grand jury was not impressed by the activities of the commissioners. They said the commissioners had obtained a piece of property without also getting the title to it . . . that the price of $12,000 for the whole deal had been illegally exceeded . . . that the jail would be "a safe place for keeping prisoners only by first securing them with irons."

Well now, this did create a stir.

One of the commissioners (not Henry) resigned. The county stopped paying on the purchase of the new public structure. Henry did what any other self-respecting property owner would have done—he repossessed the property and turned the jail into an office building which was rented to somebody who would pay their just debts.

And ever since that time, the folks have been a bit difficult about requiring the county to obtain clear title before erecting structures on a piece of land. You see, Henry not only sold the county that little plot for $3,500 . . . he sold them the plot when it was all tied up in a mortgage for money Henry had borrowed.

And how much was the mortgage?

Just $21,657.62!

Well, Ah'll be hanged!

January 18, 1882 was just about the finest day Henry ever had in his whole, entire life. He got his picture and a nice quote in a national magazine . . . a quote that was Henry's first, last and only recorded joke. There was a lot of excitement in town and he was the only leading citizen who took part in the action. And he had a memento of the occasion that he kept for seven years.

January 18 was the day a mob, with an assist from Henry, lynched three suspected murderers.

The folks did Henry the honor of staging the lynching in his own yard. Henry hadn't seen a lynching since he had observed the vigilantes in action thirty years before in San Francisco and he felt it was high time Seattle started measuring up to the forthright action in the big Bay City.

The thought never entered his mind that six years before he had planted the seed that finally erupted in this violent action. Historian Thomas Prosch reports that with the advent of Henry's lottery in 1876 there descended upon Seattle the nearest thing to what would be called a bunch of gangsters today. They were hot to get into the lottery business along with Henry, but their presence also served to awaken public consciousness of the lawless elements in town. And for the next six years there was a growing conflict between the law-less and lawful elements.

Judge Lewis was a handy man with the gavel and heavy on the sentences but the assassination of President James A. Garfield in July, 1881 and the fatal shooting of a policeman in Seattle in September had created an underlying hysteria in the community.

It was sparked into mob action on January 17, 1882 when a grocery clerk enroute home from work was shot, killed and robbed. A mob was summoned by three slow and ominous taps on the fire bell.

Two characters were found hiding among bales of hay in the Harrington and Smith Wharf. One of them had a pistol from which a ball had been discharged. They were turned over to Sheriff Wyckoff who produced them in court in Yesler's Pavilion. In the meantime the mob had ascertained that the pistol ball in the victim's body was made by the company which had manufactured the other balls in the pistol. One of the men's shoes fitted a footprint in the mud near the scene of the crime, which the amateur detectives felt was conclusive proof he had committed the crime.

The mob reconvened the next morning before the two suspects appeared in the Justice Court. A scantling from Yesler's mill was stuck between the crotch of two maple trees in the civic leader's side yard. The point of progression is of importance in that the apparatus for a hanging was erected and the mob had collected before the prisoners were bound over by the Justice of the Peace to Superior Court for trial.

The mob immediately overpowered the officers of the law and hauled the two men to the next corner for the ceremony. Judge Roger Greene attempted to cut the men down after they had been strung up, but was pulled back and hauled away.

In its enthusiasm, the mob then decided to string up the man who was being held in jail half a block away on a charge of having killed the policeman. Sheriff Wyckoff died two days later of a heart attack presumed to have been brought on by his efforts to restrain the mob.

We had four deaths on our civic conscience as a result of illegal action.

It dawned on the folks that the lynchings didn't exactly portray the image the city had been seeking to project about itself to the rest of the world . . . that it was sort of the Boston of the Pacific Northwest and the cowboys and Indians didn't periodically ride into town and shoot the place up. A grand jury, summoned to investigate, quashed things as best it could by stating that the three men were probably guilty anyway and the lynchings saved the state a lot of money.

Perhaps the most interesting of the city's efforts to expunge the triple hanging from its record came with the ingenious wording about the action as it remains today in the official files of the health department.

The cause of death of the three men is listed as: "Irate citizens."

Henry kept the hanging apparatus in his side yard for seven years as a memento of the occasion . . . and when it was stolen shortly before the fire of 1889 he irately presumed it had been taken by them danged University kids.

His Sunday punch, however, came in *Harper's Weekly* which did a featured and illustrated article on the lynchings. Yesler, former auditor, mayor, and county commissioner, was the only identifiable man in the picture. He was standing there whittling. And his quote had the greatest impact in the story.

He said, "That was the first fruit them trees ever bore, but it was the finest."

He who laughs last—laughs last

Was retribution ever visited upon this bastard? Did the wheels of justice which grind so slowly but so fine ever catch him up on their machinery? Did this outstanding example of the Sons of the Profits die in ignominy and shame?

Well, let's see.

By 1883, with an assessed valuation of his land at $318,000, he was clearly the richest man in town . . . beating out his nearest competitor for that honor, Arthur A. Denny, by about $75,000.

In 1886, he had no personal friends among the rest of the "Sons"—most of whom he had euchred out of a lot of money one way or another. But they represented a minority group and the grateful folk of the city elected him mayor again.

But by that time, senility had begun to set in and Henry became a sucker for any promoter that came down the pike. This proved to be an entirely distressing situation to J. D. Lowman, the son of Henry's half-brother—the heir-apparent to what looked like the largest fortune in the Territory. Henry was seventy-six years old at the time, and considering his hardy constitution, it looked like he was going to live forever—or at least die in the poorhourse.

The system that was being worked on Henry was diabolically simple. He got his kicks out of low characters in the first place. For example, author Jack London was conceived in Yesler's home at First and James by the housemaid and a travelling phrenologist. A quack doctor was using Henry's residence as an office from which he delivered nostrums of no proved medical value to ignorant but critically-ill patients.

Isolated from the more reliable people of the community by his somewhat unorthodox methods of making money, Henry found himself surrounded by people with get-rich-quick schemes. He got into the habit of co-signing notes with these characters. And when they blew town, Henry got stuck with enough attachments to paper his living room.

With the aid of Jacob Furth, the town's leading banker, Lowman got himself named Henry's business manager. Lowman had Henry sign over his property to Furth who in turn signed it over to Lowman. Henry became known as a bad bet to the con artists because he didn't have any property to back up his co-signed notes. Lowman started instituting sound business management of Henry's real estate holdings in 1887 when all of Henry's holdings were mortgaged to the limit and there was virtually no cash to be had.

But Henry still had a few surprises in store for his dedicated nephew. As an opener, after the death of his wife in 1887, Henry decided he needed the biggest mansion in town. For the previous thirty years he had been perfectly satisfied living in a structure that originally had been built as a store at First and James.

But now that he was alone in the world he had to have a $50,000 house. It was erected where the county courthouse is now—a delightful monstrosity of wood that taxed the ingenuity of the best carpenters in town. He kept it populated by a collection of strange characters . . . most of whom were people he'd never met before. He had a cheerful disregard for the fact that they were there for one reason—to get his money.

But it was a continuing nuisance to Lowman who had to keep a spy or two on the premises at all times to make sure the other residents of the mansion didn't succeed in their purpose.

Lowman was protecting his own flanks at the time. He persuaded Henry to give him some buildings outright—and it was well he did because he was destined for financial troubles with the Yesler estate after the old man died. But there wouldn't even have been an estate if Lowman hadn't managed it for the last years of Henry's life.

And Henry, who figured that what Lowman didn't know wouldn't hurt him, had negotiated a most interesting transaction with a man named Gamma Poncin. From time to time, when Henry needed money he didn't want Lowman to know about, he borrowed it from Poncin. As a part of his agreement, Poncin would not heckle Henry about repayment, but would pick up the amounts owed, plus interest, from the Yesler Estate. Poncin's first receipt after Henry's death was a check for $37,540.06. Later on when the creditors of the estate had to form a corporation to prevent everything from going to the lawyers, Poncin was the biggest stockholder and was named president of the Henry Yesler Estate, Inc.

But Henry sprang an even more interesting surprise for Lowman. He sprang it in 1890 when he was eighty years old. Henry got married again. This time it was to a maid in his own home. His first wife was only twelve years younger than Henry. His second wife, Minnie Gagle, was *fifty-five* years younger than Henry.

Some of the scandal mongers in town refused to believe it was a love match.

Henry was supposed to be the richest man in town . . . and Minnie was a strong contender for being the poorest woman.

The suspicions of the suspicious became more marked when Henry died two years later and Widow Minnie was arrested after Henry's death and charged with feloniously destroying his will. Henry's attending physician, who also happened to be a resident of and have his office in Yesler's mansion,—not only was charged with the same felony, but was thrown in jail. There was some testimony at the trial that he was Minnie's boyfriend.

I don't think he was a member of the City Council at the time . . . it was a couple of years later that he got elected . . . and about twenty years later the State Supreme Court barred him from the practice of medicine.

When Henry departed for wherever he went it was at two thirty in the morning of December 16, 1892, surrounded by his new-found wife, mother-in-law, a couple of nurses, his quack doctor friend and a real doctor who had been brought in at the last moment to avoid possible questions about the exact cause of death. . .

The newspapers mentioned that strychnine may have aided him along his way, but the real doctor declared he died of natural causes —which was not unnatural at his age.

The newspapers encountered considerable difficulty digging up men among the Sons of the Profits who would make a statement that they mourned his passing. Hillory Butler, who built the tunnel for the Northern Pacific, was prominent in the Mosquito Fleet, and constructed the Butler Hotel probably expressed the most kindly opinion that could be found among the "Sons." When asked to say something about Henry's passing, he said:

"No comment."

But Yesler's was a familiar name in town. A series of "no comments" would fail to fill the amount of space needed for the obituary of a man who was so well-known.

One ingenious reporter answered the problem by printing in full, the twenty-six-year-old obituary to Henry's cook house to bulk up the obit. Within a week, a squabble that would last ten years was initiated over Henry's estate.

Not needing money where he was, Henry must have been amused.

IV

Let Lux Sit*

If the Reverend Mr. Daniel H. Bagley is not listed as the Father of the University of Washington, then we'd better stir our stumps and get his name stuck in some prominent spot . . . a job that might be taken on by the students who put green paint on the statue of George Washington out there on the campus every February 22 . . . to "Keep Washington Green."

Bagley was not a Son of the Profits, which was a sad thing, because had he been he would not have come so close to being thrown in the penitentiary. Nonetheless, he was the first one to initiate an economic system that has been perfected in the ensuing years.

He instituted our first program of federal government largesse.

Mr. Bagley was born in Pennsylvania on September 7, 1818 and ordained in the Methodist-Protestant Church in 1842. He was as "ept" in the wilds of the Pacific Northwest as the Rev. David Blaine was inept. He arrived in Salem, Oregon, in 1852 and during the next eight years was never home more than twenty days at one time.

But he got two and a half churches a year built in Washington and Oregon in those eight years, for a total of twenty churches.

Daniel was the father of Clarence, Seattle's most comprehensive historian, who had this to say about why the family came to Seattle: "During all their married life Mrs. Bagley had been an invalid, and in October, 1860, the family removed from near Salem to this place, hoping the change of climate would prove beneficial. . ."

---

* Note to grammarians: If Lux wants to Sit, let him. That's the pioneer philosophy of individualism. For non-grammarians, *Lux Sit,* meaning "Let there be light," is the motto of the University of Washington.

We should all be the kind of invalids Mrs. Bagley was.

She lived to the ripe age of ninety-four. . .

By the time the Bagleys showed up, we had developed into quite a metropolis. There were twenty families in town. The forests had been cleared back 250 yards from the waterfront.

But we've *got* a church!

Bagley arrived in town prepared to produce his twenty-first church . . . and encountered the first stunning reversal in his spectacular career.

The town fathers informed Mr. Bagley that we already had a church.

It was that little structure built by the Blaines before they left town a half decade before. You know . . . the one with the tobacco juice on the floor.

But that, Mr. Bagley explained, was a Methodist-*Episcopal* Church. He had to have a Methodist-*Protestant* Church. He produced plans of what a Methodist-Protestant Church looked like. . .

To our settlers it looked a lot like the church that had lain vacant around town for the past five years.

Bagley explained that if he didn't build a church it would ruin his record. The townsfolk were sorry about that, but in view of the shortage of money which had laid blight on the land they thought they'd look pretty ridiculous with two churches in town . . . especially when they hadn't been able to begin to fill the first one.

They told him he'd take the Methodist-Episcopal church or nothing.

Bagley was too enterprising to take a reversal like that lying down. Did the town have a university?

Well, we'd never really given that much thought.

As far as Bagley was concerned no town he planned to settle down in for the rest of his life would be without a university . . . and did they mind if he got them one? To Bagley, half a loaf was better than none, and if he couldn't erect an edifice to The Lord, he could at least put together something dedicated to higher education.

Bagley was a good promoter and he had to have something good to promote. He'd never built a university before, but he'd seen one and it didn't seem like it would present a more portentous problem than an over-sized church.

Before he was through, he wished he had stuck with churches.

The sugar plum trees

Prior to Bagley's arrival in Seattle some forces had been at work in the Legislature laying just the groundwork he needed to get his new program underway.

A lot of backing and filling had been done by the legislators of various counties over three financial plums the federal government dangled in front of the noses of the hungry settlers. They were particularly hungry in this era because the Indian uprisings, while they didn't kill many people, did serve to scare the entire population almost to death. And during the Indian trouble, nobody would risk constructing buildings that the Indians might burn down.

As far as the capitalists were concerned, it was bad enough to risk scalps; they were not about to risk something important like *money*.

Wages were running from $2.50 to $4.50 a day . . . if you were lucky enough to find a job.

One financial plum that could bring jobs and prosperity was the $30,000 appropriated by the federal government for the construction of buildings in the territorial capital. Olympia was serving as the capital—but on a somewhat tentative basis. From time to time, efforts had been made to wrest the territorial capital away from there, but the Thurston County delegates to the Legislature had always been able to muster enough strength to hang on to it.

The rest of the Legislature, however, saw to it that Olympia got no part of the $30,000 for the actual construction of buildings for the capital.

The location of the state penitentiary was another plum on which any politician kept a vigilant eye. You couldn't have penitentiaries all over the place. Building a penitentiary in a particular location would mean that money subscribed from all over the Territory would be spent in that location. It would be a highly desirable economic addition to the community. The Legislature also had kept that hope circulating around the Territory.

The third great political plum was the possibility of a university. On July 17, 1854, President Franklin Pierce had placed his signature on a bill which provided that there should be set aside for each of the Territories of Washington and Oregon, "two townships of land of thirty-six sections each, to be selected in legal subdivisions for university purposes under the direction of the legislatures of said territories respectively."

Oh, boy . . . money!

Now, let's see—two townships . . . that was 46,080 acres . . . at $1.25 an acre (that's what government land sold for), that's, let me see, that's $57,600!

There was one little problem. . .

Nobody in the Territory of Washington was qualified to attend a university. The older folks had brought whatever formal education they were going to get with them when they came, and there was too much wood to be cut for any of the younger generation to waste its time learning Latin. Everybody figured the university was something that would come in the dim and distant future along with the railroads and statehood. In the meantime it made a fine political football that could be kicked around from place to place as a demonstration of political power for the local constituencies.

Arthur Denny was serving his seventh term in the Legislature by now. But he lacked Bagley's audacity and vision. It was his theory that the city of Seattle should shoot for the university—on paper, of course—for trading purposes. Get the university allocated to Seattle, he reasoned, and then when we build up enough strength to swing it, we can swap it for enough votes in the Legislature later on to get the capital and a shot at that $30,000.

Accordingly, on January 29, 1855, five years before Bagley turned up, he introduced a bill which would locate the university in Seattle. The Big Boys in southwest Washington—where the heavy population was at that time—let him have his dream, but tacked on a little provision that there would be a branch of the university (together with one of the two townships that could be sold) at Boisfort Plains in Lewis County. It was all in good fun anyway, but just in case anybody ever got a bright idea about *really* producing a university, they wanted half.

Three years later, largely as a method of demonstrating their political muscle, the southwest Washington forces moved the right of selling both townships and construction of the university to Cowlitz Farm Prairie.

Denny got around to adding a clause that the university could be built there if someone first contributed 160 acres of land for the site . . . which, of course, nobody in his right mind would do.

The triple play

By the session of 1860-61 the southwest Washington forces figured they had enough marbles to shoot for the big agate in the middle of the ring. They went after the territorial capital and the $30,000.

The political power structure of the Territory was this: The big three, Clark, Lewis and Pacific Counties, had eight representatives. Thurston had four and Pierce three. King, Island and Jefferson Counties had one each. The Big Three had four out of the nine members in the Upper House (Council). Thurston had two. Nobody else had more than one.

By tying up with King and Jefferson counties, the Big Three counties in the southwest practically owned and operated the Legislature. The night before the session opened in December of 1860 they put together a coalition with King and Jefferson with a neat plan in mind.

Vancouver would get the capital.

Seattle would get the university.

Port Townsend would get the penitentiary.

The Big Boys had tried this the year before without any outside help, but the Thurston County delegates had destroyed the dream by pointing out that Vancouver was mightly close to Portland . . . and did the people of Washington *Territory* want the far more powerful Oregon *State* controlling the destinies of the Territory?

This time in 1860, the Big Boys didn't take any chances. They followed that important adage of politics . . . kill flies with sledge hammers.

The first day they rammed through legislation that moved the capital from Olympia to Vancouver.

They throttled debate and had the bill signed into law by the Governor before the delegates from Thurston County could catch their breath.

They passed two other bills providing Port Townsend with the paper penitentiary and Seattle with the paper university.

Daniel . . . in the lion's den

The capital was the big deal and the lions of the Legislature paid scant attention to a mild-mannered Methodist minister who honeyed around the halls looking pleasant and lobbying for some teeny-weeny changes in the bill . . . or perhaps "pleased" was a more apt description of Daniel Bagley's expression. And who cared about a couple of minor changes their good friend Arthur Denny had suggested that made the bill slightly different from the one that had been passed two years before?

Denny wanted the stipulation about a gift of 160 acres as a condition of creating the university reduced to ten acres. The Southwest Washington Boys also became broadminded about a little item they had been hot for in 1855 . . . the bill failed to mention anything about a branch of the university (carrying with it the sale of one township) at Boisfort Plains.

By this time Arthur's father, John, had given up Oregon in favor of

Washington. He had run against a Democrat for governor, but he was just two years too early for a Whig to make the grade.

Naturally, he ran for and was elected to the Territorial Legislature. Father John was, fortuitously, chairman of a committee that nobody else wanted to even serve on.

He just happened to be chairman of the Committee on Education.

On January 21, a companion university bill slipped smoothly and quietly through the Legislature and was signed into law. It provided a commission of three men to "clear and improve" a site for the university, and to sell "any and all lands."

The seemingly bumbling minister who had been hanging around the halls of fame somehow got named to the commission.

As a purely precautionary measure which nobody really felt was necessary, some "i-dotter" in the Big Three delegation provided that the expenditure for clearing the land for the site should never at any time exceed the amount of money on hand. There was no money on hand, so nothing could ever get started.

But the real protective clause was one which provided the lands could not be sold for less than $1.50 an acre.

Who in his right mind would spend $1.50 an acre for the government land, reserved for university purposes, when the government itself was selling all of its other land for $1.25?

The Big Boys wasted little time over the university. After all, moving the capital was the plum . . . and it was a *fait accompli*.

At least, it was a *fait accompli* until the final day of the legislative session when the citizens of Olympia—who had plied the legislators with liquor and their favorite delicacy, the Olympia oyster, at countless suppers—made a suggestion. On that day the kindly disposed winners agreed to an election the following summer when the people of the Territory would vote on where *they* thought the capital should be located.

Such an election would really be nothing more than a popularity contest because it would have no legal standing. This still was a Territory and that kind of an election didn't count. So it was a cinch—

southwest Washington had the capital and the privilege of spending the $30,000.

They thought.

Here beginneth the first lesson

Very shortly after the Legislature adjourned, there began to be an uneasy suspicion on the part of the Big Boys from southwest Washington that they had been had.

On Washington's Birthday, a month and a half after he had been named to the three-man commission, Bagley met with the other two commissioners in the County Auditor's office at Third and James Street (later the C. C. Terry home and today the site of the Public Safety Building) and went through the formality of having himself named chairman of the group.

And it was in this role that Bagley made history.

Don't kid yourself that those legislators were stupid when they considered the stipulation of a donated ten acre gift of land a sufficient deterrent to prevent the construction of a university in Seattle.

They figured they had it made if they had stipulated one-tenth of an acre.

Nobody in Seattle gave nobody nothin' . . . for nothing.

They reckoned without the persuasive talents by which Mr. Bagley had caused the erection of twenty churches in the west.

Since Arthur Denny was the only man in town who felt ministers should be happy in Seattle, the Reverend Mr. Bagley put the pressure on Mr. Denny about that land. He was pleasant, but persistent. One day in February, Denny caved in and told Bagley he'd go with him and see if they couldn't find the necessary ten-acre gift so the university could get going.

Denny and Bagley got out some surveying instruments and plowed around in the dense underbrush on the side of a cliff at Western Avenue and Battery Street. It was the punkest piece of property Denny could find in his claim.

Bagley placed his faith in the Lord and went smilingly along. He didn't mind the brambles or those low-flying branches that caught him in the mouth or the slick mud on the side of the mountain. This was God's green earth and he loved every inch of it.

Denny, however, was not as appreciative of the conditions. The more he worked, the madder he got.

Suddenly he threw down his surveying instruments and submitted to the power of suggestion that Bagley, as an instrument of a higher power, had been hexing him with all along.

Denny uttered these immortal words: "Bagley, I'll give the knoll!"

I certainly don't wish to take any credit away from Arthur Denny's gift to the university. On the other hand, the phrases of tribute for this generous gift have been astronomical and have made him a man of great generosity, which simply isn't true. This was the biggest piece of anything he ever gave away. It hadn't cost him anything ... and even though it was five blocks up a steep cliff through virtually impenetrable forest, he knew that if his city grew, it would become tremendously valuable.

He was a man caught between two fires: he was strongly religious— and his minister wanted that hunk of ground; he also was a Son of the Profits, who saw an immediate and enormous income to his then destitute town. The existence of the university would force the community to build roads from downtown at First Avenue and Yesler Way to the university.

The value of his other 310 acres would be vastly enhanced.

At any rate, on April 16, 1861, Denny deeded to the University of Washington the eight and one third acres he held on the knoll. Bagley quickly pressured Terry and Lander into coughing up the balance necessary to create what today is known as University Properties and has on it such impressive structures as the Olympic Hotel, the IBM and Washington Buildings and soon will be developed into one of the biggest and most effective central core properties in the United States.

On May 20, 1861—a year after Bagley came to town—the cornerstone for the University of Washington was laid.

Manna . . . from heaven?

By this time the Sons of the Profits in Seattle realized they had a better thing going for them than any old $30,000 building fund for a capital. Jesus may have fed the multitude with two little fishes, but the kind of fish the Lord's disciple was producing for the hungry people of Seattle were manufactured in the United States Mint.

And Bagley's fish were negotiable.   .

Bagley started selling government lands and paying from $275 to $316 an acre for the grubbing and clearing of the university site. John Pike, who had come across the country with Bagley, was architect of the new university building. He acquired the land where the Montlake Bridge is now located as his fee. Bagley bought lumber from Henry Yesler and from the mills at Port Madison and Port Gamble, and foundation stone from a quarry near Port Orchard. Cement, paints, oils and hardware came from Victoria—giving the shipping fraternity a piece of the action. Surveying, masonry, plastering, window frames, desks, chairs, platforms, rostrums, flooring, shingling and painting all were done by Seattle people. There was nobody in town who understood the business end of a plane, a saw, a shovel, hammer, ax or pick who didn't have employment. The university was manna from heaven.

Remember, there were only twenty families in the whole town.

They were diving into a pot that could run as high as $60,000—or about $3,000 per family—in one year. Of course it didn't ever run to that much money, but it did average out at over $1,300 for the blue collar families.

By contrast, a university president could be hired for $600 a year at that time.

The University stood for Prosperity with a capital "P" in Seattle, but the "P" stood for Panic in the rest of the Territory. The acres which "couldn't" be sold for $1.50 each were melting away like snowballs would in that place to which some of the territorial officials would have enjoyed consigning Bagley.

Carry me back to ol' Virginny

I don't know whether or not the Irish are lucky, but I do know that Seattle was at that point and it wasn't because of any brains on Seattle's part.

The good luck started with an unknown lady in the state of Virginia—of all places. Washington Territorial Governor Stevens had been replaced by Governor Fayette McMullin of Virginia, who had come west for a "quickie" legislative divorce . . . the kind of proceedings to which the other party wasn't even invited. Having accomplished his mission, McMullin returned to his girl friend in Virginia. He, in turn, was replaced by a Governor Richard Gohlson of Kentucky, who returned for a visit to his home state when the Civil War was getting under way and decided to stay.

While Bagley was getting Denny's name affixed to the quit claim deed in April, W. H. Wallace, Lincoln's appointee to fill Gohlson's shoes, was getting himself elected as the territorial delegate to Congress. He therefore disqualified himself as Governor.

William Pickering, who was to be Lincoln's next appointee as the Territory's governor, hadn't arrived . . . and one L. S. J. Turney, the Secretary of State, was Acting Governor.

Mr. Turney was no Isaac Stevens. If Stevens hadn't liked what was going on in Seattle the Legislature would have found itself in a special session before Bagley could draw a deep dollar out of the public well . . . which would have enabled the Big Boys from the southwest to bring an end to what they considered a disaster.

Acting Governor Turney scarcely qualified as a member of the Seattle Booster Club, but he didn't know how to knock that obstreperous kid down. He was a bookkeeper type—happier with a column of figures and the "word" of the law, than he was in tossing martial law around or calling special sessions of legislatures. And with real governors dropping in and out of the executive mansion like a bunch of yo-yos, he was very unsure of himself.

While Turney was fooling around trying to figure out what to do, Bagley happily proceeded with the construction of the University.

To Turney he might as well have been called Danny the Flea—the Acting Governor could never catch him.

Finally in August, Governor Turney wrote Commissioner Bagley a letter couched in polite terms but asking what the devil he thought he was doing with the public lands, saying in part . . .

> and as I doubt your legal authority to dispose of the lands in question, I hope you will pardon me for asking to be referred to the law which in your judgment invests you with the power to sell.

Legally, Turney was quite correct . . . and Bagley was way out in left field.

The Law and the profits

The rules of their game originated in 1850 through the Donation Act of that year. Congress *donated* two townships to the Territory of Oregon for university purposes. In the act of 1854 by which Congress took comparable action for the Territory of Washington it only *reserved* the two townships for university purposes.

Bagley had the legal right from Congress to set aside certain lands that could not be sold to anyone else pending their uses by a university. There was nothing in the act of Congress which said he could sell the lands—much less start constructing buildings with the proceeds of the sale.

But Bagley had a few things going for him that clouded the otherwise clear-cut situation. After all, the Legislature had passed a law granting him the right to sell lands. (There was nothing in the Organic Act which created the Territory giving it permission to do something like that, but they did it anyway.) He also was operating in cooperation with the man who recently had been appointed by Lincoln as Territorial Register of Public Lands.

The man's name was Arthur A. Denny.

Armed with advice from Denny, who had been in correspondence with the land commissioner in Washington, D. C., Bagley argued with Turney that the intent of Congress would be the same for one Territory as for another and that in such a case the word *reserved* should be disregarded and that the interpretation would revert to the Donation Law of 1850 which said *donated.*

Bagley also had a couple of other things going for him.

In this frontier community the only wealth there was lay in the land that a man could put his hands on. Lands that were reserved from public sale, for whatever reason, were a source of deep resentment to the individualists who came west in the first place because they *were* individualists. Withheld lands usually were choice and therefore represented the best chance for the frontiersman to succeed in a country which was difficult to conquer even under the most optimum conditions.

As a clincher, Bagley said in his reply to the Governor, "The acutest and most eagle-eyed Mill Companies have purchased extensively and had no hesitation in doing so."

Now there Mr. Bagley had something that bookkeeper Turney could understand: naked power . . . the big lumbermill outfits.

They needed a lot more land than the 640 acres the government permitted as a maximum that could be bought by any individual at the price of $1.25. They also knew the location of the choice pieces of timber lands which they wanted. They were glad to pay Bagley the $1.50 an acre for that land.

For instance, Bagley sold Puget Mill 6,500 acres . . . Meigs Mill 3,000 acres . . . Washington Mill 2,500 acres . . . Renton and Howard Mill 1,000 acres.

Turney could stare down the most independent homesteader standing in the governor's office in his muddy boots and with his hat in his hand, but the mill owners from the major centers of the country didn't wear boots or hold their hats in their hands.

They were pretty good at staring right back.

Our mild-mannered minister knew that.

The oratory of the "silent, succulent oyster"

Governor Turney, with the less than selfless backing of the gentlemen from the southwest counties, was not about to let Bagley off the
hook with the brief question and answer period cited above, but
prior to the convening of the Legislature, he and his friends had their
hands full with yet another crisis.

During the summer the "popularity contest" election was held and
the folks voted hands-down for Olympia as their territorial capital.
The election may have been unofficial, but the wetted finger the
politicians held up in the air showed them which way the wind was
blowing and there was grave danger a majority of the legislators
would show up at Olympia for the annual session of the Legislature and vote the capital from Vancouver back to Olympia.

This was a fire that had to be put out at any cost, and they went to
work to convene the legislators in Vancouver. It resulted in a draw.

In December exactly half the legislators showed up at Vancouver;
the other half arrived in Olympia.

There wasn't a quorum in either place. No business could be done.

The matter went to the Territorial Supreme Court which had to determine which city was the seat of the Territorial Government. Our
Edward M. Lander was a member of that tribunal. The judges were
presidential appointees, but they also owned political forefingers.
However the real reason for their selection of Olympia as the capital
was neither legal nor political.

It was gastronomic.

Vancouver, Washington in those days was at least a day's journey
from Olympia. But the Olympia oyster is found only in Olympia . . .
out of all the places in the whole wide world. It's about the size of
an oyster cracker. When taken fresh, its flavor is unmatched by any
oyster anywhere.

The judges liked their oysters fresh.

It was the Olympia oyster that saved the capital for the city of the same name. After the court decision, an Olympia paper said jubilantly: "The oratory of the silent, succulent oyster is greater than that of all the lawyers combined!"

The Case of the Calloused College Boys

Even before the convening of the Legislature, it was not a secret that B. C. Lippincott, the Superindentent of Public Instruction, had taken a totally unreasonable position on the question of putting together a university. His position was that they were getting the cart before the horse . . . that they should begin by creating elementary schools and working their way up to institutions of higher learning.

Preposterous!

Bagley was aware of Lippincott's position—and the importance of timing. He needed to get bodies in the classrooms before Lippincott could officially state his views to the legislators when the session opened in December. A young man, name of Asa Shinn Mercer, arrived in the spring of 1861 after having just been graduated from college. He worked as a common laborer on the foundations of the new University—but Bagley had plenty of day laborers. What he needed was a college president. To be a college president, a fella had to have been graduated from a college.

So Bagley hired Mercer as the first president (acting) of the University, at no salary, and used him in an ad which appeared in the newspapers on September 16 announcing that school would commence on November 4.

Mercer's real job was to get out in the boondocks and see if he couldn't scare up some pupils, so he visited the logging camps around Puget Sound. He was to get students even if he had to hire them. A month later Mr. Lippincott told the legislators that there wasn't a single man, woman or child in the Territory with the qualifications to enter a university. Bagley denied the allegation. They had dug up one freshman. He was being paid to attend school, but there he was . . . cutting cordwood for his living, but not classes.

Bagley was psychologist enough to know that when the legislative investigating committee—and he knew there would be an investi-

gating committee—arrived on the premises he'd better have more
than one body about the University buildings.

He needed bulk.

So he lowered the entrance requirements and offered common
school subjects in the University. This brought a big howl from the
citizens of Seattle, especially from Henry Yesler, who lacked higher
education himself and looked with awe on that sort of thing. He declared it would be undignified for the University to teach those
lower branches of education. The protest meeting at which Yesler
spoke took place in the halls of learning before the University was to
open, but his suffering sensibilities subsided when Bagley stood before the protesting group as living proof that there *was* a Santa
Claus. Henry, who had sold a lot of lumber to Bagley, could see the
marks of his own saws in the boards behind Bagley.

The school board agreed to produce the happy voices and pattering
feet of little children in the new "University".

And the band played on

Nobody who thinks about that sort of thing would ever deny the
enormous cultural contribution that the University of Washington
makes in our community today. It is therefore only fitting that the
first cultural effort of the University of Washington and the reason
it happened should be recorded in our city's history.

It was all part of a plot.

When Acting Governor Turney mounted the podium on December
10, 1861 to address a joint session of the two houses of the Legislature, he delivered of himself a few choice words (that had not been
thought up on the spur of the moment) about a Methodist minister
who was not mentioned by name.

As far as he was concerned, the act which created Bagley's commission was illegal and void, the "action of the commissioners was hasty
and unwarranted" . . . and their action should not be ratified, on
grounds that it was illegal. He urged a rigid and faithful observance
of the law. He said that those who were entrusted with the selection

of "these lands, and the disbursement of these funds arising from their sale should be held to a strict and scrutinizing accountability ... Wrong-doers who would squander any part of these lands should be frowned down by an enlightened and patriotic sentiment."

That the Acting Governor's feelings were a lot more intense than the above words might suggest was indicated when one of the newspapers published an editorial stating that Turney had attempted to bribe the editors to take out against the commission ... and when he failed, he attempted "threat followed by punishment."

Superintendent Lippincott backed up the Acting Governor by protesting the "hasty expenditure of the funds." He said, "We hold that the public good should never be sacrificed for individual interests."

It looked like the two fellows were getting together backstage.

So it came as no startlement to the residents of Seattle that a committee composed of members of both houses was formed to investigate the university matter. It came as no surprise because John Denny, that shifty old politician, was the one who suggested the investigation.

And who better was there to make such a suggestion than the chairman of the Committee on Education?

Nor was it particularly astonishing to Bagley to find that the co-chairmen of the committee were H. L. Caples of Clark County, and Paul K. Hubbs of Jefferson County. The atmosphere of good fellowship that had existed among the co-conspirators of just twelve months before was not present on the trip up the Sound to Seattle from Olympia on New Year's Eve. The gentleman from Clark was supposed to have gotten the capital, which he did not ... The gentleman from Jefferson the penitentiary, which he did not. It was the first, but not the last time, that Seattle had out-finagled the people from other parts of the Territory.

The presence of Superintendent Lippincott as a member of the little group failed to advance the possibility of levity.

In that intervening year Bagley had successfully sold 20,000 acres of school land, and had, with equal success, spent within a few hundred dollars the $30,000 the land sales had brought in.

Knowing that the group might add a somber note to the successful conclusion of the year's work, the residents of Seattle had prepared a welcome designed to cheer their spirits. This is where the first cultural efforts of the University came into play. As a special honor to their visiting legislative friends, the men who had participated in the construction of the University had devoted some of their profits to the purchase of musical instruments, and for weeks they had been practicing. The legislators were greeted at Henry Yesler's wharf by the music of the first non-military brass band in the history of the Territory of Washington.

The music may not have been perfect . . . but it was loud. There was bunting on the pier. Flags waved. The streets leading up the hill to the University were decorated. The entire populace—and every ringer they could involve from the surrounding countryside—was on hand wearing his or her best finery. As they stepped down from the gangplank, the legislators were apprized of the reason for all of the festivity.

They had come to kill the possibility of a university in Seattle.

They learned, instead, that they were just in time to attend the formal dedication of the University of Washington.

They were taken on a tour of the university grounds. They saw the students eagerly straining for knowledge in the brand new class rooms. Finally they were escorted to their seats of honor on the grandstand which was located on a piece of land presently occupied by the Olympic Hotel.

The Seattleite sitting next to Mr. Hubbs reminded that gentleman that the choice timber land he had purchased up in Jefferson County for a mere $1.50 an acre had added immeasurably to the educational opportunities of the young people of the territory. We were sure he would take pride in the institution that was made possible by the land he got so cheap.

John Denny, chairman of the Committee on Education and keeper of the keys to Superintendent Lippincott's budget, was seated strategically behind the superintendent, who could feel Denny's warm breath on the back of his neck on that cold day. Mr. Lippincott was asked to say a few choice words at the dedication.

Mr. Lippincott said a few choice words.

That was the occasion of one of our famous historic anecdotes. The committee was staying at a hotel on Pioneer Square just across the street from Henry Yesler's wharf. The committee was to return to Olympia on the steamer "Eliza Anderson". There was, of course, no street lighting. And at five o'clock in the morning, they heard the whistle blow.

Racing across the street, struggling into their clothes as they ran, the members entered what they thought was the engine room of the "Anderson." After waiting around for a while they asked the engineer when they would be leaving port for Olympia.

"I'm sorry," that worthy gentleman is alleged to have replied. "but this sawmill doesn't sail to Olympia."

Upon its return to Olympia, the committee reported favorably on the fine work that had been done to create the Territory's splendid University.

A short time later, the *San Francisco Call-Bulletin* was moved to make the following comment about the town of Seattle:

> Seattle is situated about equidistant between Steilacoom and Port Townsend on the east side of Puget Sound. It has three or four stores, one sawmill and about two hundred inhabitants. The only attraction of the place and the object of general comment is the university which has just been completed. It is a fine building located on a beautiful eminence and commands a grand view of the Sound.

The Minister . . . of Finance?

At the time that Bagley was putting together the finest building in Washington Territory, the United States was being torn apart by the Civil War. In the course of that conflict, the federal government manufactured paper money in vast quantity. They flooded the market with it, and the value dropped to as low as forty cents on the dollar, creating yet another problem for our Methodist minister.

All might have been more or less jolly if the city of Seattle hadn't already begun to flex its muscles and make itself generally obnoxious to the rest of the residents of the Territory or if the Democrats hadn't needed to cast suspicion on the financing of the University as a method of embarrassing Republicans.

But they did and that was life . . . the kind of life designed to make Bagley miserable—and scared.

Bagley's bookkeeping system was one written in pencil on the backs of envelopes and filed in the various pockets on his frocked coat. It was admirable from the standpoint of confounding adverse accountants desirous of proving that he was a crook and sending him to jail. It was also complicated due to the problem of the greenbacks and the imaginative ways Bagley went about making deals.

In the main business of getting the University built, Bagley sold land in exchange for services rendered . . . he sold land on credit . . . he sold land for materials and construction . . . and in consequence a lot of the building costs were out of line. He also sold land for greenbacks.

And he just plain lost some of his records.

Entering into this picture was the "code of the hills." All business among private individuals was done on what was called "coin" basis as opposed to a "greenback" basis. All business done with any branch of government was done on a greenback basis—after all, it was *their* money and *they* had to honor it. If somebody went to Olympia to pay taxes or buy land or do anything else, he first went to a bank and swapped his coin for greenbacks. As far as the University was concerned this was a government operation. Bagley attempted to keep track of this monetary difference. He tried to keep everything on a coin basis. So, if he got $240 for a quarter of a section in greenbacks, he reduced it to the value of coin at whatever was the current rate. If paper was sixty cents on the dollar, he entered $144 for the $240 in his books. If it was worth fifty cents, he entered $120 and if forty cents he entered only $96.

This seemed suitable at the time, but not during election campaigns four and eight years later when hostile, Democratic-inspired committees had him frying on the witness stand.

Double trouble

However, Bagley's most troublesome problem came from another area. His ability to sell the land above the $1.25 government price hinged on two major points: the first was the interest of the previously mentioned mills; the second was the land he sold in fractional sections. He was charged with letting his friends in on a good deal now and then. One of the friends, and a mighty handy one, turned out to be William Pickering, who was appointed by Lincoln to take over the reins from Turney.

Pickering acquired a nice piece of property near Issaquah.

It was obvious that the people who bought the fractional sections— or even the big hunks, for that matter—selected their own lands, described them legally and handed the description to Bagley for his signature. He sold pieces of land as small as an acre-and-a-half and he sold land in some sixty-two different townships, including some choice lots around Lake Washington.

The big problem cropped up in the wording of the law under which federal lands were sold. The requirement was that the land be sold in "legal subdivisions" or in quarter sections of multiples thereof. He totally disregarded this detail.

Now, as Bagley learned, it was one thing to sell the land, collect the money and build the University. It was quite a different kettle of fish to get the United States government to honor the sale. Deeds could not be supplied nor final title conveyed until the transactions had been cleared by the U.S. Land Office.

When the entries were forwarded to Washington, D.C., the reply came back that no deeds—*no* deeds—could be issued under existing legislation. If a fractional tract had been selected, the Land Office must charge to the university grant the entire section in which the piece of land was located. To make things even more sticky, the Land Office informed Bagley that no titles could be supplied because the law specified that the lands were only to be *reserved* for university purposes.

Bagley decided a trip to Washington, D.C. was in order.

Fortunately, he had a friend in Washington, D.C., a friend who cared just as much about a little bit of real estate in the northwest corner of the United States as he did about the real estate which was used by the northern and southern armies in their titanic struggle . . . and he probably was the only man in the nation's capital with this divided interest.

His name was Arthur A. Denny.

The omnipresent Denny had relinquished his job as land register for the Territory of Washington when he was elected as the Territorial Delegate to Congress. The nation's capital was far more interested in the conduct of the Civil War than it was in keeping an improbable Methodist minister out of the penitentiary . . . but Denny and Bagley were a pair of resolute young pioneers.

Superintendent Lippincott, who was not as friendly as he sounded when he welcomed the University on December 31, 1861, attempted to skewer Bagley in the halls of Congress. But John Denny went back there, too, and was busy on the other side. Unlike John, Lippincott hadn't jumped out a committee room window with Abraham Lincoln. The Land Department stood firm on the matter of fractional sections, which caused the University to acquire a lot of land it may or may not have wanted or needed.

The main problem—providing deeds for the land that had been sold—was resolved when the U.S. Land Department endorsed legislation that subsequently was passed honoring the work that Bagley had done.

Later on, when he was on the hot seat with the State Legislature, he wrote his historian son, Clarence, "There does not seem to be any *danger* in my case except my removal . . ." (as University Commissioner.)

At another point, Bagley wrote his son about the local in-fighting: "Concerning the university, I think the design of McGilvra is to get up a *fuss* in the hope of getting a fee, of father Denny (John) to injure me and get his son David to be treasurer, and of H. K. Hines to get control of the institution to help the M. E. Church."

Normalcy had been restored.

We were back to bickering among ourselves.

Still later, when the whole uproar had subsided and the University had stopped hiring students, Bagley enjoyed saying, "I am the man who stole the University."

But what did he do right after the University was built? He remembered he hadn't yet built a church. So, in 1865 he turned to and raised the money to build Seattle's second church.

He was not about to do business any longer in a Methodist-*Episcopal* church.

V

Immorality and Immortality

I find no statue in any public square, nor any park, street, public school, hospital or building commemorating the name of John W. Pinnell. Yet John played his unique role in the development of Seattle with all the fervor, enthusiasm and dedication for making money as the other Sons of the Profits like Colman, Denny, Bell or Yesler whose names pepper our public places.

To date, John's role as Horatio at the bridge has been deleted through a process of polite blackmail in most of the subsidized history books. Those were the books that were paid for by the people whose names appeared in the biographical sections. They wouldn't let their names appear if John's was also there.

As a result, they left us with an official historical heritage about as rich as a bowl of broth made from the shadow of a chicken.

Prelude to Pinnell

John put in his appearance here in 1869. Seattle had recovered from the desolating influence of the Indian War. Great lumber operations were booming all around us. Coal, rich in quality and quantity, had been discovered in King County. Engineers for the Northern Pacific Railroad were surveying Snoqualmie Pass.

Seattle, a busy, bustling town thundering on the heels of Olympia in pursuit of population and ideally located geographically, was the obvious choice as terminus for the railroad.

The railroad survey crews lived in Seattle. Their findings in Snoqualmie Pass were regularly reported in the newspapers. And their findings had created a real estate boom. Town lots that had sold for $50 in January on the Portland and San Francisco real estate markets were commanding $500 in late summer.

The town populations weren't much. Olympia headed the list with 1,100. Seattle and Vancouver were neck and neck with 1,000 each—and the latter wasn't even on Puget Sound. Port Townsend was fourth at 800. Steilacoom, Port Gamble, Port Ludlow, Port Madison and Mukilteo were also-rans.

Tacoma wasn't even on the map.

But the logging camps were roaring. The men were getting sixty to eighty dollars a month. There must have been ten thousand men within a radius of fifty miles of Seattle. Soon half the population of the entire Territory was to be on Puget Sound. And Seattle was the geographic center of it all.

Yet, in spite of all of the busy-ness of everybody, there was an underlying unrest in the land . . . a kind of insanity that caused fights in the bunkhouses when there needn't have been fights. It was the kind of a tension that everybody felt but nobody talked about.

When Arthur Denny bundled up his charges in Illinois preparatory to the trip west, he had the necessary picks and shovels, saws and axes, transits and chains to whittle a big city out of the wilderness. But there was nothing in his do-it-yourself kit about one of the basic needs of the single male population.

His amateur standing in this necessary concomitant of building a city on the western frontier didn't matter a bit back when there were only a handful of folks populating the town. With only twenty-four people around, most of them married, everybody got by doing what came naturally. When Yesler's mill upped the population some, the fellows coped by bringing along their squaw wives.

The Indian Wars of 1855-56 virtually de-populated the Puget Sound area and postponed the problem for about a decade. Then the lumber mills began to crop up here and there across the Sound from

Seattle, and the city's population exploded to include say, ninety three, mebbe ninety four single men with energetic red blood. A lot of fellas from the logging camps started hanging around the corner on a Saturday night watching all the girls go by, and there began to build up a kind of static in the community like just before a thunder storm.

All of the girls were private property.

Editorial opinion began to reflect on the matter with such items as "A Good Wife" and even something about "The Shortage of White Women."

One editor went so far as to comment that the young men of the community had "calico on their brains." For some reason that pales my imagination, some of the community leadership concluded that the advent of the railroad would solve the problem and somehow all would be well again.

Nobody had faced up to the fact that the services of professionals were needed.

The matchmaker

At this point, Asa Mercer, the rosy cheeked, naive young man who had scoured the logging camps hiring "students" for the University, came up with what he thought was a brilliant idea. He approached the Reverend Mr. Bagley with a notion about bringing a load of decent unmarried young ladies from the East out to the town for purposes of clearing the air with wholesale marriages. To Mr. Bagley, who was a bit naive on the subject himself, it seemed like an eminently satisfactory solution. It was felt that being a young man himself, Mercer understood what was going on in the minds and bodies of the other young men in the area.

Mercer figured he had come up with a new approach to the most complicated problem, except survival, that has faced mankind since the beginning of time.

There were some skeptics, so the public subscription he sought for the trip east to the marts of marriageable women was not as great as he wished it could be, but he felt that once he demonstrated his system, it couldn't fail. After all, he was a school teacher and logic was on his side. The men were in the West and the women in the East.

All he had to do was get into the transportation business.

Accordingly, in March of 1864, he set forth from New York for Seattle with eleven young maidens ranging in age from fifteen to twenty-five years. Historian Clarence Bagley, who was a very young man in town at the time and wrote the kind of history that failed to give any prominence to the name of John Pinnell, voiced these sentiments about the venture when writing his chronicle about Seattle some fifty years later:

> They did not come West expressly to marry, as some would infer; but if, in addition to the appeal of wages, adventure, desire to help their people at home, and the true missionary spirit of benefitting all whom they come in contact with, the thought of marriage in the new country was considered, it is not wondered at . . .

Of the eleven who started out, nine actually got here and of the nine, eight got married. The ninth became the principal of Seattle's first public school.

For a long time, I wondered why she didn't get married, too . . . but in the course of further research I came across her picture and that solved the mystery, at least to my satisfaction.

Postage prepaid

Well, Mr. Mercer was a pretty popular young fellow when he produced the petticoats and the folks elected him to the upper house of the Territorial Legislature. But he had bigger things on his mind. With his "can't fail" formula, he persuaded a number of young men to invest three hundred bucks apiece to finance a second trip to the East.

He had an additional argument going with him when he left with the proceeds of the second public subscription. Over 360,000 young men had died as a result of the Civil War, and there were war widows until they ran out your ears. He was planning to return with about five hundred of those widows—a monumental task but a target worth shooting for. At $300 apiece he could gross out at $150,000. And if the five hundred worked out, he could shoot to provide a wife for every one of the ten thousand single men on Puget Sound. And with that many widows as a potential ...

There were millions in it!

Unfortunately, James Gordon Bennett of the *New York Herald* simply didn't believe that the distillation of naivete that was part and parcel of Asa Mercer could exist in the breast of any man . . . and the *Herald* started screaming "white slavery." Mercer's recruits fell off like flies.

A year after his first triumphal return with nine girls, Mercer came back with forty-six eligible young ladies. Make it forty-five . . . he married one of them himself. And he was broke. Though the mathematical education of the young bucks in the community was rudimentary, they were able to figure out that forty-five eligible girls was a substantially lower number than the five hundred that Mercer had promised.

And snuggling up to an empty promise on a cold winter's night was small satisfaction for the rosy dreams that had been allowed to grow while Mercer was in the East. That was the end of Mercer in Seattle. The young men of the town would have tarred and feathered him and ridden him out of town on a rail. But Sheriff Wyckoff wouldn't let 'em.

Free delivery

The next guy to take a run at solving the problem of the imbalance between the sexes was one Benjamin Sprague, captain of a boat called the "Gin Palace Polly," which sought to deliver wine, women and song to the logging camps around the Sound. He operated on a franchise granted by the Legislature for a price of $1200 a year.

On a rotation basis, he delivered sin to the logging camps seven days a week, and while it was highly popular with the men who took the day off whenever Sprague's jolly crew put in an appearance, it was less than enthusiastically received by the operators of the camps. Any day he showed up the men deserted their jobs and joined the fun. So two days were lost—the one when he arrived . . . and the next while the men were nursing their hangovers.

However, it didn't take long before Sprague found himself in residence at the state penitentiary for two years for selling liquor to Indians and on Sunday. His ship was confiscated and the "floating palace" business died fast.

So neither Mercer or Sprague—operating from opposite points of view—had been able to solve the problem. It lingered on as a blight in the land, defying the best attempts of anybody to dissipate the emotional smog so depressing to the soul.

Then the Lord, moving in his inscrutable ways, tapped John W. Pinnell on the shoulder and directed his calm, sure, experienced footsteps to the shores of Puget Sound. John answered the call, and the services of a master craftsman were made available to the little settlement on Elliott Bay.

The old master at work

Nearly forty years ago, when some of the men who had known John Pinnell personally were still alive, Jim Stevens, the venerated creator of the Paul Bunyan stories, interviewed a number of them and came up with the following description of Pinnell in an article in *American Mercury Magazine,* entitled, "The Natural History of Seattle":

> On a summer day . . . John Penell [*Editor's Note: All official county records spell his name Pinnell*] debarked from a San Francisco lumber schooner, landing on the Seattle sandspit. Tall, saturnine and suave, wearing a flowered waistcoat and a plug hat, he was a character right out of Bret Harte . . .

John clearly made a favorable impression on Sheriff Wyckoff, who had struggled with the abortive efforts of Mercer and Sprague and welcomed Pinnell. The latter produced his credentials, which clearly showed that he'd had a long and favorable relationship with the San Francisco Police. He was a man of stature in his field and he felt he had the right answer to the problem of unrest in the community that had been plaguing Wycoff for years. Unlike Asa Mercer, Pinnell had no degree in liberal arts.

On the other hand, he had graduated *summa cum laude* from the school of experience in the Barbary Coast in San Francisco and knew his way around when it came to taming the unruly elements in a growing city.

Also unlike Mercer, Pinnell did not propose a public subscription to initiate his enterprise. His program was not only self-liquidating, it would add desperately needed funds to the public treasury. Pinnell proposed to take a heretofore untaxed product and channel the income from it into programs for schools, roads, law enforcement and other civic betterments. As a clincher, he proposed to confine his particular brand of public assistance to an area of town that heretofore had been considered wasteland and thus brought in no taxes.

Wyckoff blessed John for putting in his appearance in the little settlement's hour of need and told him to hop to it. That Wyckoff was a man who exercised the kind of judgment appreciated by the public was evidenced by the fact that although the Legislature first appointed him to public office, the people returned him to office both as city councilman and sheriff for five consecutive terms—which was the period during which John Pinnell made his most effective contribution to the growth of Seattle.

Later on, when the "good" element had Pinnell under attack and blamed Wyckoff for his role in admitting Pinnell to the bosom of the community, Wyckoff smugly dismissed the charge with a succinct, "Mr. Pinnell's activities have never come under the scrutiny of the police court."

Being aware, from experience, that on occasion misunderstandings arose about the importance of his particular brand of dedication to a sound principle of society, John retained civic leader John Leary as his attorney. Leary was in the forefront of all laudable community developments and Pinnell's was no exception.

As has been indicated, 1869 was a bonanza real estate year for the city of Seattle. Lots in the main retail business district of the city— from Yesler Way to Main Street along First Avenue South—reached a high of $66.66 per front foot. Indication of Pinnell's business acumen, sagacity and pioneer spirit comes from the fact that he bought up the west side of Fourth Avenue South from Washington to Main

Street—within easy walking distance of the most expensive property in town—for a mere $2.50 a front foot.

According to the records in the county courthouse, John made his first appearance on the boards of Seattle's historical stage when he purchased his first two lots in Maynard's donation claim for $300 on July 5, 1869. The truth is that prior to Pinnell's purchase, the land was not considered desirable. John was a pioneer of the eastern frontier of the town. He was the first man to establish a business on the fill land that has since wiped out Denny's island. He was a man of imagination who could visualize the day when the lagoon just east of his establishment could be the location of fine buildings . . . when the hills would be pulled down to fill hollows . . . and one day fine restaurants, hotels and even railroad depots would grace this area. It was a proud piece of land to John—and it was his.

The other folks called it the garbage dump.

The Illahee

John named his first establishment the "Illahee," which is a rough translation of the Indian word for a home away from home. The name has since been selected by the State of Washington as the name for one of its folksy ferries. To the thousands of loggers who occupied the outposts of civilization on Puget Sound, the Illahee came to represent warmth, friendliness, women and the chance to kick up their heels a little and forget that most desolate of all emotions—the feeling of not being wanted.

This was a basic problem of the frontier that men like Denny with their cozy little cabins on the heights never had to face. They were incapable of comprehending the need that John Pinnell filled. Witness the backing they gave to the absurd efforts of Asa Mercer, which could be likened to bailing out a sinking battleship with a tin teaspoon. They were able to understand, however, that whatever product it was that Pinnell was purveying brought lots of people into town and those people spent their money with other merchants as well as Pinnell. The tradespeople rejoiced in the presence of Pinnell. The landowners also rejoiced. As he prospered, others in his field, although of a lesser caliber, came to locate in the same tideflats. The folks who owned the land in the area found that by filling it with garbage and dirt from the surrounding hills they could lease otherwise worthless property at a handsome profit.

Frugal, thrifty, far-sighted and clear-thinking, John realized early that the economy of the Puget Sound region could not support—and did not need— rare imported French wines ("Red Eye" was the stuff they drank) or the other more elegant kinds of merchandise often purveyed in his kind of business. He quickly realized it would be necessary to improvise with the homespun products near at hand. Like that great humanitarian Doc Maynard, Pinnell recognized the plight of the Indians in the area. They lived in squalor with scarcely enough food, clothing and shelter to keep body and soul together. He would remove a number of the mouths the impoverished tribes had to feed.

He descended on the Indian chiefs like manna from heaven.

He would rent Indian maidens from them in exchange for warm Hudson Bay blankets. He would then remove the maidens from their squalid surroundings. He would provide them with an education, gainful employment, food, clothing, shelter and even baths. They would advance themselves on both the economic and social scale. They would be taught a trade. They would lead a life of pure pleasure. Like the vestal virgins, of course, only the finest of the girls could qualify, but they could send some of their earnings home and all Indians would benefit.

Within the Indian reservations there was joy without reservation.

There was also competition.

When the "horse" Indians of eastern Washington Territory (as opposed to the "canoe" Indians in the western part of the Territory) learned of the splendid new educational and economic opportunities that were being offered in Seattle, their chiefs immediately entered into negotiations with John.

Natural laws of economics began to apply.

As the discrimination and economic position of the loggers increased it became economically sound to import the handsome, erect, limber-limbed ladies from the eastern Washington tribes.

Among the Indian tribes and among the loggers, John was looked upon as a saviour. Among the businessmen of the community, he was regarded as the city's greatest single economic asset. Some idea of the relative importance of John's establishment in the community may be derived by pointing out that when the Legislature incorporated Seattle the city's debt limitation was $5,000. Pinnell's license fee alone would amount to $1,200.

He not only started our first anti-poverty program, he was the biggest single contributor to public works.

Generous of impulse though he was, Pinnell perforce remembered the pledge he had made to the sheriff: neither he nor his would become a public nuisance. It therefore was incumbent upon him to study the mathematics of the situation and to charge a small service fee for his hospitality to the "forgotten man." Like Asa Mercer, he, too, was able to figure out there must have been about 10,000 unmarried men in the area. Of these only a miniscule minority dwelled within the city limits. The men in the woods received their money via drafts on San Francisco banks. Local bankers charged a 10 per cent service fee for cashing their checks. Captains of the Mosquito Fleet charged 20 per cent. Pinnell cashed the checks for nothing giving a man a free $7 to $14 to spend on pure pleasure. In response to such generosity, many of the men stayed on to visit for awhile with drinks at 50¢ and the solace of Indian maidens running from $2 to $5.

John was not a greedy man, but he did have to keep up the payments on his property, put out the $1,200 annual license fee and maintain order in a place where men were like big friendly Saint Bernard pups . . . or should we say bulls . . . released from a month's captivity. His charges were reasonable, his results fantastic and happiness succeeded despair in the woods as well as in town.

His became the most profitable industry in town . . . even more so than Henry Yesler's mill.

The loggers spent their money at Schwabacher Brothers, our biggest retail store, during the day and at John's at night.

Between them they brought in about $70,000 per month and dug the channels of trade deep for Seattle.

The sine qua non

John, like any other human being who had arrived in the Pacific Northwest by any route other than his mother's womb, had a deep appreciation of the importance of rail connection with the rest of the continent. It should be remembered that the people on the Sound had reached this remote location the hard way. Those who'd had five hundred dollars took the comparatively easy ship trip which involved a rollicking ride around the rough edges of Cape Horn or a steaming trip across the Isthmus of Panama. Those who didn't have the simoleons jarred their teeth loose on the hard seats of covered wagons or horses across the cholera-infested Oregon Trail. The idea of riding on cushions and being pulled by a steam locomotive was considered sissy stuff. But the kind of sissies who would come that way were sissies with money, which was even in shorter supply here than women.

It further was the sine qua non accepted by everybody that the town on the Sound which became the terminus of the railroad automatically would become the metropolis of the area, and people owning property in that town would become richer than they had ever dreamed was possible. The little settlements which had dreams of glory on this front were Olympia, Steilacoom, Tacoma, Seattle, Whatcom, Mukilteo, Fairhaven, Anacortes, Holmes Harbor, Penn's Cove and Port Townsend. There was no Everett then to even have aspirations.

Which town would it be? That was the question asked by the burning newspaper headlines in the summer of 1873.

There was booster conversation in the other towns about their chances of becoming the terminus of the railroad, but there wasn't much doubt in the minds of about 99 per cent of the people in the Territory that Seattle was the one that would get the bid.

As dispassionate an analysis of Seattle's relative position as there is was that which appeared in the 1873 Puget Sound Business Directory—which didn't even list Tacoma as a town.

Seattle's recent advances were described in that publication in 1873 as follows:

Seattle is the county seat of King County, has a population of about 1,500 and a commerce and business equal to that of a city treble its size, being, as it is, a centre of trade for a considerable agricultural population, and for many of the logging camps and milling points on the Sound. Its population is nearly thrice as large as it was four years ago and it can safely be put down as the leading and largest town in the Puget Sound country. It has a large steam sawmill, a grist mill, a soap factory, two breweries, a tannery, two shipyards, a sash and door manufactory, machine shops, seven wharves and warehouses, thirty-three stores, and about a hundred business buildings.

Oh yes, Seattle was the town all right.

Seattle's darkest hour

Unfortunately, the Western Representatives of the Northern Pacific Railroad—R. D. Rice and J. C. Ainsworth—didn't get their advice from the Puget Sound Business Directory. They got it from a committee composed of the railroad's board, which included themselves. The board members had just completed a deluxe tour of Puget Sound with more of an eye to the distant jingling of the cash register than the relative importance of the biggest frog in what they considered a small pond.

While they were taking their tour, they concluded that there was nothing wrong with any site on the Sound that $2,000,000 wouldn't fix.

And $2,000,000 was fixed as the amount the railroad would spend in developing a company town at the western terminus for the road.

It was their judgment that a tiny spot like Seattle, with or without Pinnell, would present no competition. On the map, the harbors of Seattle and Tacoma were identical. They figured that while they were here they could obtain complete control of the Tacoma harbor and they initiated the formation of the Tacoma Land Company for that purpose. Rice and Ainsworth were left behind, to wind up the details.

On June 30, 1873, Rice and Ainsworth sent in code to the home office the telegram that cast the die. The telegram pointed out that while Seattle had made the biggest offer in terms of land and cash, the pledges of land were scattered all over the landscape. The railroad would be important to Seattle, but the railroad could not "own" Seattle. In Tacoma, on the other hand, they could acquire two solid miles of waterfront in one bite. The telegram concluded with the following: "To carry out plan of company city on $2,000,000 basis with any prospect of success, as now advised, shall unhesitatingly decide in favor of Tacoma."

On July 14, Rice and Ainsworth sent the blow that was supposed to kill Seattle in the form of a telegram to Arthur Denny reading:

"We have located the terminus on Commencement Bay."

The unsung hero

It was quite natural that the telegram be delivered to Arthur Denny rather than, say, somebody like John Pinnell. Denny was the guy with whom the railroad had been doing business. He was the venerated "father" of Seattle. John was just a dues-paying member of the town . . . a solid citizen who had justly earned the respect of his fellow businessmen.

John made the largest single cash pledge to the "kitty" that was raised to entice the railroad to our town.

Several million words have been written about the heroism of the people of Seattle in the fracas with the railroad, and I will be adding to the supply substantially in this book. According to the legendeers, Seattle reacted angrily, effectively and instantly to the action of the railroad in selecting Tacoma as the terminus. The truth is that at first we were stunned by the shock and didn't react at all. Then we got angry—among ourselves. And finally almost a year later we got sore at the railroad. During that hiatus, John saved the town.

Irony compounded irony.

Seattle went into the railroad business—where it had no business.

The Northern Pacific went into the town business—where it had no business.

While this was a normal procedure on the part of the railroad and had been worked with considerable success elsewhere, the company never before had encountered a leader with the qualifications, strength, vision, perseverance, capitalization and intimate know-how of John Pinnell.

He was the man who staved off the legions of the enemy until the good guys could regroup and carry on a fight that was to last for the next twenty years. Author Jim Stevens touched upon Pinnell's importance nearly forty years ago . . . and now Pinnell is being given the proper recognition he deserves in Seattle's history—almost a century after he loyally performed his greatest service to the city he loved.

Tacoma booms

The Northern Pacific pulled the "people" plug in Seattle with its July 14 announcement about the terminus. The boom that had been building in Seattle transferred itself to Tacoma. H. A. Atkins, who recently had completed two terms as Mayor of Seattle, was one of the first to go. He got the contract for building Tacoma's first hotel.

Before the railroad announcement was made, Tacoma consisted of ten business houses including the Hanson and Ackerson mill. Immediately after the announcement it became a tent town as men hastened in to set up business. An enterprising shoemaker put a three by twenty foot roof between two houses, paid nine dollars a month rent and did a roaring business.

Thomas Prosch, who later became one of Seattle's leading historians, set up Tacoma's first newspaper less than a month after the announcement. Johnstone Brothers, Seattle merchants, moved over. Others came from Olympia. Before the end of the year advertising had been placed in Prosch's newspaper by a tailor . . . two livery stables . . . a title abstract company . . . teamsters . . . builders . . . three doctors . . . a restaurant . . . a blacksmith shop . . . job printers . . . an architect . . . a bank . . . wood dealers . . . lumber dealers . . . boat renters . . . Wells Fargo express agents . . . a wagon maker . . . a fish dealer, and a lot of saloons.

While Seattle's population dropped from over 1,000 to about five hundred, Tacoma's jumped from a hundred to 1,500 or more. Two hundred and ninety-three new homes were built. The assessed valuation of Pierce County land jumped from a few thousand dollars to $702,017 in less than six months. The school population went from about twenty to two hundred and forty three. Ministers flocked in and churches were built for the purpose of saving anybody who had time for that kind of luxury.

The Tacoma Land Company, backed by the $2,000,000 that had been set aside for the purpose of building a town that would put Seattle out of business, went about attaining that objective by putting prices on downtown lots that were enough to set the Seattle land-owners' teeth on edge. Corner lots were listed at $250, a tenth as much as the same lots in Seattle . . . bringing forth editorials like the following in the *Seattle Intelligencer* (aimed at Denny, Bell and Yesler):

> The cheapest lot on Fifth Avenue back of the University, was held at $1,150, with more than 50 big stumps on it. An adjoining lot, half cleared, was held at $1,400, and would cost $175 to grade.

> That our city is growing is very evident. It never will grow while men who paid nothing for their town lots ask San Francisco prices for them . . . the three principal owners of this city were donated their land by the federal government. These men, who always want their pound of flesh in advance, are driving out transient capital by their exorbitant demands.

Next, the Tacoma Land Company started selling the timber rights along its projected rights-of-way to loggers at a dollar a thousand board feet. (Legally, the railroad was not supposed to sell anything on its land grants until it had proved up its claim by constructing rails along the rights-of-way.) This funnelled loggers' money into the new townsite along with the wages that were being paid to construction workers, who got half their wages in cash and the other half in credit at Hanson and Ackerson's mercantile store.

By December 16, 1873 the last spike was driven connecting Tacoma with Kalama. Travel time between Portland and Tacoma had been slashed from a week to two days. The passenger took a boat out of Portland early in the morning, arriving at Kalama at 2 p.m. He stayed overnight in Kalama and caught a train that landed him in

Tacoma that afternoon. If he wished to go on to Seattle he stayed
overnight again and got to Seattle the next afternoon by boat.

The company had the world by the tail and a downhill pull. All
traffic on Puget Sound would funnel through Tacoma to Portland
and the East. And Tacoma automatically would become the trading
center on the Sound.

The big mistake

A month after Arthur Denny got the terrible telegram from Rice
and Ainsworth, the railroad told John Pinnell that he, of all the
Seattle businessmen, was the only one not welcome in Tacoma. This
was a less publicized message than the one that Denny got, but it
sure caused the railroad a lot more trouble than the first one.

As a Son of the Profits, John had opened a subsidiary of the Illahee
in Tacoma while the railroad was building north toward Puget
Sound. It was an example of good business and the pure unselfish-
ness that made John a great man. His heart overflowed with love
and he sought to establish a chainstore operation not only to fill
the voids of lonesomeness in the men of the Pacific Northwest, but
to give employment to deserving Indian maidens.

Then—three weeks after the wire to Denny—a fellow was accidentally murdered inside of John's Tacoma store.

The railroad kicked Pinnell out of Tacoma.

Loyalty to Seattle in John's great heart was now joined in marriage
to a dedicated hate of Tacoma and the railroad. He figured the railroad's action was entirely out of keeping with the spirit of the west
where a murder or two every day or so occupied about as much public attention as the arrival of a mailman today.

The genius that made him the undisputed ruler of his field on
Puget Sound never was more clearly demonstrated than in Pinnell's
first, swift, decisive counter move against the railroad in the fall of
1873.

Perhaps, if the railroad had had a vice president in charge of vice,
things would have been different. Of course, there were practical

problems involved in creating that kind of a position—important though it might have been. It is questionable that such an office, even though created, could have been passed by the board of directors. And the chances are that such a man would be so fouled up he couldn't reach a decision in time to do any good.

After all, what could a guy in an elegant, wood-panelled office in New York do to stop a drunk who was about to shoot up a back bar 3,000 miles away?

The conventional business leaders in Seattle visualized the Northern Pacific as it one day would be—a huge transcontinental railroad system. They foolishly turned their attention to the construction of a competing system—or at the very least a connection of their own across the Cascades with such a system. But John was a man with experience and sound judgment. The fact that the Union Pacific had terminated at Sacramento had not put San Francisco out of business. There was no reason why the Northern Pacific should put Seattle out of business.

John saw the Northern Pacific railroad for what it really was—a local line less than two hundred miles long connecting a little sawmill town with an equally small river port called Kalama. There were no tracks between Bismarck, North Dakota, and Kalama. He rightly concluded that the Northern Pacific was a paper dragon and would be for a decade or more to come.

John was a man who faced the here-and-now problems.

Until then, he had exercised a virtual monopoly on Puget Sound. Now, thanks to the precipitous and unwarranted action of the railroad, (after all, it was an *accidental murder*) competitors were luring some of his best Indian maidens to Tacoma. John realized it was a free country and the girls had a right to work where they wished.

As a man of sharp business acumen, John saw that the competition in Tacoma marked the beginning of the end of an era. The time was right for derring-do.

John sent for shock troops.

The old order changeth . . .

Writer Jim Stevens provides us with the following priceless prose describing the entry of the troops into Seattle:

> One fine day a lumber schooner from San Francisco tied up at the sandspit dock, and there appeared before the incredulous eyes of the hangers-on a marvelous parade. Down the gangplank tripped a dozen *white* damsels, all dazzling in form-fitting bombazine frocks, French-heeled shoes, silk stockings, and the war paint of their profession. The parade, escorted by Pinnell, marched daintily on to Illahee . . .
>
> Recovering from its first surprise and enchantment, Seattle whooped in jubilation, shook hands all'round, and bellowed a new defiance at Tacoma. Again, stirring news grapevined up the skidroads into the deep timber . . . an overwhelming tide rolled for Seattle . . .

The arrival of the ladies from San Francisco was greeted with as much enthusiasm as the arrival of the Mercer Girls. But the objectives of the two sets of girls were different. The Mercer Girls came here to get married.

John Pinnell's girls did not.

They were professional and business women.

They knew their business and their profession was an old one. Like the other Sons of the Profits, they were here to make the desert blossom . . . and to make money. John even bought new property to provide them a better showcase. Comparing their operation to the amateur Indian women in the Illahee would be no more fair than comparing the Wright Brothers' first efforts at flying to a supersonic jet . . . yet each, in its time, had enormous impact.

Other proprietors of lesser establishments were forced to meet the competition. The land down around where the railroad stations are today was filled in and bloomed. A new district called Whitechapel came into existence. It was not what you could call fine residential property, but it sure boomed. It even moved west and started pushing the retail center of the city north to Pioneer Square.

The bright lights burned and Seattle became the Las Vegas of Puget Sound.

The fruit stand

Let it not be said that John Pinnell licked the railroad all by himself. He would be the first to file a modest disclaimer of that tribute, even though the other folks in Seattle weren't doing much to help him. No, John couldn't have done it without a major assist from the Board of Directors of the Northern Pacific.

The company employed Frederick Law Olmstead, a great New York landscape architect, to draft a model town for Tacoma. The plan proposed to make Tacoma the most beautiful city in the world. The contours of the land had been studied carefully with an eye to beauty. The streets were sixty-six feet wide instead of forty-eight. The boulevards were eighty feet wide. The alleys were thirty-six feet wide instead of eighteen. Pick any model real estate development of today, with its graciously curved streets and its built-in park areas and you have the Olmstead plan for Tacoma in 1873.

Olmstead selected street names such as "Manoca" and "Orinoco." As Tacoma's historian Hunt put it, he "robbed geography all the way from the equator to the poles for his street names." He laid out seven parks ranging in size from two to thirty acres right in the heart of town.

Hundreds of purchasers with dollars in their hands were lined up at the offices of the Land Company preparing to acquire their own hunks of property in the Pacific Northwest's newest bonanza. But the Land Company held up all sales until the Great Plan arrived from the New York offices. The whole thing, meanwhile, was being kept hush-hush. The railroad wanted to spring the great surprise on Puget Sound when it would make the greatest impact . . . when it would deliver the *coup de grace* to Seattle.

Late in 1873 the plan was revealed to the frontier community.

The people of the Puget Sound country took one astonished look at it . . .

And started laughing.

Editor Thomas Prosch reacted to the Olmstead Plan in the following manner:

> In three months he had devised and put on paper the most
> fantastic and astonishing plat of a town that ever was seen. It
> covered a thousand acres . . . there wasn't a straight street, a
> right angle or a corner lot . . . The blocks were shaped like
> melons, pears and sweet potatoes . . . One block, shaped like a
> banana, was 3,000 feet in length . . . In general, it condemned
> itself as a city.

Historian Hunt reports that the sarcastic settlers vowed that everything that "had ever been exhibited in an agricultural show had its
counterpart in the shape of lots in this town, from calabashes to ice
boxes . . ." A state of emergency was declared. General James Tilton,
the fellow who had a fracas with Arthur Denny but retained the
title of "General" the rest of his life, was hired at the exorbitant fee
of three hundred dollars a month *cash* (as opposed to those half-
priced greenbacks) to junk the multi-thousand-dollar plan and give
the folks what they wanted—square lots.

While the rest of the Puget Sound people were laughing Tacoma
out of countenance, the railroad compounded the felony by setting
the folks within the Tacoma area at each other's throats.

The railroad established its own town about two miles from the old
town. In other localities across the continent, the old towns had folded their tents and moved to the new towns.

In Yakima, for instance, they packed up the old town at what now is
Union Gap and trundled across the prairie to the new location
where the center of town is today. The whole town, hotels, restaurants, saloons and retail stores, conducted their normal operations
while they were being hauled to the new location.

Quadruple trouble

In Tacoma, however, the railroad company had some stubborn people, each trying to make his area the biggest and best. Before they
were through there were four warring communities . . . each more
interested in destroying the other than providing a generally hospitable atmosphere for trade. Nobody with the leadership capabilities of

John Pinnell rose to the surface. And John, operating with deadly precision, continued the monopoly for his particular product on the Sound.

Thanks to this monopoly an axiom that had been held by everyone concerned went down the tube. Tacoma got the terminus of the railroad and by the laws set down by the prophets, she was supposed to become the major city on Puget Sound. But she never did make an appreciable dent in the trade that went to Seattle.

The time was out of joint for Tacoma. A few months after she had been named as the terminus, the country went into a financial tailspin sparked by the failure of Jay Cooke & Company. Both Seattle and Tacoma lost population as a result of the ensuing depression. Neither of the towns had a population over 1,000. And nobody in either of the towns had any money. The people living in their glad-rags on view property found themselves swapping music lessons for the butcher's daughter in exchange for pork chops.

Construction on the railroad had been halted as a result of Cooke's failure, so there were no construction workers. There was no measurable amount of traffic on the road between Tacoma and Kalama.

There was some money in the area. It was the wages paid to the 10,000 or so loggers in the lumber camps around the Sound. But where they worked there was no place to spend their earnings.

It was this kind of a stand off: Tacoma had the railroad; Seattle had John Pinnell's girls . . .

And when the loggers came into town to spend their money, it wasn't for a railroad trip to Kalama.

Brown and out

In the light of history, it seems incredible that anyone in Seattle could fail to recognize the fantastic contribution made by John Pinnell to the healthy growth of the city of Seattle. But Seattle had, and probably always will have, Bluenoses who fail to realize that some of the people in a seaport town like to kick up their heels once in a while. Beginning with Arthur Denny, they have represented one half of Seattle's split personality.

Beriah Brown was the first to capitalize on that half. He was the first of the important professional Bluenoses . . . the advance man for the Blue Laws that were finally passed in 1909 making it illegal to have fun in public on Sunday. But—we must take the bad with the good if we're going to present an honest history, and that means Brown must be included in our chronicle.

For a time, Brown was the publisher of a long-since defunct newspaper called the *Puget Sound Dispatch,* which he used as a sounding-board for his bitter attacks on Pinnell. His were the scurrilous kind of charges that best were answered by calm, intellectual editorials like the following, which appeared in the opposition paper, the *Intelligencer:*

> Old Molly Brown gloats over an opportunity for a diatribe on obscenity . . . and is as corrugated with fatty tissues of pruriency for unclean things as is possible for anyone.

Brown's short-lived paper came into existence on September 19, 1872 with the fearless pronouncement that it would begin a campaign for "Christian Decency." By November 21 of the same year it had concentrated its attack on John Pinnell as the leading citizen in his field, saying that he must be stopped . . . "peaceably if possible, but by force if necessary."

The failure of Brown's paper can clearly be traced to his abysmal inability to grasp the significance of Pinnell's work. It is especially deplorable that he concentrated his attack on Pinnell between 1873 and 1876—the very years when John was performing his greatest service to the community . . . at the time when John was securing Sattle's position as the trading center of the Sound against the awesome opposition of the railroad.

For example, in 1873 when John was the boy with the finger in the dike, Brown came roaring forth with headlines announcing there were five squaw brothels in the city of Seattle. "Seattle," he pointed out, "has a population of less than 2,000 people. That's too many squaw brothels for a town of less than 2,000 people . . ." Actually, it would have served Brown's purpose better if he had used the true figure of less than 1,000 instead of the Seattle booster figure of 2,000.

There, I say, is ignorance in action . . . an example of the total breakdown in civic unity that has given Seattle a split personality ever since.

What did he mean, "squaw brothels" in Seattle? Those were hospitality centers. Like the Travelers' Aid, they weren't there to serve the needs of the folks living in town. They were there to provide a service for the people from outside of Seattle . . . the visiting firemen —or loggers in those days. Besides, they had been superceded by the professional and business women . . .

They were the predecessors of the trading stamp!

While Brown's sanctimonious paper harangued the public to drive out people like Pinnell, John's part of town forged ahead. The recreational palaces of pleasure joined forces with the butcher, baker and candlestick maker and all prospered together. A prognosticator of gloom and doom, the *Dispatch* languished for lack of advertising revenue, but continued its futile fustations in direct opposition to the economic lifestream of the city . . . and finally, on July 13, 1874, one day less than a year after the Northern Pacific had arrived, the *Dispatch* felt it could deliver the blow that would kill Father John Pinnell.

How now "Brown" cow?

It was election time. For years Brown had been trying to oust the county commissioners, who took a realistic view of Pinnell's importance in town, and Brown felt he really had evidence of hankypanky in connection with the county farm, which was located out near Georgetown.

In the sixties the farm had reverted by escheat to the county from an estate and was supposed to be the "poor" farm. The description was adequate because they never had been able to get the poor to farm it and after Pinnell got into a financial position where he could start breeding thoroughbred race horses, he offered to rent the land from the county for $150 a year—which was $150 a year more than the county had been getting for it.

In the meantime, John had become buddy-buddy with one of the other Sons of the Profits, banker Angus MacIntosh, and Angus cast a covetous eye on a rock quarry that occupied part of the farm. He figured there was money in that rockpile if the ground could ever be separated from county ownership.

The commissioners handed MacIntosh the chore of finding a new site for the courthouse. MacIntosh talked the matter over with Pinnell and jointly they came up with a proposition to the commissioners.

The Illahee wasn't doing very well at that time—due in large measure to the existence of other more profitable spots on additional land that John now owned. John would accept $1,000 in cash and a deed to the county farm, which he had been leasing for the past several years, in exchange for the two lots he had bought for $300 when he had first come to town.

Brown charged that Pinnell had added a further and secret fillip to the transaction . . . he had agreed to sell MacIntosh the rock quarry. The paper went on to charge that MacIntosh "who now with Mr. Dexter Horton is endeavoring to make a raid on University lands" was using his position as a public official for private gain.

Whether or not this is true, I don't know. It becomes suspect when you consider the charges were made on Election Day when it was too late for any rebuttal. On the other hand subsequent events proved there might have been just a grain of truth in them.

Pinnell came out with a rebuttal in the *Intelligencer* the next day in defense of the deal that had been made with the county . . . and levelled the charge that the *Dispatch* "deliberately lied!"

Brown failed in his efforts to oust the commissioners, but he did get one little tag line stuck in before the transaction between the county and Pinnell was completed. It stated that the county would get 10¢ a cord royalty if the rock on the farm was ever quarried.

So the county bought the site of the Illahee for a courthouse. And when you think of some of the things that have gone on in the courthouse since, it could have been a delightful living memorial to our first major pleasure palace . . . a thing we could point to as a part of Seattle's colorful past . . . a perfect place for a plaque to Pinnell.

Unfortunately, this was not to be. The deal with Pinnell fell through in 1875 and today the Great Northern's Empire Builder thunders into a tunnel about where the courthouse would have been. John got his property back . . . and the county got back its farm.

There was one little difference that apparently went unnoticed at the time. The rock quarry wasn't included in the land the county got back from Pinnell.

That piece of property had been sold to MacIntosh.

The passing of Pinnell

I am indebted to Howard F. Grant's unpublished manuscript, "Skid Road," for information concerning the ultimate fate of Citizen Pinnell and for what might be called the traditional view of the passing of this unsung hero of our history.

On February 17, 1883, the *Seattle Weekly Herald* notified the world that John Pinnell, proprietor of a small saloon in Ellensburg, had gone along to his great reward.

Mr. Grant sums up John's life with these words:

> So passed the man who taught . . . Seattle the value of catering to man's illegitimate desires. With the profits he derived from that education, he opened a jewelry store, a stage line to Lake Washington, a restaurant, a skating rink and developed one of the best strings of local race horses.

> Like many a man even of the present day he had tried to establish himself financially and thereby socially on the proceeds of vice. Had he not been singled out for the principal scapegoat in Seattle's first moral awakening he might well have become one of the civic pillars . . .

With all due respect for Mr. Grant, I feel he is reflecting a minority view of the relative importance of John's contribution to Seattle's history. Who is to judge. for instance, whether or not the vital human needs served by John's hospitality houses were legitimate or illegitimate—Beriah Brown?

I'd like to hear the case for John Pinnell presented by some of his contemporaries like Bailey Gatzert, John Leary, Henry Yesler, Thomas Burke, Orange Jacobs, and all of the others whose names appear so prominently in our history of that time. The shadow cast by John Pinnell was as big if not bigger than that of the others.

I also would like to ask Rice and Ainsworth whether they would kick John out of Tacoma if they had it to do over again. It is quite untrue that John retired in disgrace . . . much as the moralists would like to think so. And I must disturb their complacency.

John married Annie Murray, one of the professional and business women, in 1875. And, instead of leaving Seattle in disgrace, John left Seattle because he had bought an estate in eastern Washington. After selling the county farm back to the county, John had no place in which to breed his thoroughbred horses.

If he did not initiate the program under which this state is a great breeding place for thoroughbreds, he at least was one of those who helped create that excellent enterprise.

John was not the kind of guy who would fold and give up.

And after all, he had the proceeds from the jewelry store . . . the stage line . . . the restaurant and the skating rink to provide him and Annie with the little luxuries that make old age a graceful time of life.

VI

The Colman Cometh

While John Pinnell was modestly moving mountains to preserve Seattle's position as the trading center of Puget Sound against the threat of the Northern Pacific Railroad, Arthur Denny & Co. were off on the wildest goose chase in the city's history.

Out of this chase came the wonderful myth about the May Day Picnic of May 1, 1874. That was the day when all of the folks in town decided to build a transcontinental railroad with volunteer labor.

If you're going to have a myth of any stature at all, this is the kind to have . . . long on emotion, short on fact.

Describing Seattle's reaction when the Northern Pacific picked Tacoma, one homespun historian said:

> Seattle was furious. We had fighting ancestors here. This city decided that if the Northern Pacific would not come here, it would build its own railroad, the Seattle & Walla Walla, through Snoqualmie Pass to a rail connection with Walla Walla.

> At dawn on that memorable Friday, cannons were fired, bells were rung, the town band paraded playing louder than it ever had before. All business houses were closed . . . Something big came into being in Seattle that day—the Seattle Spirit!

> That May Day was a demonstration to the world, to the Northern Pacific and to themselves, that the citizens of Seattle were not to be beaten by the mere loss of a terminus.

This myth is rich in the tradition of the original settlers who "gladly" moved their stakes to make room for "Doc" Maynard and later for old Henry Yesler . . . and most purveyors of nostalgia hold that the May Day Picnic outclasses the stake-moving example of selflessness nearly a quarter of a century earlier.

Well, that's the way the Seattle Spirit bounces—check any of the older history books. It's true that they did have a dandy picnic. But I'm sort of in the business of checking out some of our favorite legends, and that picnic didn't add up to building a railroad. Those railroads are kind of hard to build, and doing it with volunteers— that really stretches the imagination.

So once again we went to the sources to find out what actually happened, and once again we find the true story is not only more interesting but also more important to the development of Seattle than the myth. Still, if it hadn't been for the myth we wouldn't have checked it out in the first place. So who's to say it should be expunged from the record?

Lover's quarrel

A nine year-old love affair between Seattle and the Northern Pacific Railroad ended on July 14, 1873, when Arthur Denny got that telegram from Rice and Ainsworth in Kalama informing him that the terminus of the railroad had been located at Commencement Bay. The people of Seattle promptly blew a fuse.

The railroad scandals that had been rocking the nation gave our folks a stimulating breath of outraged virtue. Maybe we should have pledged our land and money to the railroad speculators instead of the railroad! we said. The pledges we made were greater in value than the whole of Pierce County! we said.

And the time was ripe for saying those things.

Congressional hearings revealed that the railroad barons had bought the Republican majority in Congress. Funds had even been tucked into the hip pocket of the Vice President of the United States. Revelations of exhorbitant rates had the Granges up in arms in the Mid-West. There had been repeated reports that the railroad directors and their friends—armed with the foreknowledge of where the railroad stations would be located and where towns would grow—had bought up all the choice real estate in advance of the public announcements.

Now they had done it in Tacoma.

Now it was brought home to little old Seattle.

Seattle's ensuing wrath and its decision to build its own transcontinental railroad found ready sympathy in the rest of the territory because ours weren't the only toes getting trod on. Under the railroad land grant system the railroads could project lines around the compass, and the land on either side of the projected lines was withheld from settlement until the railroad decided in its own sweet time which of the projected lines would be used for the actual track. As a net result, millions of acres of valuable timber, mineral and agricultural land in the Territory were being withheld from settlement.

A map of proposed Northern Pacific lines looked like a purse seiner's net closed at Spokane but hauling in all the land from Vancouver to Everett. As long as the Northern Pacific could keep that loop intact, it owned the territory and the settlers there were so many fish.

It was our theory, on the other hand, that if we could get a line actually going we could get a railroad land grant of our own from Congress and connect with a transcontinental railroad either in Canada or some place to the south or east of us.

It was the objective of the railroad to keep the net closed.

It was our objective to break out.

The S. & W. W.—a glint in Arthur Denny's eye

The laying of the keel of the Seattle & Walla Walla Railroad and Transportation Company took place at the behest of Arthur A. Denny exactly one week after he had received the bad news from the railroad. None of the valuables like choice land and real money that had been pledged to bring in the Northern Pacific had as yet been *un*-pledged. It seemed like a shame for all that wealth to be lying there on the books—going to waste. Why, there were people on that pledge list who had never before done anything for *anything* civic. Here was some Seattle Spirit in the making. All it needed was a little nudge.

As has been mentioned, the Northern Pacific had surveyed a route from Walla Walla through Snoqualmie Pass into Seattle. The engineers who had done that survey for the Northern Pacific were at loose ends at the moment. They had copies of the survey and literature telling about the traffic potential of such a road. The people of Walla Walla had a tough time barging their grain past two portages on the Columbia River to Portland. Why, men with imagination and courage and a little cash could push through a railroad to Walla Walla . . . and then when the Union Pacific came through from Salt Lake to Portland as they were intending—we'd be hooked up to a transcontinental railroad! And the Northern Pacific could go whistle after a kite.

Who would step up and switch his pledge from the Northern Pacific offer to the Seattle & Walla Walla?

Arthur Denny initiated the re-pledge program by switching his pledge of $21,000 worth of land to the new project. Others like the C. C. Terry Estate . . . the W. N. Bell family . . . David T. Denny . . . William Renton all followed suit with pledges of land. John Pinnell headed the list of people who pledged cash, with his $3,500. All in all, some $500,000 was pledged—but only an infinitesimal portion of that was in coin of the realm. And the next day the news hit the headlines that two thirds of the pledges originally designated for the Northern Pacific had been switched to the Seattle & Walla Walla.

The inevitable mass meeting was held in Yesler's Pavilion a couple months after the fateful telegram. Seleucius Garfielde, our delegate to Congress, was the main speaker. He pointed out that the Northern Pacific had tied up with the Oregon Steam Navigation Company and never would go for a road across the mountains. Half a million bushels of wheat were sitting in Walla Walla at the moment and couldn't be shipped before the winter blockade of ice. It was worth only 40¢ a bushel in Walla Walla. Wheat was selling in Seattle for a $1.25. Here was 85¢ that could be split between the farmers and the railroad. Because the government was subsidizing railroads with land grants, they would get free land valued at about two million dollars as a railroad grant. On this enough money could be borrowed to get the road well underway.

As a result of this meeting the company was formed. Stock was subscribed to. Arthur Denny was named president of the road and J. J. McGilvra the attorney.

Pie in the sky

Denny and McGilvra went to Walla Walla. The folks there asked only that they have representation on the board of directors and that whatever money they raised be applied to the section of the railroad that ran from their city to Wallula, the connection with the Columbia River. There were two notable exceptions in the main line of Walla Walla enthusiasm. One was Dr. Dorsey Baker who had planned a small railroad with wooden tracks as far as Wallula; the second, the *Walla Walla Statesman*. But other than these, the project was off to a good start.

In the meantime the Legislature passed an act which permitted the four counties through which the railroad was to pass to issue bonds to the extent of $500,000 each provided the proposition was approved by 60 per cent of the voters . . . for a potential total of $2,000,000. The engineers who had been retained to survey the route came up with the thought that two and two make four. They pointed out that a standard gauge railroad would cost $8,000,000, but a narrow gauge railroad could be built for $4,000,000. If we got $2,000,000 from federal government land grants and $2,000,000 from county bond issues, we were home free.

On the income side of the ledger, it was estimated that the Kittitas, Yakima and Walla Walla valleys and the Blue Mountain foothills would generate traffic valued at $1,600,000 annually. For a coefficient of safety they cut that estimate in half. Interest on the bonds would run to $600,000, giving them a safety margin of $200,000.

In the meantime the Northern Pacific Railroad had passed into the hands of a receiver. It was flat on its back. On paper, the Seattle & Walla was already making money. And the people rejoiced. The newspapers printed millions of words about the rejoicing on their front pages. But those were the only papers that showed the rejoicing. A depression was in the land and the kinds of papers like stock certificates indicating that people had bought stock in the railroad were not in evidence.

We couldn't sell our railroad stock.

In short, there was an emergency. Something had to be done in a hurry or the patient would expire. What could they do to prove there really was going to be a railroad? Why not a ground-breaking ceremony? That'll jingle the money loose. After all, they practically had a $4,000,000 railroad built . . . and one that would turn a $200,000 profit the first year. Ground-breaking? Ground-breaking, my eye, let's start building the thing.

They had millions in prospect, but there was a small problem— there wasn't a dime in the till.

May Day! May Day!

"May Day!" is a modern method of hollering for help. In 1874 it just happened to be a good day to start a railroad, but the main idea was the same. The chief engineers in charge of promoting their paper railroad had moved the folks into action. They had turned on en- thusiasm in Seattle so many times in the past they could do it in their sleep. Why not a picnic? That would be a good gimmick. Shut down the businesses to show that everybody meant business. There were enough businessmen on the committee to handle that phase of the operation . . . and close down the schools . . . a touch of genius! The kids would love it.

What about money for the food?

Don't be ridiculous. The women in the community were old hands at putting together the necessary groceries for a church social . . . why not for the start of a transcontinental railroad! That oughta grab 'em. So while the men provided sweat, blisters and aching backs, the ladies provided baked ham, chicken, pickles, jellies, hot biscuits, pies, cakes and coffee toward the grubbing out of a roadbed for the railroad-to-be.

All morning, the butcher, the baker and the candlestick maker bent their backs to the chore. After a wholesome lunch, Henry Yesler, who had occupied his time whittling while the others entertained themselves with picks and shovels, provided us with a quote that has since rung down the long corridors of Seattle's history.

He said, "Quit your fooling and get to work!"

And that's what they did. They worked the rest of the afternoon. According to the theory of the promoters, so much public spirit would be generated at this point the men of the town would set aside one day a week for the building of the railroad. Just to make the project more enticing, they would be paid off for that work in railroad stock. They would show the world the kind of spirit the city of Seattle had!

And they did.

A couple weeks later a small group of volunteers assembled at the site. They got a little work done but that was the end of the line as far as volunteer railroad builders were concerned. The bells weren't ringing and the cannons weren't shooting and the newspaper reporters weren't there to write the story. The old Seattle Spirit was willing, but the flesh . . .

Ah, that was weak . . .

A case of spirits

The lovely thing about local spirit is that nobody outside of the area pays any attention to it. So a community can be as spirited as it likes and nobody else challenges it. We, for example, have wallowed for a long time in the positive knowledge that we were the only city with a local spirit. We're like the descendants of our own pioneer forefathers. All they either know or care about is the history of great grandpa or grandma—and what *they* did to build the city. This is a common ailment of both frontier towns and the sons of the Sons of the Profits.

I'd heard about the Seattle Spirit ad nauseam, so I thought it would be fun to find out how some of the other towns reacted when the Northern Pacific chose Tacoma as its terminus.

How did Olympia react?

How did Olympia react? Well, they had a big picnic and started to build a transcontinental railroad of their own. The men provided sweat, blisters and aching backs and the ladies came through with baked ham (or was it roast beef?), chicken, pickles, jellies, hot biscuits, pies, cakes and coffee . . .

How did Port Townsend react? Well, they had a big picnic . . . etc.

And what do you bet that somebody in each town didn't get up after lunch and say, "Quit your fooling and get to work!"?

On the other hand, we got a railroad and they didn't. We became the biggest city and they didn't. Why Seattle and not the others? Their "spirit" stories were no more nor no less foolish than ours. So what happened in Seattle that made the *difference?*

For one thing, Seattle's leaders were either too stupid or too stubborn to give up, no matter how tough things looked. In spite of the fact that the railroad project practically folded in the next few months, they kept at it.

May Day plus one

Undaunted, Arthur Denny's next stop was Washington, D.C. He went prepared to do the same yeoman service on behalf of the Seattle & Walla Walla he had performed for the University of Washington and Daniel Bagley nearly a decade before . . . and by effective politicking, he got the route for the new railroad approved.

It took two years for the rest of it to happen, but at the end of that time, the following events had taken place: Congress refused a federal land grant—that was the first $2,000,000 down the drain; Congress repudiated the action of the Legislature permitting the counties to issue railroad bonds—that was the second $2,000,000 down the drain; Oregon congressmen pushed through legislation facilitating shipping on the Columbia River; Dr. Dorsey Baker built his own railroad to Wallula . . . and the *Walla Walla Statesman* turned against Seattle, fought to get Walla Walla on the main line of the Union Pacific and to eliminate any "branch" road to Seattle.

By the beginning of 1876, the board of directors of the Seattle and Walla Walla Railroad and Transportation Company concluded they had some kind of a problem or something.

Congress was not about to grant land to any railroad headed any place. A reverse trend had set in and they were starting to take land away from railroads.

Politics in Washington, D.C. didn't vary appreciably from what they are today. And at least the fellows back there were honest . . . once bought, they stayed bought. The Northern Pacific had long since paid out good money for its congressional merchandise. After all, it did have track as far west as Bismarck, South Dakota, and just because it was on its financial back at the moment was no reason for deserting it.

Besides they knew one day the Northern Pacific would be back in business—and who could say the same for a small dot on the map called Seattle?

At this end, however, we found it difficult to overlook that long, long gap between Bismarck and the proposed terminal at Kalama, Washington Territory—it was a 1,287-mile gap, with no track in sight.

On the front pages of our newspapers there still was a big whoop-de-doo about the Seattle & Walla Walla Railroad. Somebody had been at work on the hot air machine and the big balloon it sent up had the newspapers in Portland nervously trying to pop it.

Suppose there was a miracle and Seattle could get track laid across the Cascades to a hook-up with the Union Pacific in Walla Walla?

The Portland papers worried aloud that traffic down the Columbia River might be diverted across the Cascades to Puget Sound . . . so they put on a campaign urging Walla Walla to secede from the Territory and profit by the obvious advantages of being part of the State of Oregon. The "obvious advantages" consisted primarily of the fact that a State could get more federal money than a Territory.

Don't hang your hat on Seattle, the Portland papers advised, it will never survive.

The Board of Directors of the Seattle and Walla Walla were so heartened by this adverse publicity out of Portland that they committed the cardinal sin of believing they had a real threat going.

But money was the problem.

The easy money . . . the public money . . . was on a shelf a little too high for the Seattleites to reach and they had to go into the tough market place to get their dough. It was to be had in San Francisco, but they were not the men to get it. So they looked around for the most promising candidate in the place and their eyes fell on a newcomer to the city by the name of James M. Colman. Colman had only been around town four years, but he'd had a lot of contact with San Francisco capital for the previous fifteen years and he'd shown enough interest in their railroad to be elected as a member of the board, himself.

Colman would get them to the promised land.

The man with the Midas touch

Even then it was beginning to sound like Seattle had its own anthem called "The Man with the Midas Touch." Henry Yesler provided it during the fifties. Daniel Bagley brought it into play in the early sixties. John Pinnell assumed the mantle in the late sixties and early seventies. And Colman took the helm in the late seventies and early eighties.

Colman was forty-four years old when it came his turn to change the course of the city's history. He was born in Scotland on June 17, 1832 and migrated to the United States in 1854 with a technical education as a machinist and engineer—a field for which he had a native talent. He went to work in a machine shop in Wisconsin and it was typical that within six months he had become the superintendent.

Colman's first job after arriving in the Puget Sound area in 1861 was that of managing a huge mill at Port Madison for some San Francisco capitalists. While Colman did the managing of the mill, Mrs. Colman did the cooking for the mill hands. As usual, they tucked their combined earnings in the savings bank. During the next three years, Colman impressed the San Francisco investors with his ability to make money for them. Mrs. Colman impressed the mill hands with her cooking and both of them impressed the bankers with their thrift. So that when Colman decided to buy his own mill at Port Orchard, he carried the good will of the San Francisco men with him. And the bankers loaned him the money that together with his own enabled him to get started in his new enterprise. His wife's reputation as a cook provided the mill with top hands.

It was not startling to find that Colman was not satisfied with the mill the way it was and completely rebuilt it in 1867. In 1868, fire removed the Colmans from both their mill and their investment, leaving them penniless.

Colman's reputation as a mill manager, however, had made itself known in San Francisco financial circles. The Hanson, Ackerman and Company of San Francisco, which owned a mill in Tacoma put him to work enlarging it. His meticulous attention to detail produced such an excellent mill that the San Francisco group persuaded him to stay on and manage it. He again made the owners so much money he was offered the chore of enlarging and operating the Yesler Mill in Seattle, which had been leased by J. J. McKinnon, another San Francisco financier.

It was at this point that historian Frederic Grant took note in his *History of Seattle* (published in 1891) that "for the next ten years from that time, the history of Mr. Colman is the history of Seattle . . ."

Within three years, Colman not only had made a lot of money for McKinnon, but had saved enough, himself, to make McKinnon such an excellent offer to take over the lease that McKinnon couldn't afford to turn it down. Colman determined to increase the capacity of the mill from 15,000 to 50,000 board feet per day which would have kept an ordinary man busy. But Colman wasn't an ordinary man, and when the owners of the nearly defunct Seattle & Walla Walla approached him about bailing them out, he thought he saw a way to do it and the challenge was more than he could resist.

You run your railroad and I'll run mine

The proposition the board offered Colman was the same type that had been offered him three times before by San Francisco capitalists . . . for the mills in Port Madison, Tacoma and Seattle. He would be the boss. In this instance, Arthur Denny would remain as president and the other officers would retain their titles. Colman would get the work done.

There was one unsubtle difference.

In each of the previous propositions, he had been placed in charge of a going concern. He was asked to perform a service. They had money and he would be paid.

This time, however, he was to be superintendent of a piece of paper.

The Seattle & Walla Walla had no track, no rolling stock, no roadbed, no dockside facilities, no land—but most of all the thing they had most of was no money. Next only to that, they had no credit either. They had spent their small cash sums, the ones handed over by men like Pinnell . . . and the rest of the pledges, the ones to be paid for with land, had been withdrawn.

Look at the wonderful articles in the Portland papers, the board members said. We've got Portland scared to death. Now all you have to do is build the road to Walla Walla and we'll mow 'em down. Colman sounded the board out on the money part of the proposal. He would throw $10,000 into the pot. Would the other five members of the board match it? If they would, a bond issue of $30,000 could be floated and backed by $60,000 worth of the railroad's stock.

The board wasn't *that* heartened by the adverse publicity in Portland.

Colman then suggested that he would up his ante to $20,000. They could sell the $30,000 in bonds if all of the present stockholders of the company together would put up $40,000. He didn't request cash on the barrel-head, so why not?

The board agreed this was a splendid idea.

They were great hue-and-cry experts, and within a short time Colman had been built as the savior of the Seattle & Walla Walla Railroad. The public gobbled up the $30,000 bond issue, and with that money added to his own and a mortgage, Colman went out and bought up land along the right-of-way to Renton. He thoughtfully bought the land in his own name, not that of the railroad. As it turned out it was well he had done so, because the stockholders only came through with $2,500 of the $40,000 that they had pledged.

It is ironic that the public bought the bonds because it thought that Colman intended to build a railroad to Walla Walla, and that the stockholders failed to produce their pledges for the same reason.

The latter had "had it" on that Walla Walla business. They'd had two years of batting their heads against a stone wall consisting of just about every powerful interest in the Territory. If the mountains didn't provide an insurmountable barrier, the financiers and Congress did. If Colman wanted to play Don Quixote, it wasn't going to be with their money.

Colman, on the other hand, was not interested in a pie-in-the-sky proposition. He was an intensely practical man. His vision was not obscured by any day-dreams of getting to Walla Walla with a railroad . . . and once again Seattle had the right man at the right time in the right place.

There was coal in King County, millions of tons of it. It was excellent coal, and at the right price there was a market for it in San Francisco. The fact that it was fifteen or twenty miles from dockside with only half-baked methods of getting it from mine to market was merely an engineering and financing problem.

Colman was an engineer. He knew a lot about building logging railroads. He had a few bucks of his own, and he had the confidence of a lot of moneyed men in San Francisco. He had proved that when he said he could do something, he could do it. He entertained no high-flown thoughts like that of building an $8,000,000 standard gauge railroad that maybe would link up with a major transcontinental system three hundred miles away.

His thoughts ran more to $80,000, fifteen miles . . . and coal.

Old King (County) Coal

Colman had not previously become involved in the great coal controversy that had raged in the county for the previous decade. It was a resource that was every bit as valuable as the timber that he had been dealing with and the Newcastle mine near Seattle was queen of them all and at the center of the struggle.

By engaging in massive, free-for-all throat-cutting among themselves, the businessmen in Seattle had lost the coal fields to outside interests.

Bagley, who is normally a kindly man, was moved to make the following editorial comment in his *History of Seattle:*

> Had the money wasted on this project been invested in providing transportation from the Newcastle mine to Seattle, the history of the coal industry in King County would have been vastly different from what it is. It could have remained in the ownership of Seattle people and would not have passed to San Francisco capitalists, who later furnished the money for its development and absorbed the profits...

Speaking to that point, coal got so costly in Seattle with the profits being taken out by the San Francisco owners of the mine, many a fortune was made in the city by shipping the stuff here from as far away as New Zealand . . . making the carrying of coal to Newcastle something less than an idle phrase in this city.

The San Francisco capitalists were bright enough to get their hands on the coal-bearing property, but they could have used some lessons in transporting it to market.

And Colman was just the teacher for the job.

The story of coal on Puget Sound began twenty-five years before Colman's arrival in the picture with the discovery of coal at Bellingham. It was close to the water, but pretty punk coal. In the sixties, an excellent brand of coal was discovered east of Lake Washington . . . at Coal Creek, just south of Issaquah . . . and at Newcastle, about seven miles north of Renton. The two fields were only a couple of miles apart.

While other coal was found around and about, the above mentioned fuel was the hottest find we had at the time Colman got in the act. A couple of other mines, one at Renton which gave birth to that town . . . and the other called the Talbot mine, about four miles out of Renton, were in operation also when Colman got dealt into the game, but they weren't the prizes that Coal Creek or Newcastle were.

It seems somewhat astonishing that two ministers, G. F. Whitworth and the irrepressible Daniel Bagley, were ringleaders in promoting these mines. However, Whitworth was a geologist and engineer with a lot of coal mining experience in his background. And Bagley was just a born promoter. In 1865, when he was headed for Washington, D.C. anyway, he learned there was some doubt about the legality of the mineral rights that Whitworth and his group had to the claims they had staked out at Newcastle.

So Bagley's seemingly naive and very cheery face appeared once more in the halls of a legislative body . . . and when he returned to Seattle, there was an Act of Congress in his pocket giving his friends the coal rights to the property they owned.

They spent the next six years and $25,000 attempting to wrestle that coal to market over a system of wagon trails three miles down the hill to Lake Washington and then by barges to a place called Flea-burg, which since has acquired the more attractive name of Leschi Park, and by wagons over the hill to Yesler's Wharf. Then San Francisco interests who were better at figures than at figuring, had taken over and really complicated the travel pattern. They rigged up a system of inclined railways that they were pretty proud of. Cables were attached to cars so that when one set of coal cars went down the hill they hauled the set of empties up.

Pretty neat, eh?

They then barged their coal in coal cars to a portage where the Lake Washington Ship Canal is today. The cars then were placed on tracks and transported to Lake Union . . . barged across Lake Union to another set of tracks which took the coal over the hill to coal bunkers at Pike Street where they were dumped into coaling ships. Teredoes got after the piling at the foot of Pike Street and every once in a while the whole business would collapse on somebody's head, which was as inefficient as all get out, not to mention the damage it did to the persons or the workers who happened to be around when things dropped on them. What was even worse, in Colman's eyes, was that it cost $5 a ton to make the eleven different transfers the coal underwent in getting to dockside.

Not so neat, eh?

To make things even more lamentable, a syndicate of business men headed by the ubiquitous Henry Yesler got their hands on the Coal Creek fields. Instead of joining forces with the ministerial group, they decided they'd become millionaires all by themselves and set about organizing a competing transportation system, and succeeded in one thing...

They dropped $30,000 without moving a ton of coal.

They achieved that highly successful maneuver in 1868. Things got no better fast and within three years they dropped the ball which was happily scooped up by the money men in the Bay City.

They got the coal moving all right—but at the $5-a-ton figure and over the Rube Goldberg system that previously had been concocted by our own local talent.

And they got it moving at just the wrong time. A building slump hit California, and San Francisco, which always had been our big buyer of coal, found it cheaper to get its coal from a field at Mount Diablo in Contra Costa County just a few miles north. It was inferior coal, like that of Bellingham, but it had the lovely advantage of being nearby.

The market for Seattle coal collapsed. As late as 1874—the year of the May Day picnic—only 9,000 tons of Newcastle coal found its way into the San Francisco market. In that same year 200,000 tons of Mount Diablo coal was bought in that same city.

The coal man cometh

Colman set about planning the building of a logging road—same as he had always done—a little longer than most, but definitely a narrow gauge logging road. He had fifteen miles of comparatively easy building across some tideflats and up a valley into Renton where he could start tapping the Renton and Talbot mines. And presumably four or five miles of that already was in operable shape. The two mines had leased part of the right-of-way of the Seattle and Walla Walla to haul their coal to Steele's Landing where it could be loaded on barges and then hauled to ocean-going ships in Seattle. By running a couple of miles of trestle across the tideflats and then grading along the shore of the Sound and up the Duwamish Valley he could put coal directly in the holds of coaling ships a lot cheaper than the owners of the two Renton mines. Once he got that deal going, and money coming in, he could turn his attention to the matter of getting to Newcastle where the real money was. Under the existing system it was costing them $5 a ton to move coal to the coaling ships. The pencil he applied to the piece of paper told him he could do it for less than half of that, and net out at 50¢ a ton personally.

True, the seven miles from Renton into Newcastle were an expensive proposition, but he could knock off a couple or three miles of that along the lake shore at little expense and building three miles or more into the mine presented no more of a problem than he had faced many times before with logging roads.

He presented the proposition to J. J. McKinnon along with another little side deal to sweeten the pot. A coal field known as Cedar Mountain had been discovered nearly twenty years before up Maple Valley from Renton. And one day a railroad was going to tap that area. Nobody had filed a claim on it until Colman had formed the Cedar Mountain Coal Mine, Inc. McKinnon could have a piece of that action as well as the proposed coal road to Renton and Newcastle.

The whole thing seemed eminently practical to McKinnon who suggested that if Colman ran into financial troubles McKinnon would bail him out.

Meanwhile, back at the newspaper offices they were setting up headlines that read like:

RAILROAD TO WALLA WALLA UNDER WAY!

J. M. Colman was the hero of the hour. An enthusiastic Walla Walla newspaperman wrote: "We of Walla Walla have been looking upon the building of this road as an imaginary vision, but, mark my word, if James M. Colman lives, he will build this road over the mountains alone unless some capitalist comes forward and takes it off his hands to build it faster. He is one of the most remarkable men of this coast. A man of active brain, and a splendid mechanic, he is always equal to any emergency . . ."

Everybody in the Pacific Northwest, including the board of directors, believed that the Seattle & Walla Walla railroad was being built from Seattle to Walla Walla—except, of course, the man who was building it.

May Day plus two . . .

It was purely coincidental, but on May Day, 1876—just two years after the historic picnic—Colman's crews went to work on a railroad. Only this time it was no picnic. The bottom had dropped out of the lumber market. Jobs were so scarce you had to have a magnifying glass to find one and nobody could afford to buy a magnifying glass.

The eight-hour day wasn't even in the dream stage yet, and a man who had worked ten hours for J. M. Colman on any given day knew he had done a day's work.

But he also knew he would be paid.

When Colman took over, he was faced with the following: the City Council had granted the Seattle & Walla Walla a right-of-way from the foot of King Street and southeasterly across the tideflats to dry land at the foot of Beacon Hill. King Street really had no foot, except on paper because it was under water and there was no pier. Touching the main land on what then was the Duwamish bottom, the right-of-way ran half a mile, wholly untouched by any grader, and then came upon the old grade. The work on that grade two years before had not been thoroughly done and had to be done over.

At Steele's Landing, seven miles from the point of origin, he met the Renton mine tracks which extended about four miles. Beyond that there had been some grading to a distance of twelve miles from the city, but this had been guttered by rains and blocked by fallen timber.

That was it.

Colman was a one man band. He was timekeeper, bookkeeper, construction superintendent, foreman, financier, paymaster. To give you some idea of his capacity for work it is pointed out that after he had completed the railroad and sold it to Henry Villard of the Northern Pacific, he stayed on for a couple of years as assistant superintendent. When he retired from that job they had to hire six men to take his place.

Overnight, Colman became the biggest employer in town. He didn't take any trips to Washington, D.C., Walla Walla or even San Francisco. But by mid-June the trestle work across the tideflats had been completed. By the end of August all of the grading, trestling and bridging from the terminal to Steele's Landing had been completed. A contract had been let for laying the tracks, building the wharf and bunkers. Then the contracts were let for building the cars, including the casting of the wheels. They'd never done that sort of thing in Seattle but they learned fast and when the road was completed, everything but the tracks and the locomotives had been built in this city.

In January an incline to the bunkers was laid and put into position. It was sixty-six feet above the tide flats and a thousand feet long. It was a facility capable of handling four coaling ships with drafts of twenty-five feet around the clock and regardless of tide. By February they had a twenty-one ton locomotive named the Arthur A. Denny, twelve flat cars, and a combined passenger-baggage-mail car with a seating capacity of about forty people. Colman told his board of directors he was in a position to move 1200 tons of coal a day. The Talbot and Renton mines, producing 400 tons a day, were setting up to double their capacities.

Problems were encountered when Colman attempted to run the twenty-one ton locomotive over the roadbed that had been installed by the mining companies, a ballasting job which delayed the first celebration excursion from March 3rd to March 7th.

The Big Day finally arrived and is described by J. Willis Sayre in his book, *This City of Ours,* as follows:

> With J. M. Colman at the throttle and two hundred and fifty people on the train, the Seattle and Walla Walla Railroad was formally dedicated by a trip to Renton. Every man, woman and child in Renton, and the town band, turned out; the Rentonites rode to Seattle and a second Seattle crowd rode out to Renton. The struggle of the years had been crowned with success; the dream of a decade had come true. Seattle at last had a passenger railroad ...

Monkey business

All of this was grand . . . just grand. But the owners of the Renton mines—some financiers from San Francisco—had a nasty surprise in store for Seattle's hero. Instead of doubling the capacity of their mines, they were going to close them down!

They figured that without the Renton coal to haul, Colman would go broke.

The Renton mines were really quite expensive to operate, they explained, and perhaps if Mr. Colman would like to spend the additional money necessary to put his railroad into their other piece of mining property at Newcastle . . . They recognized that putting the railroad into Newcastle would be terribly expensive. Going up that mountainous country was a lot more costly than that little jaunt across the tideflats and up the Duwamish Valley to Renton.

Mr. Colman wondered if they could assist the railroad financially in the further jaunt?

No, that was out of the question. On the other hand, they said, Mr. Colman had spent about $80,000 getting where he was and was deeply in debt. Perhaps they could get him off the hook for, let's say, about ten cents on the dollar . . .

There were no hard feelings, of course. This was just good business.

Mr. Colman would think it over—with J. J. McKinnon. He had the wharf and the bunkers in, he explained to McKinnon. The big expense was under his belt. But maybe those Renton-Newcastle mine men needed a lesson. They only had a lease on the road they put into Steele's Landing, so without his permission the Renton mines couldn't move their coal. He figured he could put the line into Newcastle at $6,000 a mile or a total of under $40,000. They were paying $5 a ton to move their coal. He had figured he could do it for half that, but if they were going to play rough, he figured he'd make it $2.75 a ton and let them charge the extra 25¢ a ton up to experience.

This seemed admirable to McKinnon.

Colman went back to the men who had tried to steal his road. He had the financing to move the railroad into Newcastle, he told the business men who had started the fun. He'd be glad to transport their Newcastle coal to dock side at $2.75 a ton. But he was curious —what were they going to do with their Renton coal, lay another set of tracks alongside his as far as Steel's Landing?

No hard feelings, of course . . . this was just a matter of good business.

As it turned out, there *were* no hard feelings . . . and it *was* good business. It had been costing the Renton mine owners 86½¢ a ton to put their coal into the holds of the ocean-going ships. Colman could put it in those same ships at a cost to them of 50¢ a ton.

By February 5, 1878, Colman's tracks finally reached Newcastle, and he obtained a coal transportation monopoly in King County. The Renton mine owners had paid him $175,000 for hauling coal from Renton to the coaling ships in Seattle during the time he was building the Newcastle Road. It is doubtful that he ever had to borrow one red cent to put the last segment of his road into Newcastle.

And did his monopoly help!

In the first year of Colman's first operation into Newcastle the number of tons sold in San Francisco jumped from 9,000 to 128,582— that was his first big bite out of the 200,000-ton majority that previously had been enjoyed by the Mount Diablo mines. His net profit that year was 30 per cent. Within two years, King County was producing 50 per cent of all of the coal produced in the state of Washington and 22 per cent of all the coal produced on the Pacific Coast. Steamers were burning coal in those days and Seattle became the main coaling port on the West Coast. It also became a major city.

R.I.P.

The Seattle & Walla Walla Railroad and Transportation Company never went to Walla Walla. The farthest it ever got was twenty-two miles into Newcastle, but it was the building of the railroad and its corollary functions—the work provided in supplying the mines and running the wharves—that made the Seattle & Walla Walla the most profitable railroad in the United States during the decade of the 1880's.

Colman functioned during a critical period in Seattle's growth. When he entered the scene, there was little to distinguish it from any other little logging town on Puget Sound. The development of King County coal was another major step in launching Seattle as the big city of Puget Sound.

The Newcastle Mine was the grand old lady. She produced over a million and a half tons of coal. She was the biggest, the finest, the deepest mine of them all. In addition to building Seattle, Colman's road built Newcastle into a town almost the size of Walla Walla. Colman's railroad was the lifeline of Seattle in the decade in which she was growing her 1200 per cent from 3,500 to 43,000 people. The whole operation was a major source of the vitality that breathed life into a village and at a time when it needed it most.

As I finished the research on this chapter, I was moved to go and look at the area that had meant so much to this city. I took a trip to Newcastle to see if there was anything left to show the signs of the gigantic struggle that went on there nearly a hundred years ago . . . and drove two miles past it before I realized where I was.

All visible signs of the railroad have disappeared . . . no trestles . . . no road bed . . . no loading platforms . . . no nothing. Nature has taken over completely except for one or two houses and a garage, where once there was a town of over 1,200 people. It is necessary to beat your way through the underbrush to find even the airshaft of the mine.

For nothing and for everything, I tossed a battered block of wood into the hole.

It found its final resting place 1100 feet down.

VII

The Establishment

Even as I pause to record the following priceless prose about the birth of Seattle's first Establishment, a niggling little doubt exists in the back of my brain about how it will be received by the man who built it into a fierce, fighting force.

I am presuming, of course, that there is a hereafter, that he is there and that "there" really is here, which means that he is among us at this very moment—possibly even looking over my shoulder as this is written.

Will he appreciate the posthumous honor that is about to be bestowed upon him? Has he changed his ideas since he passed into the great beyond—perhaps become a spiritual Democrat, or developed a sense of humor about Seattle?

Well, whatever . . . when I build my park in Skid Road to honor Seattle's unsung heroes, one of the targets for our pigeons is going to be a statue with the following identification:

Charles Barstow Wright
Father of
The Seattle Establishment

It also has occurred to me that this will not be a memorial to which the people of Tacoma will respond with spirited enthusiasm, because he already is listed in their history books as the Father of Tacoma. The Charles B. Wright Boys School is named in his honor. Annie Wright Seminary bears his daughter's name. He is responsible for laying out Tacoma's streets . . . for putting together power, light and water systems . . . and was largely responsible for the construction of St. Luke's Episcopal Church.

153

Wright has been big in Tacoma—very big—ever since he cast the
deciding vote that made Tacoma the terminus of the Northern
Pacific Railroad in 1873. His role in creating the Seattle Establishment is lesser known, but I figure Wright is Wright . . . Truth is
Truth . . . and the statute of limitations has not run out on our privilege of handing Mr. Wright exactly what he's got coming to him.

Mr. Wright entered Seattle's history just twenty years after our
hardy little band drove its sturdy little stakes on Denny's muddy little island, giving birth to the great metropolis. He became the first
—but not the last—outsider who tried to force us into a course of
action we didn't want to take. And for the first time, we stopped
squabbling among ourselves and presented a united front against an
intruder.

An Establishment is . . .

For the benefit of those who are not quite sure of what I mean by an
Establishment, let us define the term.

It's the power structure of the community . . . the top ten men in the
human pecking system.

It holds no regular meetings. It elects no officers. It has no constitution and by-laws. There isn't even a membership list. It's the elite
corps of the Sons of the Profits. It is necessary to be one of the Sons
to belong, but no Son is admitted solely on the basis of his ability to
make money. The membership changes from decade to decade . . .
sometimes from year to year. Individual members have their own
side projects, but these mustn't be confused with those of the main
body, which precipitate on call out of community activity.

In a way, it's like a river—sort of a fluid force that gives a little here
and takes a little there. You can't describe any part of it any more
than a blind man touching one part of an elephant can describe the
whole animal. It's the collective judgment of the most powerful men
in the community at a time when they are willing to back their deci-
sions with their dollars.

Like the "boss," the Establishment may not always be right—but it's
always the Establishment.

And where it wants the city to go—there the city goes.

Pre-clash hash

There was no C. B. Wright, nor any Seattle Establishment, in evidence on July 2, 1864 when President Abraham Lincoln signed a piece of paper that chartered the Northern Pacific Railroad and authorized it to build track from Lake Superior to Puget Sound somewhere north of the 45th Parallel.

For that matter, there wasn't even a town called Tacoma.

Seattle was picking herself up from the Indian War and was beginning to forge ahead of Olympia and Port Townsend. Newspaper reporters around the country wrote items like the following one which we reprinted and circulated far and wide. It appeared in the *Detroit Advertiser*.

> The (Northern Pacific) line would probably start at Bayfield or Superior City and run in a westerly direction . . . through the territories of Dakota, Montana, Idaho and Washington, throwing off a branch line to Portland . . . while the main line would pass a little north of west and terminate at a town or settlement now known as Seattle . . . one of the finest and most secure harbors on the globe.

Those were the halcyon days when life was simple and Seattle had no real need for a power structure. But the nucleus of Seattle's first Establishment was on hand—in the persons of Arthur Denny, who located the city in the first place; Henry L. Yesler, who gave the city its first economic foundation, and James M. Colman, who was then doing his economic push-ups in Port Orchard.

The gathering of the clan

It was in 1864 also, when a gentleman by the name of John J. McGilvra put in his first appearance at Seattle. In the 1850's he had become a buddy of old Abe Lincoln when they had adjoining offices in Chicago. The rooms had a connecting door, and each baby-sat in the other's office in his absence. When he became President, Lincoln appointed J. J. as United States Attorney in Washington Territory.

McGilvra first tried out Olympia and Vancouver—both of which were big-time towns when Seattle was just a lumber camp. Then

McGilvra read the advance publicity on the Northern Pacific, noting that Seattle was in the geographic center of Puget Sound and by one means or another had nailed down the University of Washington. He figured he'd cast his lot with Seattle and established residence here. He was 37 years old.

Five years later he gave up his government job in favor of making money and starting the Seattle Bar Association. A little later on he was personally able to subsidize the Madison Street cable car system to the tune of $100,000.

He was the first man in town to wear velvet gloves—over his iron fists. He also had a daughter who had a compulsion to steal sugar lumps from restaurants—even after she was grown up.

John Leary was another man who could read the newspaper articles about the love affair between Seattle and the Northern Pacific Railroad. He was on his way to a comfortable fortune in the lumber business in New Brunswick, Canada, when an idiotic United States government cut his economic throat by repealing a reciprocity treaty. After a try at lumbering in Maine, where they were running out of heavy stands of timber, Leary decided to cast his lot in the Pacific Northwest in general and Seattle in particular.

He arrived in Seattle in 1867, at the age of 31, and promptly involved himself in such money-making ventures as creating Ballard, opening up some coal mines, founding the *Post-Intelligencer,* participating in the formation of the Spring Hill water system, and giving birth to the socio-economic Rainier Club.

He maintained that money was more fun than marriage—until at the age of 54 he paused long enought to marry Eliza P. Ferry. She evidently was supposed to have been a boy, because her first name comes pretty close to that of Elisha P. Ferry, the first governor of the state.

What Leary didn't take with him when he went in 1905 was an estate valued at two million dollars.

Bailey Gatzert was the sixth man who was to become part of Seattle's first Establishment. He was a supreme individualist who refused to pay his way into Seattle's history books, so it's hard to find the sugary frosting for his piece of cake. His newspaper obituary hands him no exorbitant ecstasies, but does point out, however, that he worked hard as a young clerk in the grocery business, saved all his money—and then got rich when he married the boss's sister.

Gatzert was the head man of Schwabacher Brothers, Inc. in Seattle from the time he arrived in 1869 at the age of 40. He built it into the biggest wholesale and retail mercantile firm north of San Francisco. If I had to pick the biggest rock that C. B. Wright stubbed his toe on, it would have to be Schwabacher—and Gatzert. Gatzert grabbed all the Puget Sound trade and kept it in Seattle in spite of all the efforts of the railroad to dislodge it.

Denny, Yesler, Colman, McGilvra, Leary, Gatzert—there they were, the personnel that would make up Seattle's first Establishment . . . the Sleeping Beauty of our Seattle fairy tale, awaiting only the magic touch of the Wright man to spring to life.

Your friend and mine—the Northern Pacific

A proper understanding of the personality of the Northern Pacific is essential to this story . . . and like all the rest of us pre-destined souls, it had to run on the track that was provided for it. A track, as has been hinted earlier, that took it on a collision course with Seattle.

It was born into a railroad world that was dominated by the construction of the railroad which we know today as the Union Pacific.

Congress, which will try anything once, had backed the construction of the Union Pacific Railroad with $50,000,000 worth of government bonds. By the time the Northern Pacific came along with its out-stretched palms, Congress thought it would be interesting to see if a railroad could be built across the country subsidized only by a land grant. So it voted to give the Northern Pacific 50,000,000 acres of land, generously estimated at being worth about $10 an acre.

Our Congressmen thought a half billion dollar land grant ought to provide enough money to build a railroad to the moon.

The bankers didn't agree with the politicians. That "West" was pretty wild. You might make yourself a multi-millionaire buying Northern Pacific bonds, but you also might make yourself a pauper.

So the investment houses went for the Union Pacific's government-backed bonds, and the Northern Pacific had to sit twiddling its thumbs until 1869 when the Union Pacific was completed.

This opened up the railroad bond field and gave the Northern Pacific a chance to lay its hands on a little money for a change.

And Jay Cooke & Company, which was a hot shot eastern promotional outfit, came up with a bright idea for peddling Northern Pacific bonds.

The railroad needed manpower to get itself built. Over in Europe, there was a great stockpile of humanity that was used to working hard under any circumstances and to whom working hard with a chance of bettering oneself would be a sheer pleasure. The Northern Pacific had land and opportunity for these folks until it was running out of its ears.

So, the boys on Wall Street concocted the idea of providing little farms—complete with fences and houses—of forty, eighty and a hundred and sixty acres along the right-of-way. Anybody who wanted to work on the construction of the railroad to get a little stake would be given the farm of his choice at low monthly payments.

The railroad would be built and the right-of-way populated by the most industrious people in the world. A belt of civilization would stretch from Lake Superior to Puget Sound.

Now this idea was as American as apple pie and Jay Cooke & Company generously agreed to let American investors have first crack at buying the bonds. The first issue of bonds was over-subscribed. The Northern Pacific was the American Dream.

But the financial hard-heads within the company took a long look at the promotional proposition and decided that was all it was. The land was supposed to sell for $2.50 an acre to the settlers. It would take a long time to get the settlers here and an even longer time to collect their money. In the meantime, it cost money to build a railroad.

To get this kind of money, the railroad needed investment gamblers as well as tillers of the soil. So it adopted a policy of determining where it would locate its townsites before laying the track. It then would connect the townsites with rail service.

This gave the company a chance to send out real estate agents who quietly bought up the pre-selected land. Then the railroad would touch its magic wand and a town would spring up. If there already was a town in existence at a spot where the railroad wanted to be, it would touch its magic wand a couple of miles away from the existing town. Land prices would skyrocket at the new site.

This procedure resulted in kind of a round-about route for a railroad, but it was a wonderful way to increase land values . . . a little item that was not overlooked by the members of the railroad's board of directors. Since they were privy to the secret plans for townsites, they managed to make tidy personal fortunes in land speculations while the railroad itself was utilizing the money from the land sales to construct track.

The railroad usually made or broke whatever towns it liked as it made its way across the country.

When it selected Tacoma as its terminus, Tacoma was to be the pot of gold at the end of the rainbow . . . the gateway to rich trade with the Orient and Alaska. The board had voted an appropriation of $2,000,000 to make it a model town that would be the envy of all cities in the country. Its agents obtained two solid miles of waterfront.

Individually and also acting on behalf of the railroad, the board members bought up thousands of acres of land in and around Tacoma. C. B. Wright, then a vice president of the Northern Pacific, who had visited Puget Sound, was the biggest individual investor of them all. For that reason he was named the president of the Tacoma Land Company, which was in charge of making Tacoma the major city on Puget Sound.

From a purely cold-blooded business standpoint, neither Wright, because of his holdings in Tacoma, nor the Northern Pacific could afford to have a town on the Sound that was more important than its terminus. It either had to serve Seattle—in which event Wright stood to lose on his land investment in Tacoma—or kill it off.

Wright determined upon the latter course.

With him, it wasn't a question of whether Seattle would be eliminated, it was just a matter of how to do it at the least personal inconvenience.

There was a further facet of the Northern Pacific grant known as "in lieu" land. The land grant provided that when the railroad right-of-way went through land that already had been settled and owned by somebody else, the company could select an equivalent amount of land some place else. The operators of the land company, who were not behind the door when the brains were passed out, naturally selected the most valuable land in the neighborhood. In the Territory of Washington, the "in lieu" lands selected usually contained coal or some other valuable mineral or great stands of timber.

In 1872, when construction commenced, the route of the Northern Pacific approved by the United States Land Office entered the Territory at Walla Walla, went down the north side of the Columbia River to Kalama and then straight up through Western Washington and Puget Sound to the Canadian border.

The railroad owned every other section on opposite sides of its track in Western Washington to a depth of forty miles. On Puget Sound, its ownership extended from the Olympic Peninsula to the divide of the Cascade Mountains.

To all practical purposes, it owned Puget Sound.

The Wright man at the wrong place

Beginning in 1873, Charles Barstow Wright dedicated his spare time to thoughts of methods by which the town of Seattle could be aborted.

Mr. Wright was in his early fifties at the time and for thirty years he had been a wheeler and dealer in real estate, banking and railroads. He was a distinguished, albeit austere-looking gentleman with long sideburns and a partiality for the good things of life. And as far as he was concerned, the good things in life were not to be found west of his home town, Philadelphia.

He experienced no difficulty in nominating and electing himself as the sole member of the Tacoma Establishment—a role which he played from his comfortable and spacious offices in Philadelphia for the next quarter of a century. It is true that from time to time he came west in his private car to attend to his usual philanthropies . . . but on those occasions he managed to pick up such tidy items as the power and water franchise and other monetary knick-knacks from Tacoma's complaisant City Council . . . little money makers that made the trip worthwhile.

His original thought about the annihilation of Seattle was absurdly simple. He merely had the city expunged from the Northern Pacific maps and time tables. When that failed, he rearranged the railroad's time schedules so that anyone wishing to travel either to or from Seattle had to stay overnight in Tacoma.

He didn't have much of a railroad to fool with in the early stages . . . less than 200 miles between Tacoma and Kalama . . . so there had to be boat connections at either end for persons wishing to travel between Portland and Seattle . . . and the overnight stay in Tacoma added considerably to the elapsed time of the journey.

There was no such place as Seattle noted on either the Northern Pacific timetables back East or any of its literature. But at one point a terrible thing happened—a beautiful brochure extolling the virtues of the Northern Pacific inadvertently made a reference to Seattle. Wright caused the entire issue of the publication to be called back and completely redone, eliminating the reference to Seattle.

Wright was no fumbling old fool. When he inherited the presidency of the railroad in 1875, it had not yet recovered from the panic of 1873. It had about six hundred miles of track altogether. But he forced economies, made the track he had pay, and added another four hundred miles into Yellowstone Park. Within a year after assuming the presidency, he was able to write Martin Maginnis, delegate to Congress from the Montana Territory a letter that read in part:

> This enterprise is no longer in a crippled condition. It has not now another note or a dollar of interest-bearing debt. The Annual Report to be issued the last of this month will show you a condition that will command aid and credit, and if your Territory will now come forward with its credit to the extent of $5,000 per mile, as we progress, say to the extent of 300 miles, we will meet you in a manner that means business.

There's no question that he had plenty of things on his mind besides the rape of Seattle, but in the latter seemed to lie his greatest emotional enjoyment. We found that railroad clerks in the East had a habit of saying, "Hunh?" and looking blank when somebody asked about a trip to Seattle. Tacoma newspapers, which were largely controlled by the railroad, allowed that Seattle exceeded Tacoma in but one field—its death rate.

Bulk cargoes consigned to Seattle were broken up and sent piecemeal—at an increased cost. When it looked like Colman's Railroad was going to do Seattle some good, Wright built a coal road out of Tacoma to Wilkeson and Carbonado at his own expense to compete in the market. The folks in that coal region were so pleased with his pleasantness they named their richest vein in his honor.

When it looked like nothing else was going to send Seattle to the bottom, Wright came up with a bold stroke. He authorized the Land Company to offer anything Seattle businessmen wanted in the way of land for nothing or at low monthly payments if they would move to Tacoma.

That started something near a mass exodus from Seattle.

Denny, Yesler, Colman, McGilvra, Leary and Gatzert were not among those who departed. But a feeling of isolated togetherness was beginning to take shape in what had previously been an individualistic society of every man for himself.

The new recruits

Money always was in frightfully short supply in Seattle, but the Panic of 1873 was a major disaster. It was also a great leveller that touched the mighty mogul from Philadelphia as well as the tiny town on Elliott Bay. There was as yet no Establishment, but as individuals, Seattle's men had no objection to kicking the giant's shins.

Seattle deliberately utilized the highly effective talents of John Pinnell to improve its cash flow in spite of the idiotic bleatings of Beriah Brown. It also utilized to the fullest twenty years of trade connections with the farmers and lumber operators on Puget Sound where 50 per cent of the total population of the Territory lived and worked.

Schwabacher & Co. had no dependence upon the railroad. Its supplies came in by boat from San Francisco.

The construction of Colman's little railroad added to the meager stockpile of cash in the community . . . and then a freak of circumstance made Seattle the communications center of the Puget Sound area—a position which it has retained ever since.

In 1870, one Captain H. H. Hyde, a resident of Seattle, learned via the Western Union Telegraph station in Seattle that Selucius Garfielde had been elected as Territorial Delegate to Congress by a plurality of six hundred votes . . . an election he was supposed to have lost.

Captain Hyde hied himself to Port Townsend, which had no telegraphic communication with the outside world, and successfully wagered several thousand dollars that Garfielde would win by the plurality he already had won by.

But one poor sport by the name of E. S. Fowler, who had lost a mere $100, sued Hyde the following year and collected his money and court costs. This brought the communications problem in Port Townsend to the forefront and Dr. T. T. Minor, who was Mayor of that city, decided to do something about it.

In his negotiations for the telegraph, Minor got a closeup view of Seattle and its controversy with the Northern Pacific. Being a man who couldn't resist a good fight, Minor came here after he got through mayoring in Port Townsend and immediately became a member of the Establishment in the early eighties.

In 1875, while Minor was cleaning up the details in Port Townsend that preceded his move here, a couple more fellows of Establishment caliber took up residence in Seattle. They were Thomas Burke and J. R. Lewis.

Burke was only twenty six years old at the time of his arrival to become a partner in McGilvra's law firm and startle the socks off of everybody by marrying Carrie McGilvra, John's socially-prominent, sugar-stealing daughter. Burke's biographer, Robert Nesbit, points out in his excellent book, *He Built Seattle,* that Burke was "not inclined to unprofitable idealism."

Burke, who stood about five feet high and had a voice punctuated by thunderclaps, found his idealism the most profitable when he was attacking Wright. Wright didn't have to die to go to hell. Burke gave it to him right here—and it cost Wright plenty.

Although they didn't come hand in hand, J. R. Lewis arrived in Seattle the same year that Burke did. Lewis was red-headed, opinionated and dedicated to the proposition that he had always been right, was right now and always would be right. Lewis was for Seattle. If Wright was against Seattle then ipso facto he was wrong and equally ipso facto and de jure Lewis was against Wright.

A contemporary said about Lewis that he had a "radical, earnest, combative temperament, a contempt for sham and a habit of speaking his mind in a plain and piquant speech that often offended those individuals who happened to be meant . . ."

C. B. Wright frequently "happened to be meant."

The Drop Dead Department

Some time in 1876 when Wright, as president, was busy putting the Northern Pacific on its financial feet, he paused in his daily occupation to note that Seattle had failed to follow his instructions three years before when he had told it to drop dead.

Instead, the reverse was true. The corpse was livelier than ever. Railroad terminus or no railroad terminus, it was progressing pace for pace with Tacoma. And it was the general consensus around Puget Sound that one of those days the railroad would be forced to build track into Seattle.

Significantly, two-thirds of the mail which the railroad hauled into Tacoma from other parts of the United States was destined for Seattle. It was also beginning to trickle through to Wright's ivory tower in Philadelphia that while there had been a mass exodus from Seattle at first, it had petered out and Wright's attempts to induce them to move weren't working out the way he intended.

There was no concerted effort on the part of the men in Seattle to resist Tacoma's attempted raid on the business community. The community's first effort at cohesion had fallen apart as predicted when the Seattle & Walla Walla Railroad had found its proper mission in life as Colman's coal road.

On the other hand, the kind of men that Tacoma wanted and needed were staying in Seattle. Wright was all powerful in Tacoma. He had no counterpart or group of men who represented a counterpart in Seattle. Yet Seattle stubbornly hung on, and her leaders stayed there. The following story illustrates how things were going. When Wright contributed $35,000 toward the construction of St. Luke's church and the Tacoma Land Company came up with the location for the edifice, it was as natural as gravity that no Seattle firm was asked to bid on the construction.

The architect, who didn't happen to be a fan of Wright's, surreptitiously slipped a copy of the specifications to M. J. Carkeek, a Seattle contractor. Being a highly competitive man, Carkeek came in with the low bid and the short-funded vestry signed a contract before anybody could intervene.

When Carkeek went to work, Theodore Hosmer, manager of the land company, tried to talk him into moving to Tacoma and as bait offered him a good deal on the purchase of a couple of choice lots in downtown Tacoma. Carkeek said he'd think it over, and while he was thinking it over he encountered a troublesome flow of water in the basement excavation. He asked Hosmer to send to Seattle for some sewer pipe so the construction could proceed.

"Seattle!" Hosmer screamed, "I'd send to New York first!"

Hosmer then added the quote that has rung through Seattle's history. He said, "Mark me, you'll see the day when grass is growing in the streets of Seattle!" It was on a par with a quote attributed to Wright who is supposed to have said, "No locomotive will ever turn its wheels in Seattle."

When Carkeek completed his job, Hosmer renewed the offer of the downtown lots and Carkeek handed him the following exit line, "I wouldn't live in a town like this! You didn't care how much money I lost by being held up because you wouldn't have sewer pipe bought in Seattle. I'm going back to Seattle and we'll fight this thing out with you and see who wins!"

Checkmate!

Then Wright decided to make a move that would finally and irrevocably remove Seattle from a competitive position.

In its original land grant, the Northern Pacific's proposed route went through Seattle to the Canadian border. In 1873, when the railroad decided on Tacoma, an amended route was filed in which the proposed track by-passed Seattle by running up through Renton, along the east side of Lake Washington and through Snohomish to a crossing at Skagit Pass.

But everybody figured that route easily could be shifted again to include Seattle, and a preponderance of public opinion in the Territory held that Seattle ultimately would win out.

In the latter part of 1876 the railroad made its move. It quietly petitioned and got another route from the Department of Public Lands. The new route permitted the railroad to touch Puget Sound only at Tacoma. It did a hairpin turn at Tacoma and routed itself back either over Natchez Pass just north of Mt. Rainier or Cowlitz Pass just south of Mr. Rainier, wiping Seattle right off the map.

McGilvra happened to be in Washington, D.C. when this move was made.

He immediately returned to Seattle and called his buddies together. His buddies included Denny and Yesler—although they weren't on speaking terms—Colman, Leary, Gatzert, Burke and Lewis. At that time they had but one thing in common . . .

An uncommon hatred of C. B. Wright.

For years the Northern Pacific had acted and the Seattle boys had reacted, sometimes as a group—as when some of them tried to promote the Seattle & Walla Walla—but mostly as individuals.

This time, they not only reacted, they decided they would move on their own to see if they couldn't make the president's seat too hot for Wright to sit in.

In 1877, the Establishment was born, and immediately struck back.

They broadcast the news far and wide that the Northern Pacific had

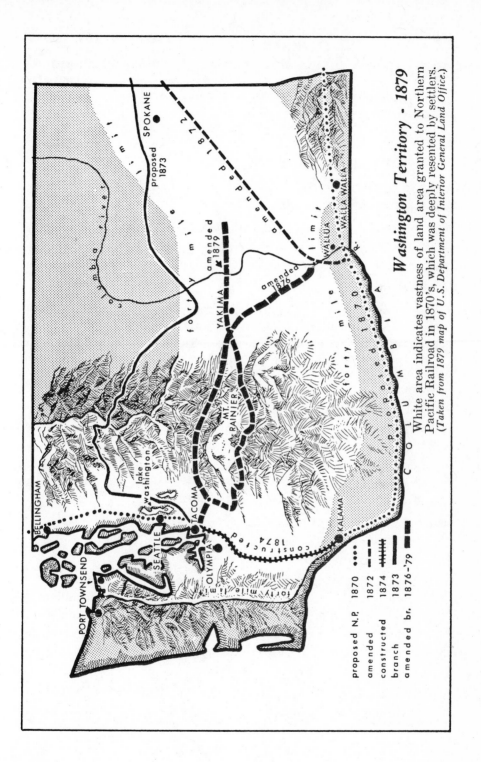

Washington Territory - 1879

White area indicates vastness of land area granted to Northern
Pacific Railroad in 1870's, which was deeply resented by settlers.
(Taken from 1879 map of U.S. Department of Interior General Land Office.)

proposed N.P.   1870   ••••••
amended   1872   ━ ━ ━ ━
constructed   1874   ┼┼┼┼┼┼
branch   1873   ▬▬▬▬▬
amended br.   1876-'79

abandoned both of its northern routes up Puget Sound and with the aid of the farmers in Skagit County, they put together a campaign kitty that sent McGilvra back to the congressional sessions of the winter of 1877-78.

The company has abandoned that route, they told Congress. We want the land opened for settlement.

In spite of the powerful lobby the railroad maintained in the nation's capital, McGilvra succeeded.

Five million acres—10 per cent of the originally projected land grant for the entire transcontinental trek—was restored to public domain. The entire Puget Sound basin was taken away from the Northern Pacific.

The following year, Wright resigned as president of the railroad. The stated reason was "ill health". I don't know whether he was in danger of dying and would rather be Wright than be president . . . or whether it was just a plain pain in the neck.

If it was the latter, I can certainly report that the Seattle Establishment gave it to him.

But neither losing the land nor the pain in the neck was as important to Seattle's history as the fact that Seattle's brand new Establishment had gone to the national capital and won its first battle against the champ. From then on the Establishment went into every fracas with the pre-conceived notion that it couldn't lose.

What price Tacoma?

The financial physician

The Seattle Establishment was still pretty much of a perky-tailed pup when a world figure named Henry Villard came into our back yard and started to give the Establishment lessons. The group had a lot to learn when Villard came along and he had to knock it on the nose a couple of times, but the education was valuable.

Villard, referred to in Tacoma's history as Gus Hilgard because it was a less attractive but probably true name, had the interesting virtue of being a railroad mogul without knowing the least thing about railroads. I like to point out that he was a writer. Born in Bavaria, he found himself covering the Lincoln-Douglas debates . . . and later serving as a war correspondent reporting the progress of the Civil War for both German and American newspapers.

I'm sure that if they were wearing spats and top hats and carrying thin canes in those days, Villard would have been in the height of fashion. And at one time or another, he most certainly must have drunk champagne from a lady's slipper. He could charm his way into any social circle in any part of the world—outside of Tacoma.

After the war was over, he got a degree in law in the United States. He looked around to see where the fighting was now and found it in the railroad business. So he became a financial physician for some German bond-holders who held paper in some sick railroads and other transportation companies in this country.

His first patient was the Kansas Pacific, where he charmed his way into the life of one Thomas F. Oakes, who was the operational vice president of that organization and knew where all the joints creaked. With Oakes' assistance, Villard cured the patient, got a reputation as a financial wizard and was sent on to Portland to see what he could do about a faltering transportation system there.

Villard felt he should have somebody in his organization who knew something about railroads, so he brought along Oakes as executive vice president. With the aid of Oakes, he put the sagging enterprises back on their feet and created a transportation monopoly in and around Portland that restored the Germans' bonds to par and put Villard himself in the limelight on Wall Street.

Villard, who had a knack for making simple things complicated—to his own advantage—created the Oregon Transcontinental Company, which in turn bought a big block of Northern Pacific stock.

Then, through the Oregon Transcontinental Company, Villard sired the Oregon Improvement Company and became the proud president of both. He generously offered some Oregon Improvement stock to Oakes, who wrote that he had no right to "burthen" Villard with "anything more for me." He further replied . . . "in ten years I ought to accumulate enough to purchase the place on the Hudson and settle down. That is all I hope to accomplish, having no ambition to rival Gould or Vanderbilt."

Villard gave him the stock anyway, because Oakes had just finished an impossible job of building a railroad track up the south side of the Columbia River, paralleling the proposed route of the Northern Pacific on the north side of the river. The Northern Pacific had barely enough money to build to Wallula back at the confluence of the Snake and Columbia Rivers, let alone run more track on down along the Columbia.

Thus, when it got to that point, it would be forced to use the Villard track on the south side of the Columbia—and feed into his monopoly at Portland.

Villard's new track served to free a bunch of ships he had been using in the river trade so he looked for another place in which to play Monopoly with the ships . . . and noted Puget Sound. By this time the Oregon Improvement Company was going great guns, buying up vast acreages in wheat in eastern Washington to keep the railroad down the Columbia busy. Villard figured this was the outfit to use when he moved into the Puget Sound picture.

The Rover Boys on Puget Sound

It was 1879—the year of Wright's retirement—when Villard moved grandly into Puget Sound with his faithful servant, Thomas Oakes, tagging along. He bought Colman's coal road and coal mines in King County for $250,000 and added another $750,000 worth of ships. The ships promptly started hauling 11,000 tons of coal a month to San Francisco—all this via his Oregon Improvement Company.

Oakes was put in charge of Colman's road and its name changed to the Columbia & Puget Sound—but Villard cannily kept Colman on as assistant superintendent, because the latter knew every inch of the road and bed—and where most of the coal in King County was buried.

It took Villard about twenty-four hours to find out who the real leaders were in Seattle. First he made Denny and Gatzert directors of the newly established Columbia & Puget Sound. A little later on, he made a proposition to Burke and Leary that if they would raise a subsidy of $150,000, the Oregon Improvement company would change the Columbia & Puget Sound track from narrow to standard gauge and extend it from Renton up the Cedar River valley and on to Green River where the Oregon Improvement Company owned the Franklin mine.

This made beautiful music to the Seattle Establishment. By the early eighties the folks realized that one day the Northern Pacific would build over the Cascades, probably at Stampede Pass. A standard gauge railroad out of Seattle would meet the main line of the Northern Pacific in the mountains near Green River. It would tap the Black Diamond and Franklin mines that were fourteen miles closer to Seattle than they were to Tacoma.

Tacoma, of course, hated Villard—both because Wright told it to and because Villard provided that city with the greatest insult of all . . . indifference. He didn't hate Tacoma; he simply had no use for it. Tacoma had nothing that could make money for Villard. Wright controlled the coal mines in Tacoma's hinterland. Wright owned the valuable property. Wright was out and so was Tacoma.

Tacoma thought enough of Oakes, on the other hand, to name a street after him . . . and I can't help wondering if they would have done that if they had known that as Villard's first lieutenant he'd coached the chief on the relative potential of the two towns by advising that "Seattle is getting all the good men and Tacoma is getting the deadwood that want us to feed them . . ."

Trouble at Wallulla

When C. B. Wright retired from the presidency of the railroad, his place was taken by a friend, Frederick Billings, who was—of all things—a bonafide railroad man. Billings had a burning desire to build track not only down the north side of the Columbia but also up through Yakima and across the Cascades.

As long as he didn't have any money, he was forced to agree to use Villard's track along the Columbia. But in 1880 the money market loosened up a little. Billings laid his hands on $40,000,000, reneged on his contract with Villard and prepared to lay his own track. This presented a real threat to Villard's ambitions. Instead of being associates, the two men were now to become competitors.

Villard saw his monopoly falling apart. He couldn't begin to match money with Billings, but he sure could match wits—and he countered with the greatest coup in railroad history. He organized something called the "Blind Pool" . . . $8,000,000 which his Wall Street buddies entrusted to him without knowing how it was going to be used. With this, and an additional $12,000,000 developed via pledges from his own holdings, Villard bought controlling interest in the Northern Pacific Railroad.

Billings was left with his $40,000,000—and his mouth hanging open.

By 1881, Villard was president of the Northern Pacific and told Oakes to quit fooling around with the Columbia & Puget Sound in Renton and go finish the transcontinental railroad he had started when he built track from Portland to Wallula.

The return of the native

Villard had made friends and influenced people in Seattle with little thoughtful details like keeping the University of Washington from folding by handing it a liberal gift, and sending a dozen red roses to the prominent Mrs. Burke.

So his return to.our city as president of the Northern Pacific was like old home week for our boy who made good in the big time, and he was given a gilded wooden key to the city.

His return to Puget Sound did not meet with the same degree of enthusiasm in Tacoma where downtown lots had been selling at as much as $4,000 a front foot prior to the time that Villard became president of the Northern Pacific.

But let's let Historian Hunt provide us with the doleful details:

> Here in Tacoma, buildings that had begun were left uncompleted. About forty structures were under way or construction was under contemplation. Work stopped; plans were pigeonholed. Many newcomers who had expected to settle in Tacoma went to Portland or Seattle. The tide of travel shifted, leaving Tacoma merely a point of transfer and no longer a stopping

place. There was no manner of computing how much the young
city lost in the paralysis of its prestige by the Villard schemers ...

What caused the panic? Tacoma still was the terminus of the railroad. There was no track of any kind extending to Seattle. There
was the same glorious harbor extolled in the Northern Pacific
brochures.

What had happened?

Tacoma was the little rich boy on the right side of the railroad
tracks who had taunted the tough kid down the street from a safe
position . . . now the fence had been torn down and he was facing
that tough kid on his own.

The business of the railroad business

The truth be told, and of course it is, Villard was presenting nothing to Seattle on a silver platter. He was still wearing two hats, the
one that had President of the Northern Pacific in the lining . . . and
the one that said Portland Monopolist. And the latter was a better
fit.

Seattle raised the $150,000 subsidy for standard gauge track on the
Columbia & Puget Sound out of Renton and up to Green River, but
the Oregon Improvement Company seemed to possess a singular inability to get the construction going.

Impatient at the delay and still determined to hook up with a trans-
continental railroad someplace, the Establishment incorporated the
Seattle, Walla Walla & Baker City Railroad in March of 1882. This
was to be another narrow gauge road that would go over Seattle's fa-
vorite pass, Snoqualmie, and follow the general route of the former
Seattle & Walla Walla. It would connect with the Union Pacific.
Among the incorporators were J. R. Lewis, Henry Yesler, John
Leary and Thomas Burke.

This was the second time the Establishment acted on its own as a co-
hesive unit and let somebody else do the reacting. Tacoma bleats
that Seattle got preferential treatment out of Villard. But Seattle
wasn't sitting back with a basket in its lap waiting for the apples to
fall in. It was doing something.

In this instance, Seattle was saying to Villard: We love you, and we honor you, but we don't trust you.

John Leary reported he could lay his hands on some money from the San Francisco owners of the Black Diamond mine. Other members of the Establishment realized that in addition to getting track into the interior, the new line would open new coal fields tributary to Seattle, tap extensive timber lands—and best of all move a step closer to tapping the iron deposits in Snoqualmie Pass that Denny had held for years and that Burke more recently had acquired.

J. R. Lewis reported that he'd been to Tacoma where the Oregon Improvement Company was building larger coal-handling facilities, which he read as a clear indication that the Northern Pacific was planning to extend its Puyallup spur into Green River in competition with Seattle. Our mistrust of the Northern Pacific or any of its affiliates was never far below the surface.

John Collins, another one of the incorporators, stoutly declared that if Seattle could raise $10,000 to build the original Seattle & Walla Walla during the depression of 1873, it easily could pull together $250,000 in 1882.

As a member of the board of the Columbia & Puget Sound, and as a propagandist for the Seattle Establishment, Denny reported to Villard that the animals were becoming restive and if Villard didn't do something they were liable to go ahead with their new railroad scheme.

Nesbit reports that Villard scribbled the following note on the bottom of Denny's letter: "Simply nothing in all this. It would be suicidal for the Seattle people to build a foot of RR. in opposition to our interests. No."

Villard knocked the Seattle, Walla Walla & Baker City in the head while it was still a-borning, but he got the point. He suspected that we were out talking with railroad moguls somewhere beyond the Seattle city limits about getting a transcontinental rail connection with somebody, and that somebody didn't necessarily have to be the Northern Pacific.

Villard thought: those wild-eyed idiots might just be lucky enough to make some other connection . . . and that's all that one of the other big railroad outfits would need as an excuse to move in on my monopoly.

So he made a counter offer.

The franchise for the Columbia & Puget Sound took it on trestles across the tide flats to the south of the city to the coal bunkers that Colman had erected and Oregon Improvement had improved at the foot of King Street. If Seattle would provide Columbia & Puget Sound with a franchise across its waterfront to University Street, the Oregon Improvement Company would build a standard gauge track as far as Stuck Junction (Auburn, to you and me) at a cost of about a million dollars. And the Northern Pacific would build track north of Puyallup some seven miles to meet it.

It was kind of a haywire arrangement with the Northern Pacific owning seven miles of track and the Oregon Improvement Company owning another fourteen, but it did give Seattle a transcontinental connection immediately through Puyallup and Tacoma . . . and through Stuck Junction and Green River if as or when the Northern Pacific went over the Cascades.

The million dollar price for building track through the Kent Valley was not something Seattle could casually write a check for, so the boys went along with Villard.

It took some doing to browbeat the rugged individualists owning property on Seattle's waterfront into giving up part of their land for a right-of-way. But the Establishment pitted its strength against the other Sons in the city and got it—for free. There was one problem. Some of the owners gave land on the water side of their property. Others gave it in the middle. And others gave it at the back. All in all, it ran a crooked mile and because of that, it was dubbed the "Ram's Horn" railroad.

The Establishment would live to regret that achievement.

All hail the U. S. Mail

For years it has been the consensus of historians that the Klondike gold rush of 1897 made Seattle the major city of the Pacific Northwest.

True, true . . . but a great basic is overlooked in this oversim-
plification of the case. Seattle was in the right geographic location
for the gold rush, but we'd been defrosting Alaskans for fifteen years
before the rush was on. And that came about as a by-product of our
long fight to get a transcontinental railroad.

When John Leary was in San Francisco looking up cash for the proposed Seattle, Walla Walla & Baker City Railroad he discovered
what a lucrative deal the steamship firm of Goodall, Nelson and Perkins had in hauling mail to Alaska. They took a small bag or two of
letters to that outpost twelve times a year from Portland and got a
whopping $26,000 annually out of it.

So John put in a bid to haul it at $14,000—only he proposed that
the southern terminus for the mail be Port Townsend instead of
Portland He figured he could charter a steamship some place for
that amount of money and whatever it carried in addition to the
mail would be pure profit.

But Goodall, Nelson and Perkins was a big outfit and they figured
they'd teach our boy John a lesson. So they chartered every steamer
on the coast that was seaworthy enough to make the trip and John
found himself with a nice contract and no craft.

Scouting around for something—anything—that could make the
voyage, he encountered the Reverend Mr. James R. Ludlow, who
had a ship, the "Evangel" under construction at the Hammond Shipyard in Seattle. Ludlow planned to use the ship to deliver the message of the Lord to the natives between Seattle and Alaska . . . and
Leary persuaded him to add twenty feet to the length of the ship
and deliver the United States Mail as well.

On March 20, 1882, at 3:30 in the afternoon, the 14.9-ton steamer
slipped down the ways in the presence of a large assemblage. No
champagne bottle was cracked to launch *this* ship. Instead, an open
bible was lashed across the bow. Gospel bells sounded. A Baptist
choir sang "Dare to be a Daniel" . . . "Pull for the Shore" . . . and
"Hold the Fort". A little girl tossed biblical tracts on the water.

A group of seafaring men present predicted that no good would
come of these shenanigans . . . and they were so right.

The Portland Board of Trade shared the opinion of the seafaring men, and the Portland newspapers, still smarting from the loss of the contract, joined with the Portland Board of Trade. A lot of static emanated from that town and the U. S. Steamboat Inspectors were moved by both the facts and the political pressure from Portland to take a long look at the proposed mail carrier.

Leary couldn't do anything about the facts. The "Evangel," good, bad or indifferent, was what she was.

When it came to the political pressure, however, Leary figured Seattle could easily match the Portland Board of Trade.

What we need, Leary told the other members of the Establishment, is a Chamber of Commerce!

That seemed like a good idea at the time, so the boys quickly threw one together. They had J. R. Lewis take on the presidency, Bailey Gatzert was installed as vice president and Thomas Burke as corresponding secretary. They didn't want anybody to get any false ideas about democracy in the organization. If Lewis got sick, Gatzert could take over. Burke was on hand to see the group didn't get any notion about making any statements the Establishment didn't want made. It was okay to have a Chamber of Commerce. It was *not* okay for that group to come up with any bright ideas of its own.

The Chamber was instructed to emit a loud scream at Portland.

The promptly-emitted scream pointed out that the Portland Board of Trade's protest against entrusting the U. S. Mail to the "Evangel" was an "unwarranted intermeddling in a matter which in no wise concerns it . . ." The resolution further pointed out that "upon the most careful inquiry and investigation, it was clear that Mr. Ludlow had the ability and was ready with the most ample facilities for the transportation of the mail in accordance with the requirements of the contract . . ."

The engine of the "Evangel" responded to this pronouncement by blowing up out of Victoria on its first trip north.

Leary bounced back by chartering the steamer "Yaquina," which Goodall, Nelson and Perkins had overlooked when they tried to freeze Leary out.

A load of lime on the "Yaquina" responded by catching fire out of Portland and causing the ship to be scuttled.

Leary appealed once more to the Establishment. The "Evangel" was limping back to Seattle. Leary had to have something to move the mail or he would lose the contract. Burke bethought himself of the sea-going tug, "Mastick." It was owned by John Ackerson, partner in the Hanson and Ackerson mill in Tacoma. Perhaps they could charter it.

Burke, who loved to do things with his coattails flying anyway, hopped on a Tacoma-bound boat with Leary to talk things over with Ackerson only to find that the latter was staying at his summer place somewhere near Puyallup.

"We'll have to get horses and ride out," Burke said.

"I was on a horse once," Leary replied, "And I wouldn't get on another if I got the contract for all the mail in the world and the 'Mastick' thrown into the bargain."

So Burke undertook the horseback ride and later related his thrilling midnight trip back to Welford Beaton who chronicled it in *The City That Made Itself*:

> He could not see his horse's head, much less the road, so he made no effort to guide its movements. It was an animal of spirit, and it had been held in the stable without its evening meal, so it decided to get back to its livery stable home in the shortest possible time. Burke was satisfied that he could ride as fast as the horse could run, so he settled himself in the saddle and let 'er rip. It was a great ride. Burke had the sensation of great speed and could feel that the animal was eating up the road with long strides that brought her belly almost to the ground, but he could see nothing and at no stage of the journey except at its end did he have the remotest idea where he was. Covered with mud, wet to the skin, he at last pulled up at the livery stable, where he was informed by its irate keeper that he had almost ridden to death a race horse which he had in training for some approaching meet, and which an addle-pated stable attache had rented out by mistake . . .

It was a grand ride. Burke had the charter for the "Mastick" in his pocket and the old Seattle Spirit rode along with him. However, the tug was even smaller than the "Evangel" and after two attempts at hauling the mail—with the "Mastick" breaking down on each attempt —the contract was returned to Goodall, Nelson and Perkins.

There were, however, a couple of minor differences in the new contract. Instead of their former $26,000, the Goodall people had to take the $14,000 which Leary had bid, and instead of terminating in Portland, as had been the case in previous years, the southern terminus for the mail was Port Townsend.

This was the Establishment's third attempt at acting and letting somebody else do the reacting, and at the time it didn't look like we had produced a very favorable result. We did get a Chamber of Commerce . . . but Leary lost a lot of money.

So what else was new?

Well, the lousy $14,000 for the mail contract soon caused Goodall, Nelson and Perkins to lose interest in it, so Seattle got it—that was new. And the Chamber of Commerce decided it could bang away at getting that contract to Seattle without getting the Establishment mad at it—that was new.

But the biggest bonus at that time in 1882 was that Seattle and the Chamber of Commerce had their attention drawn to Alaska at the same time—and this was of critical importance—that Portland lost interest in Alaska. The Chamber kept wooing the Territory and making friends up there. The Alaska folks had a frightful inferiority complex anyway, and whenever somebody from the Chamber would pat them on the head, they'd practically burst into tears at the unexpected friendliness. So they started buying their oatmeal and their women and their pianos for their bars from Seattle, and we developed some channels of trade.

Thanks to these humble beginnings, we really hit the jackpot when the Klondike rush came through in 1897 . . . so I think we can score the Establishment's third try as a hit, instead of a miss.

Sound the trumpets, beat the drums

On September 1, 1883, the final spike for the Northern Pacific Railroad was driven in Missoula, Montana. It was supposed to be gold, but I doubt if it was, because at that time, the railroad didn't have enough money left to make a gold spike.

But the exuberance in all the cities along the line made up for a little detail like that. Villard, with the instincts of a first-class showman, had brought along a collection of barons, earls, lords, dukes and moguls . . . and as the party progressed westward, the celebrations became more magnificent.

In Portland, they had a real whing-ding. And Seattle, being the last city the travellers would visit, determined that hers would be the greatest celebration of them all. Villard was due to land at the foot of Main Street on the "Queen Of The Pacific," a fancy new iron ship just completed the previous year in Philadelphia. And you would never have known the old town.

At the intersection of First South and Main, four arches, woven with evergreens and interspersed with berries from mountain ash, formed a square. Chinese lanterns furnished illumination. The Arlington Hotel, right on the corner, was decorated with shields representing the various states touched by the railroad. The Brunswick Hotel up the street was described as being so hung with pennants and flags as to resemble a fairy palace.

There was a grand, evergreen arch thirty feet high and topped by an eagle across the intersection of First Avenue and Yesler Way. Two platforms illuminated by gas jets and covered with bunting were erected in Pioneer Square. All buildings and piers along the route were decorated with evergreens and buntings and the sidewalks were solid with rows of small evergreen trees all the way to the University of Washington, which was the smasheroo of them all.

Four thousand yards of canvas were used in the construction of a pavilion. An illuminated background behind the stage represented the rising sun over the word "Alki" and above all was the greeting: "Welcome to Henry Villard And His Guests!"

It was by far and away the most expensive public production the city ever had attempted.

Anything that could float was hidden in the lee of West Point, all be-decked and waiting for Villard's arrival so it could escort him into Elliott Bay.

They had kind of a long wait.

Enroute from Portland to Seattle the 330-foot "Queen of the Pacific" carrying Villard's party, made a premature landing on Clatsop Spit in a little smog created by a large forest fire. It took four tugs and $60,000 to get her off the spit so she could resume her trip, which interrupted schedules and caused the Villard party to zip through Seattle like the Twentieth Century Limited passing a flag stop.

Villard liked a good show, however, and paused long enough to make a few choice remarks. Miss Nellie Powell, daughter of L. J. Powell, president of the University, read a eulogy she had written about Villard who had the wit to ask for the original manuscript, which was gratefully given to him. He then introduced his family and blew.

The Committee regretted the expense of the Japanese lanterns and the gas lighting jets, neither of which were used because of Villard's hurried departure.

It must have occurred to somebody like J. R. Lewis to ask, "What in blue blazes are we celebrating?"

Although Villard had promised that his third visit to Seattle would be by rail in his own private car, he had come by boat from Portland. The track between Tacoma and Seattle had not been completed.

We didn't even have a line running from Renton to Green River.

The King is dead! Long live the King?

On December 17, 1883—just ten years, five months and three days after Arthur Denny got the bad news that the Northern Pacific terminus was to be on Commencement Bay, the Establishment got the bad news that Villard had been bounced.

"They" had finally got him. One of "them" was C. B. Wright—retired, but still the principal stockholder in the company. And boy, had they fixed Villard! They took away his big panelled office and his private railroad car. They also took away his monopoly in the Pacific Northwest. He was down to his last yacht.

They had fixed him for good—well, at least until 1889 when he showed up again as chairman of the board of the railroad.

They also had fixed Seattle.

The Establishment had given away the waterfront to the Columbia & Puget Sound Railroad, but neither the road up from Renton to Black Diamond nor the connecting road from Green River to Stuck Junction had been completed. Neither of them was more than six months from completion, but if Wright was the power in the railroad again, they might as well have never been started.

The Establishment was not quite back where it began, though. It had done a lot of growing-up during the Villard regime. Instead of emoting, it was calculating.

The Union Pacific was honeying around looking for a chance to jab some iron into the Puget Sound region. The Canadian Pacific was a little less than a year from providing Vancouver, B. C., two hundred miles away, with transcontinental track. And the biggest railroad news of the year concerned a young, Canadian-born promoter by the name of James J. Hill.

He had welded the St. Paul & Pacific Railroad and a few other odds-and-ends of transportation trivia into the St. Paul, Minneapolis & Manitoba. The St. Paul & Pacific had bravely started out for the Pacific Coast in the early seventies and had foundered at Breckenridge, Minnesota in the Panic of 1873.

Mr. Hill had plunged into the murky depths of high finance and had come up with $27,000,000 for the St. Paul, Minneapolis & Manitoba. He certainly didn't need that much just to replace worn out railroad ties.

Hill was thinking big—and big meant a transcontinental railroad. The word was around that the new road was headed for Puget Sound across the northern tier of states by the shortest, fastest, cheapest route.

So there was some place else to go if the Northern Pacific proved totally intractable.

On the other hand, Black Diamond and Stuck Junction were by all odds the nearest plums and a bird in the hand being worth several in the underbrush, the Establishment figured it had better take a long look at the Northern Pacific's new president.

And what they saw gave them cause for consideration in depth.

His name was Robert D. Harris and he was a railroad man's railroad man. Unlike Wright whose judgment was influenced by his real estate holdings, or Villard to whom the railroad was just one tool among many in his various stock manipulations, Harris saw the railroad as a functioning, economically sound unit in the development of the West.

Harris proposed to build track down the north side of the Columbia . . . to exercise the railroad's influence to finish the lines to Black Diamond and Stuck Junction . . . but most important of all to us, he planned to construct a Cascade Division which would give the Puget Sound a direct shot at the transcontinental track.

He had radical notions for his time—like paying a living wage and giving trainmen Sunday off. He retained Oakes as executive vice president on the ridiculous grounds that although Oakes had been Villard's right-hand man, he knew how to run a railroad. And, in spite of Wright's influential position on the board, Harris dismissed favors Wright sought for Tacoma by saying, "It is highly objectionable to agree to anything as to one point of the line that it (the railroad) is not willing to extend to any point . . ."

Reform had set in.

The problem, however, lay in the fact that the rest of the world had not as yet been informed. To date, the Northern Pacific had spent $90,000,000 of somebody else's money without fulfilling the terms of the charter it had been granted twenty years before.

The Establishment was impressed with Harris, but a lot of other people in the country were disenchanted with railroads in general and the Northern Pacific in particular . . . and a bill was dropped in the congressional hopper calling for forefeiture of the land upon which the railroad had failed to construct track.

This was Harris' first major crisis.

Seattle's position on that question suddenly became vitally important to him. The Northern Pacific already had Walla Walla plumping for it because that town was assured of rail connections . . . and the same was true of all of Western Washington as far north as Tacoma. Most of the rest of eastern Washington was violently opposed to the railroad because it was holding up land settlement. But Puget Sound was the big population center and Seattle was the biggest town on Puget Sound.

On February 11, 1884, Harris' emissary, Paul Schulze, showed up in Seattle.

Schulze convinced the folks that Harris intended to build track across the Cascades and give Seattle equal treatment with Tacoma. His argument: "Whichever town generates the most traffic will get the most service. Meanwhile, it behooves us on Puget Sound to break the Portland monopoly by building across the Cascades. Let's work together now and fight about details after the main line is completed."

In order to sell its bonds, the railroad pointed out, it couldn't have land grant forfeiture legislation hanging over its head.

If we sent anti-forfeiture letters to Congress as the people who would be served by the railroad, Congress would listen.

John Leary and J. R. Lewis, two of the men who heard Schulze appeal to the Chamber of Commerce, agreed to write an anti-forfeiture resolution which read in part, "for the best interests of the people of the Territory of Washington . . . we oppose and respectfully protest against any action by Congress tending to the forefeiture of said land grant . . ." This was passed almost unanimously by the Chamber.

The boys got busy, and a couple of days later, a similar resolution emerged from the City Council . . . and both of them were forwarded to Congress. The Oregon Improvement Company explained to Leary, Burke and Yesler, the members of the Establishment who had raised the $150,000 subsidy for the extension of the Columbia & Puget Sound beyond Renton, that it was temporarily low on funds . . . and would they extend the time limit of the subsidy.

The gentlemen checked with their cohorts and reported they would be more than happy to extend the time limit of the subsidy.

That was on February 15, 1884.

The schmaltz of Schulze

Paul Schulze had the biggest mouth in the world. He had to, otherwise he couldn't have put his big foot in it and changed the course of Seattle's history.

He figured he had it made. Resolutions from the Chamber and the City Council had gone to Congress. And then, after it was all settled and he was lifting a few with the boys he allowed as how this wasn't the only mission he had successfully accomplished on behalf of the Northern Pacific...

Why, only two years before he had gone to Portland and superintended the burning of the steamer "Yaquina"...

The burning of the "Yaquina!"

And Leary was one of the men who had written the anti-forfeiture resolution for the Chamber of Commerce! John would be interested in hearing about that.

It was one of those ironic twists of fate. As far as the record shows, there was nothing to indicate that the fire that burned the "Yaquina" had been anything but an accident. But the Establishment was beginning to get the impression that every time something bad happened to Seattle the Northern Pacific was involved. Maybe it had turned over a new leaf, but maybe the leaf was the same on both sides.

They decided to take another long look at the railroad.

While Harris had a lot to commend him, he did favor his railroad over anything else. Quite a logical attitude for the president of the company, but the Establishment found the company had quite a few policies they didn't care for at all. The most critical of these affected their interest in the supposed mineral wealth in the mountains.

There were evidences of gold, copper, iron, coal, marble and limestone just a hop, skip and jump from Seattle. Arthur Denny owned a piece of real estate which he called the Iron Mountain of Snoqualmie. He also had selected Seattle primarily because he believed that the logical access to the rest of the country lay over this lowest pass in the Cascades. There probably was no businessman in Seattle who didn't own mining property in Snoqualmie Pass.

But the Northern Pacific showed absolutely no interest in using Snoqualmie for either a main or branch line.

Another further bone of contention involved the question of whether the line that Wright had personally financed to get coal out of Carbonado and Wilkeson was a part of the railroad's main line or whether it was a coal road. Seattle maintained it was a branch line and could not be claimed as "in lieu" lands. The railroad claimed it was a main line and therefore gave the railroad the right to claim 750,000 acres of valuable mineral land in King country.

The railroad refused to sell mineral rights when it sold to homesteaders, and the latter could not profit in the event coal was found on their land. It also held coal lands immediately adjacent to people with coal claims. The railroad could bottle up the privately-owned coal by not hauling it and forcing owners to sell. Harris would not make any promises about whether he would haul coal from claims other than the railroad's or whether he would or would not force the others to sell to him.

The Establishment was dedicated to the proposition that Seattle would become the Pittsburgh of the West. It also reached a basic decision that no one railroad would ever be permitted to dominate the town. That meant we had to reach out for some other transcontinental; if we figured this move right and made a connection, it would bring the Northern Pacific in time.

I've always been taught that it was the Northern Pacific which picked a fight with our poor little town—but we're the ones who picked the fight and it was in the last two weeks of February, 1884 that we did it . . . deliberately and objectively and with a clear idea of where we were heading.

Sidney Dillon, president of the Union Pacific, long since had informed some of our leaders the Union Pacific was anxious to enter the Puget Sound region but had been deterred by the overwhelming advantage the Northern Pacific had in its land grants.

The Establishment's first move would have to be in favor of forfeiture of the land grants.

The House bill forfeiting about fifteen million acres of Northern Pacific land grant across the Cascades and down the Columbia already had moved on into the Senate. Also, there was the little detail about resolutions opposing forfeiture that had just been sent to Congress by the Chamber and the City Council, but that's all it was to the Establishment, a detail.

Oh, oh—the Wright man again

On March 1, 1884, John Leary's *Post-Intelligencer* sounded the opening guns of the campaign. The Northern Pacific, which a few months before had been the big benefactor of the people suddenly was a "soul-less corporation that ground the settlers under its despotic heel . . . the sinuous snail slowly crossing the continent . . ."

This was just two weeks after the anti-forfeiture resolutions. And there sat the Chamber of Commerce and the City Council with those resolutions in their hands and the outhouse blown down by the first blast.

Leary's law partner, Henry Struve, who was the Mayor, quickly called a mass meeting at Henry Yesler's Pavilion to "discuss the question of terminating the Northern Pacific's unearned land grant now pending before congress . . ."

The meeting was held on March 22 and the pavilion was jammed. It was one of those "spontaneous gatherings" that an Establishment puts together with its own brand of economic judo.

And C. B. Wright, who had returned to the Northern Pacific's Board of Directors to vote Villard's demise, was the piece de resistance.

The Establishment had its speakers ready: Leary, Orange Jacobs, T. T. Minor, J. R. Lewis and Thomas Burke. One William H. White was called on first, the *P.-I.* reported the next day, because he was not a member of the Chamber and "didn't have to eat crow."

The theme of the meeting—and subsequently of the anti-Northern Pacific campaign—was that the company had been chartered for twenty years and never had fulfilled the commitments of its charter.

White's comments included the following:

After a time, certain men went before Congress and asked to be entrusted with the building of this road.

For C. B. Wright?

No. For the People!

The first thing the people know, by some hokus pokus, the main line is changed from Puget Sound and laid down the Columbia River . . . Whenever I see a man build a church for his own aggrandisement (St. Luke's in Tacoma), instead of for the cause of Christ, I put him down as a fraud . . .

From that opening gun, the "press" was on and Wright was the goat. For a long time Tacomans had ridiculed Seattle with such little ditties as "Seattle, Seattle . . . death rattle, death rattle" and by referring to our majestic town with such belittling terms as Yeslerville. And ever since Wright had arrived, there'd been a fight between the two cities over whether or not Mt. Rainier should be called that or Mt. Tacoma. At one point in this fight, which lasted until 1925, the *Argus* in Seattle inquired of its readers, "Will some kindly disposed person tell, if they can, why the inspired idiots of Tacoma insist on calling the beautiful mountain after their dinky little city?"

But Wright had done a greater thing for the Establishment's purposes than that. Within the past two weeks he'd introduced a bill in Congress requesting statehood for the Territory *and changing its name from Washington to Tacoma!*

And his timing was fantastic. The story hit the newspapers the very day of the mass meeting!

Well, friends, how's that for co-ordination?

From the time of his ascendancy to the presidency of the railroad, Harris had poured several million dollars worth of oil on the troubled waters by way of concessions that would keep the settlers in their seats. The folks in Seattle temporarily were lulled into the thought that Harris was really running the railroad.

Then, with one masterful stroke, Wright blew the whole stew.

T. T. Minor took full advantage of that timing with the following:

Fellow Citizens of Yeslerville and the future state of Tacoma . . .
(wild catcalls and protests) . . . We have seen the broad, fair-
minded Villard displaced by the narrow and bigoted Wright, and
today we learn that the great commonwealth is to be named after
one of his hobbies—Tacoma . . .

With friends like that, Harris needed no enemies at all. Judge Lewis
expressed the prevailing sentiment with a little poem that wouldn't
have won a Pulitzer Prize, but brought down the house:

Railroad, railroad, Ichry Am
Northern Pacific railroad, you we dam

For badder or worse

When Seattle got mad, somebody got stung . . . and Seattle was good
and mad.

On April 17, the Chamber of Commerce not only repudiated its
original resolution against forfeiture, but ordered that resolution
forever expunged from the record of the Chamber's activities.

We wrote the President of the United States demanding that an investigation be made of the Northern Pacific's claim that its coal road
to Wilkeson was a part of the main line when its real purpose was
robbing King County of $7,000,000 of mineral lands.

We said the railroad was "a black cloud over the Territory developing a system of floating its grant over about three quarters of
the land by filing 'general routes' . . . 'trial routes' . . . 'proposed
lines' and 'amended lines' over an area equal in size to the state of
Ohio . . ."

The Chamber of Commerce produced "black cloud" maps showing
the tangled web of railroad lines and sent copies to Congress, the
newspapers of the country and anybody else it could think of.

James McNaught, resident counsel for the Northern Pacific, kept
firing distress signals to Harris, but he was too busy building a railroad to pay any attention to them until June 30, when the Senate
Committee on Public Lands reported "Do Pass" on the house bill in
favor of forfeiture. The arguments supporting its position were

taken in their entirety from various and sundry resolutions written in Seattle.

The bill called specifically for the forfeiture of 214 miles of the land grant between Wallula and Portland. The committee pointed out that Villard already had built a road that could be used—without any subsidy of any kind from anybody. The Northern Pacific was using that road as part of its transcontinental system and there was no need for the land grant.

It also called for forfeiture of the 180 miles over the Cascades on the grounds that the railroad had dilly-dallied for twenty years and nothing had as yet happened.

It dawned on Harris that he was in imminent danger of losing 15,000,000 more acres of granted land . . . and without that grant he never would be able to construct his road over the Cascades. He finally acknowledged McNaught's frantic telegrams. He agreed to attend a meeting of the Seattle Chamber of Commerce that McNaught had succeeded in having called together for July 17.

Meanwhile, at the behest of Thomas Burke, the Establishment had put together a kitty of five hundred dollars. It was used to send Daniel H. Gilman on a hunting expedition to the wilds of Wall Street and environs for capital to build a railroad out of Seattle connecting with one of the transcontinental railroads in the United States or Canada.

The late Mr. Harris

After it was all over, the Tacoma papers said that Harris had come to Seattle "bearing the olive branch, hoping to convince that city that the railroad intended to be fair . . . But instead of opening the gates of peace, he only invited a torrent of abuse. Judge Burke denounced him most bitterly to his face, accused the company of deceit if not worse . . ."

Nesbit had a nice way of putting it, too, when he pointed out that the meeting seemed to confirm the hostility to the Northern Pacific. He said there was little effort to placate that hostility over the next five years, and added "Nor was there much reason for such conciliation in the face of the inspired rancor toward the railroad and its management..."

Inspired rancor.

Mr. Nesbit said a mouthful.

Harris failed to endear himself to the members of the Chamber by being two hours late to the meeting—an oversight in public relations that was duly noted on the front page of the *Post-Intelligencer* the next morning.

Actually, he was walking into a stacked deck. The Establishment was off and running on its own railroad project and it planned to use Harris' own words in whipping the public into line behind it.

Leary met Harris in Tacoma and came over to the meeting with him. At that time, he presented Harris with a set of questions concerning the deals Harris was willing to make on coal and the connections that would knit Seattle with the outside world.

Harris fell into the trap by using the questions as the basis for his speech.

Harris refused to make any commitments on coal because policy had not as yet cleared his board. He couldn't make any commitment on connections with the outside world because he didn't control the Oregon Improvement Company.

The Establishment knew in advance he couldn't answer those questions. They also knew he was an honest, blunt, outspoken man who inevitably would antagonize the people. Seattle was pretty emotional about railroads at that point. Our folks figured it was a matter of but a short time before the railroad's land grant would be snatched from it.

Harris was supposed to be in the role of a supplicant. Instead, he expressed thoughts like the following: "I don't feel I should reveal my hand during negotiations (with Oregon Improvement) . . . If the people expect to get a $200 deal (on hauling coal) for $20, they would be mistaken." He said that Snoqualmie Pass was not even being considered as the route across the Cascades . . . that under any circumstances it would be three years before there would be a year-around railroad across the mountains. He also said he understood some gentlemen in Seattle thought that if the Northern Pacific was out of the way somebody else could do it quicker. He added:

> Seeing, as I do, that the future of Puget Sound is intimately connected with the railroad across the Cascades I would urge whether it would be wise to throw away a pleasant position and trust someone else to take it up under other and worse circumstances to carry it through . . .

He brought down the house—on his own head—when he concluded his remarks by pointing out that any time anybody wanted to take a railroad trip they could always "Come to Tacoma and be sure of catching a train."

He was absolutely right in everything he said . . .

And 100 per cent wrong for saying it at that meeting.

The British are coming! The British are coming!

Then Burke mounted his white charger and woke up the meeting. He referred to "the evil hour" in which the United States Government had given the Northern Pacific railroad about half of the Territory of Washington. "The government reduced its gift to the pioneers from 320 to 160 acres to open up its frontier", Burke roared, "yet no amount is too much for a company that promises to build a railroad no matter whether it does or not . . ." His further remarks did nothing to relax the crowd, either:

> Their contracts are the most atrocious and most villainous ever drawn up for the conveyance of land . . . we have built our own towns and cities and railroads and developed the country. After all this was done, along comes the Northern Pacific and demands half the country . . . for what? Broken promises? For retarding the growth of the country? For holding it in bondage? . . . As a simple illustration shown by the Company toward Seattle, I refer you to the course of your Company when some advertising literature referred to Seattle as the Queen City. The Great Corporation was instantly stirred to its lowest depths and promptly the whole edition was suppressed and once more peace and quietness reigned through the councils of the Company . . . Today your

trains are run so as to cause this city and the traveling public coming here as much inconvenience as possible.

Leary, who was the last speaker to attack Harris, ended on a glorious note. He said: "Give me Seattle or give me death!"

Harris attempted to oblige him by cutting off all railroad service to Seattle a month later.

The March of Dimes

The railroad's lobby in Washington, D.C. got the forfeiture bill killed in the Senate and Harris went about building a railroad across the Cascades at Stampede Pass. At the same time, he started construction on the Stampede Tunnel, without which the Cascade branch never could be considered a year-around route. The track was aimed directly at Tacoma.

No trains ran on the track through the Kent Valley to Seattle.

Because it had no single owner and really went from no place to no place, Harris dubbed this the "Orphan Road." Its tracks lay rusting in the farmers' fields as the months raced by.

Meanwhile, Gilman was living high on the hog at company expense, smoking big black cigars and rubbing elbows with the rich while he hunted for an angel for the Establishment's railroad. He was looking for an angel with the right color of harp. He found all kinds of angels who never came through and even one phoney angel who tried to get money out of him ar.d the fellows back home who were footing the bills started getting a little impatient with Mr. Gilman and his angels.

Viewing the actual construction that had begun on the Northern Pacific, Leary and Lewis were for forking over the $150,000 subsidy the city had offered the Columbia & Puget Sound. It was obvious that the railroad was going to build through Stampede Pass, and a favorable connection would be made with the Northern Pacific at what was called the "Common Point" . . . a spot near Black Diamond where the Green River leading to Stampede Pass came down out of the mountains and nearly merged with the Cedar River Valley. Gatzert, too, was for making peace with the Northern Pacific and getting use out of the rusting track on the Orphan Road.

But Burke was still itching to build a railroad and wouldn't be deterred. With the aid of some of the new members of the Establishment like Angus MacIntosh, George Kinnear, J. W. Currie, G. M. Haller and F. H. Osgood, he held the line until the following spring when Gilman wired that he'd found an angel . . . and this one had a harp of gold.

On April 15, 1885, the Seattle, Lake Shore & Eastern Railroad was incorporated with the old Establishment and the new names mentioned above. Our friendly historian, Mr. Bagley, put it like this:

> This was entirely a Seattle enterprise, and introduces into the history of the city several new names, representing chiefly what might be termed the second division of the pioneers. All of them realized that the only way to bring the Northern Pacific to time was to make an aggressive stand, as a decade of appealing to the company had gained Seattle nothing.

Gilman, who always did things enthusiastically, enthusiastically reported that the new backers, who included among them the president of the New York Stock Exchange, were prepared to put up a million dollars as a starter on a transcontinental railroad originating in Seattle.

If you don't think that made a splash in Seattle, you just aren't familiar with splashes. And just by way of providing a basis for judgment, the total receipts in the General Fund for the City of Seattle during that year were $38,974.53.

A million dollars!

Burke hurried back to New York to take care of the details and learned that the bankers were willing to fork over half of the million immediately. Seattle of course, would advance 10 per cent as its share of the enterprise. And once more I feel it incumbent to turn the description of the situation over to Bagley, who was living at the time and got the information straight from Burke's mouth:

> "We will organize a building company to construct it and subscribe $500,000 ourselves if you will put up $10,000 yourself," Burke was told.

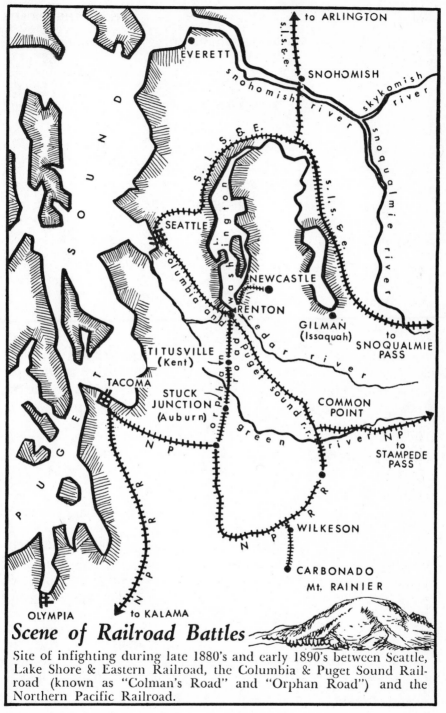

Scene of Railroad Battles

Site of infighting during late 1880's and early 1890's between Seattle, Lake Shore & Eastern Railroad, the Columbia & Puget Sound Railroad (known as "Colman's Road" and "Orphan Road") and the Northern Pacific Railroad.

"Good heavens, man!" exclaimed the Judge. "I haven't $10,000 cash and never had."

"If you people out there cannot raise at least 10 per cent of the money, I'm afraid we cannot entertain the proposal," was the reply of the banker.

Burke scurried back home in a panic and managed to borrow his $10,000 from banker Angus MacIntosh, the same fellow who had worked out the real estate deal connected with the rock quarry on the County Poor Farm. MacIntosh, Leary, Kinnear and Currie each took an additional $10,000 to make up the $50,000, but that's really beside the point.

And the point is that originally the Sons of the Profits really thought they were going to get a transcontinental railroad built out of Seattle without putting up a thin dime themselves.

No wonder Seattle is the major metropolis of the Pacific Northwest!

Later on the Seattle quintet had to fork over another $10,000 apiece to get a total of a million dollars invested in their own railroad . . . and according to my arithmetic that's getting nine bucks invested by someone else for a proposition that largely involves a profit for the man who put up the one dollar.

And don't think that isn't what the boys had their eyes on.

Real cash and real estate

I don't suppose anybody will ever know whether our boys ever really thought the Seattle, Lake Shore & Eastern was going to live up to its advance billing. Burke might have, because he'd never done this before. But all the evidence indicates they talked transcontinental and bought "local." They never had any thought beyond providing a local network that would be bought by one of the other transcontinentals looking for a feeder line.

For example, the original capitalization of the line was only $5,000,000. That wouldn't get them over the Cascades, let alone provide local terminal facilities. At best they hoped they might get as far as Denny's Iron Mountain in Snoqualmie Pass.

It also is interesting to note that all three of Seattle's paper transcontinental roads proposed to go east via Walla Walla. Nobody from Seattle goes to Walla Walla these days unless he is sentenced to take the trip to the Penitentiary by some judge. And no transcontinental road goes through there today.

On the other hand, another circumstance would indicate their interest in reaching Seattle's hinterland with the S. L.S. & E. The easy logging, on the shoreline of Puget Sound where the timber rolled easily into the water for transport to market, was peaking off. But there was money in those hills from logging . . . and, they hoped, from mining. They never figured Seattle as the distribution center that it is today. They were born and brought up on making it an industrial town.

So, while the S. L.S. & E. was designed to connect with one of the other transcontinentals, its primary purpose lay in tapping the city's hinterland. Leary and Burke decided to add another little fillip to this philosophy via a project called Gilman's Addition to the City of Seattle.

Leary had bought the D. W. Crooks farm on the shore of Shilshole Bay in 1882 and once their railroad was under way, it seemed like a bright idea to develop the seven or eight hundred acres as a major suburb to Seattle. The theory, which later became a profitable fact, was that commuter trains could run along the S. L.S. & E. track and be only twenty scenic minutes away from the center of the city.

And ever since, every suburb around the perimeter of the city has been advertised as only "twenty scenic minutes away from downtown."

So Burke and Leary pulled in William R. Ballard and Boyd Tallman to do the work that created the West Coast Improvement Company which in turn developed the town of Ballard into the most successful real estate promotion in the early history of Seattle.

It was so successful that similar projects were attempted in West Seattle, East Seattle, Columbia City and Kirkland—all of them with disastrous financial results for the promoters . . . especially West Seattle which went under on as grand a scale as Ballard went up.

Take all to Titusville

While some of the others were doing about the S. L.S. & E., Judges Cornelius H. Hanford and J. R. Lewis were busying themselves with the problem of the rusting track of the Orphan Road.

Then Judge Hanford encountered a former bookkeeper for the Northern Pacific who had no love for the company when he departed, but had retained a set of books showing the profit and loss statement for the Orphan Road during the one month it had been in operation.

It occurred to the Establishment that the farmers in the valley were annoyed at the non-use of the rusting track that bisected their farm lands, and that it was about time for another "spontaneous" mass meeting.

And on September 26, 1885—just 13 months after the order had gone out from Harris shutting down rail operations on the Orphan Road—a gentleman with the delightful name of "Foghorn" Green called a protest meeting in Titusville, which we all know today as Kent. The farmers showed up with unkind words about the Northern Pacific. Judges Lewis and Hanford were on hand as amicus curiae. And John L. Howard of the Oregon Improvement Company was on hand to howl about hard times.

Judge Lewis appeared with the pleasant news that he had got himself elected to the Territorial Legislature with but one plank in his campaign platform—that if the Northern Pacific couldn't get together with the Oregon Improvement Company and re-establish rail service along the Orphan Road, the Territory would be glad to solve the problem by taking over the operation of the road. Judge Hanford explained their legal position to the farmers. He pointed out that their land had been condemned as a right-of-way for the Oregon Improvement Company road on the grounds of eminent domain. Hanford said:

> Railroads are for public use. A railroad is a tangent; it takes a slice out of meadows, orchards and gardens; where houses and barns were obstructions, they were removed to make room for a

railroad. If you farmers did not consent to have your improved land cut to ribbons, the law of eminent domain gave consent . . . the same reason that justifies condemnation of public land for public use likewise sanctions condemnation of an existing railroad that is not serving the public. If whoever had proprietary interest in this road cannot, or will not operate it, you farmers can acquire possession of it rightfully and put it to work.

Mr. Howard then rebutted that this was all well and good, but if the farmers thought they had troubles now, they'd really get themselves in the financial wringer if they tried to operate it. Howard pointed out that operating that short railroad was economically unsound . . . and how would they like to lose their shirts?

Hanford said I'm glad you asked that question—and that's where the bookkeeper came in. His books showed the line had made a 50 per cent profit during the month it was in operation.

Two weeks later, trains started running on that track, and they've kept it from getting rusty ever since.

The Weakly Reeder

Although the Northern Pacific found itself forced to use the track of the Orphan Road, there was no law that said when and how they had to use it. And for the next four years, it showed the little hick town what it was like to play in a major league ball game.

The Northern Pacific, itself, was racing against time and the St. Paul, Minneapolis & Manitoba in establishing itself as the major railroad on Puget Sound. Harris was aware that he not only needed track across the Cascades, but a tunnel through them to make his year-round road.

Harris had no hope of wooing Seattle, so he set about breaking her. If he could move fast enough, he could force Seattle into line through sheer economic pressure and encourage Hill to tap tidewater somewhere further north on the Sound.

The one train a day that ran to Seattle usually ran there during the middle of the night. It usually consisted of one car and a locomotive which didn't begin to handle the traffic. Mail to Seattle was held over twenty-four hours in Tacoma, for months—until Seattle finally got to the Post Office Department and had that one corrected.

Wheat shipped from eastern Washington was 50¢ a ton less to Tacoma than to Seattle. Freight headed as far east as Mandan, North Dakota—which was about as far as any appreciable amount from the Pacific Northwest sent—cost $80 a ton more from Seattle than from Tacoma. Carloads consigned to Seattle were broken up into small lots and shipped on from Tacoma. Southbound passengers were forced to stay overnight in Tacoma. Seattle passengers headed for St. Paul were required to get up at three o'clock in the morning to make connection at Puyallup with the crack passenger trains from Tacoma.

The newspapers of the time stated that the railroad could have saved over half a million dollars by constructing track from Auburn to Stampede Pass instead of from Puyallup, but that the railroad chose the latter because it was ten miles closer to Tacoma.

The Seattle, Lake Shore & Eastern was a pretty weak reed for Seattle to cling to. We blew a lot of money on that railroad and when we were through, it had only been built as far east as Rattlesnake Prairie above Snoqualmie Falls and as far north as Arlington. But it was the only hope we held out to ourselves for a connection with a transcontinental system.

On the other hand, the side benefits of the S. L.S.& E. enabled us to hit the jackpot with the Great Northern. For one thing, the Seattle railroad immediately started spending a lot of money in Seattle. It acquired six hundred acres of land at Smith's Cove and announced that it would push north to Vancouver and east at least as far as Issaquah where Burke and Gilman had the Seattle Coal and Iron Mines.

The Establishment was somewhat embarrased by the fact that it had acquired the Ram's Horn right-of-way across our waterfront for Villard's Columbia & Puget Sound Railway. Now it wanted a right-of-way for its own S. L.S. & E. Burke proved adequate to answer that one. He pushed an ordinance through the City Council providing for the construction of Railroad Avenue, 120 feet wide and entirely on piling over water, to the west of the Ram's Horn. The S. L.S. & E. got a franchise for the first thirty feet. The Northern Pacific was offered but turned down the second thirty feet, so there was an additional ninety feet awaiting the arrival of the first transcontinental railroad.

The creation of Railroad Avenue was easy for the Establishment. And it was the most important contribution to the development of Seattle, in the light of subsequent events, that the Seattle, Lake Shore & Eastern made.

Other effects of the S. L.S. & E. were having a vital impact on our economy at the time. The folks could *see* the piling being driven. They could *see* the tracks being laid. They could *see* work trains moving out to the head of construction and trainloads of logs and coal returning. They could take pictures of people swarming from the Ballard commuter trains. It didn't matter that the whole track only went forty-three miles or that the folks from Ballard only paid 15¢ a head.

Real estate could be bought for five bucks and sold five days later for fifty bucks a front foot in downtown Seattle. It was a boom town when according to the time schedules of the Northern Pacific it should have been busted. Money flowed into town from all over the country. In addition to seeing what was happening, we could feel our pocket books bulging.

And don't think the flint-faced fellows in the black Homburgs who came from James J. Hill's headquarters looking like agents in a Vienna spy movie weren't impressed.

Seattle's boom was real and the bank clearings showed it.

And those were the details the Hill agents paid attention to.

After the S. L.S. & E. left Ballard, it wound around the north end of Lake Washington with the twin objectives of heading north to the Canadian Pacific and east to Issaquah. And it was in the construction of that northern leg that Burke made an important contribution to the education of one Eugene Canfield of Fairhaven (Bellingham) and eliminated a major obstacle to the selection of Seattle as the terminus for the Great Northern.

Fairhaven considered itself a pretty strong contender for that terminus. The Great Northern was plowing along through Montana enroute to Puget Sound. Should the railroad decide to cross the Cascades via Skagit Pass, it would be a very strong contender indeed.

Canfield evolved a scheme for building a railroad called the Fairhaven & Southern from Fairhaven to Seattle and with this in mind went to Congress where he obtained the right to cross all of the rivers between Fairhaven and Seattle. Mr. Canfield allowed as how this congressional action gave him an exclusive on crossing rivers and when he was tentatively approached by the S. L.S. & E. about working out a deal, he expressed the thought it would cost the Seattle people about a million dollars for the franchise.

Bagley says that Canfield was encouraged in his delinquency by the Northern Pacific and that this little technicality about who had the right to do what worried the S. L.S. & E. bond-holders enough so that they declined an opportunity to buy more bonds.

Burke, who never enjoyed being on the giving end of a million dollar conversation, decided he would see whether Canfield's thoughts would stand up in court . . . and in the process gave rise to one of our wonderful Burkean legends.

The S. L.S. & E. built track to the south side of the Snohomish River. Canfield went to Tacoma where he got an injunction against the Seattle railroad prohibiting it from crossing the river . . . and when the process server was standing in the S. L.S. & E. station at Western Avenue and Columbia Street waiting for the northbound train to leave, Burke and the irrepressible Leary swiped the locomotive and headed north to Snohomish. The Snohomish county sheriff and deputies were friends of the Seattle men and were easily persuaded to go hunting for a couple of imaginary criminals in the Cascades while Burke ordered the construction of a bridge across the river.

The process server finally showed up, but for the next couple of days there was nobody on whom he could serve his summons. The bridge was completed, a precedent established, Canfield's exclusive removed, and the bonds sold.

And when Hill came along a few years later, he knew he didn't have to deal with Canfield on the matter of crossing rivers enroute to the Canadian border.

The rough Mr. Clough

Unlike Harris, who had the Land Company virtually opposing him within the board of directors, James J. Hill was the supreme boss of the St. Paul, Minneapolis & Manitoba. And unlike the Northern Pacific, which waggled all over the landscape like the sinuous snail previously mentioned, Hill was following the Great Circle route—some six hundred miles shorter from the Great Lakes into Puget Sound. Also unlike the Northern Pacific, Hill's railroad enjoyed no land grant or government subsidy of any kind—nor any time-consuming federal red tape. Hill was an empire builder in every sense of the word. Before he was through his empire would include the Great Northern, Northern Pacific and the Chicago, Burlington & Quincy Railroads, which would make him one of four men who controlled all of the railroads in the United States until the cartel was broken up by the Sherman Anti-Trust Law.

His objective was Puget Sound and the Orient.

Where he touched tidewater was of vast unimportance to him.

His engineers told him the shortest route was over Skagit Pass and down into Bellingham Bay . . . and that was the route that was surveyed first. But in the course of his transcontinental construction he got thought-provoking reports on Seattle that fitted neatly into his plans. It looked like Seattle would remain the major port on the Sound. He wasn't above picking up a little local traffic on his run to the Orient. And the Northern Pacific was wearing itself a little thin in its fight with the feisty little town.

He had the same objections to the terrain that the Northern Pacific had professed in the original instance. It was all hills and water. Where would he put his freight yards and depot?

Early in 1889 he visited Fairhaven, which offered him all of the free land he wanted and the entire harbor to do with as he pleased. It offered him a right-of-way all the way to Seattle including its precious congressional franchise to cross rivers. The Fairhaven & Southern was his for the asking to use as a branch line.

He was friendly, but non-committal.

He also visited Seattle, where he was equally non-committal.

He returned to St. Paul to think things over.

Then, two months after the Seattle fire, Hill's right hand man, Col. W. P. Clough, appeared in Seattle. He had no difficulty finding members of the Establishment for the simple reason that before going with Hill in the latter's westward expansion, he had been an officer of the Northern Pacific fighting Seattle's Establishment tooth and toenail.

Mr. Clough professed to be on vacation . . . but he privately suggested that the Establishment consider the formation of a railroad called the Seattle & Montana and above all be prepared to produce a sixty-foot right-of-way on Railroad Avenue for spring delivery to the St. Paul, Minneapolis & Manitoba . . . which by that time would have changed its name to the Great Northern.

At the same time, Mr. Clough gave Burke a little lecture on the facts of life. James J. Hill required certain things in a terminus. These included freight yards and docking facilities at Smith Cove . . . a free and easy passage across the Seattle waterfront to more freight yards south of town. If these were delivered, the railroad would terminate at Seattle.

If they were not delivered—and with no problems involved—then the railroad would terminate either at Fairhaven or Everett.

The Northern Pacific's final selection of Tacoma as its terminus still was extremely fresh in the minds of the Establishment. The current obnoxious treatment the city was getting at the hands of the Northern Pacific was even fresher. Burke assured Mr. Clough the goods would be delivered.

Burke suggested to Clough that the S. L.S. & E. was ready for rape and Clough just laughed and said the Great Northern was a railroad, not a real estate promotion. He pointed out that Hill was planning to cut straight across the state into Puget Sound. He had no desire to build track down to Walla Walla and back again to Seattle. The S. L.S. & E. would do Hill no good whatsoever.

Burke suggested that he and some of the others owned a town called Wenatchee and would gladly part with half of it as sort of a maraschino cherry. Clough allowed as how that would be more interesting . . . and took it.

On March 7, 1890, just eight months later, the Seattle & Montana Railroad was incorporated to "build a railroad from Seattle to the eastern boundary of the state and branch lines and lines of telegraph; to acquire other railroads and telegraphs; to build and sail steamships; to build wharves, and bunkers; to do business in Oregon, Idaho and Montana . . ."

It's capital stock was $10,000,000.

The same day, an ordinance was drafted, run through both chambers of the City Council and signed by the Mayor giving the new railroad company a sixty-foot right of way on Railroad Avenue.

The next day, Mr. Clough bought the Fairhaven & Southern Railroad—with the objective of keeping it out of hostile hands.

The Northern Pacific was taken completely by surprise.

In a last ditch effort to keep Hill out of Washington, the N. P. countered by seizing control of the Seattle, Lake Shore & Eastern. To show Seattle what it thought of her, the Northern Pacific moved all of the S. L.S. & E. shops to Tacoma, ran schedules from Tacoma to Arlington ...

And made Seattle only a flag stop.

What the Northern Pacific didn't know did hurt her. The horse was long gone out of *that* barn!

The Establishment had its hands full with Hill's demands. The Northern Pacific was fighting him every step of the way. Headed by Burke, they went quietly about collecting the necessary parcels of land for Hill's terminal. One man noted that our boys collected a building over the tideflats into their fold and forgot to collect the rent the next month. Suspecting that they were functioning on behalf of Hill, he held out for $10,000 when it came his turn to turn in his land.

Rather than let Hill even know about the problem, Burke, Furth, John Collins, Leary, MacIntosh, Yesler, Dexter Horton, Amos Brown and Colman coughed up a thousand bucks apiece to pay him off.

Hill then decided he needed land closer to the wholesale district than what the Establishment had secured for him and asked Burke to obtain the land between Second and Fourth Avenues South, Jackson and King Street, at the lowest possible cost. Burke then went to the property owners urging them to sell their land at a price that would enable him to report he could buy the entire section at a cost lower than Hill could get it any place else on the Sound.

One owner, a friend of Hill's, refused to deal with Burke. And when the latter reported this information to Hill, the empire builder said, "Oh, I'll pay him out of my own pocket."

Burke came up with a not-on-your-tintype reply in the form of a telegram reading: "If you pay your friend more than you pay my neighbors for the same class of property please consider my resignation in your hands."

A somewhat startled Hill referred the friend back to Burke and the man cut his price to meet the going rate.

After the ball is over . . .

By 1890, the Northern Pacific had capitulated. The Establishment had won. A parity of rates was established by the railroad. A sleeper which could be boarded at the convenience of the passenger was hauled in the middle of the night to Puyallup. There was no staying overnight in Tacoma for southbound passengers. The service to the city was excellent.

Thomas Oakes, who was then president of the Northern Pacific, sold out his real estate holdings in Tacoma and with $150,000 joined with a syndicate that spent nearly half a million dollars buying land in Seattle.

But the fight was not over. It wouldn't be over for another ten years and more. And the Establishment realized that with victory comes responsibility. We had delivered the goods that had been asked for by James J. Hill, but the Great Northern found itself in a court dispute over its right to the use of that sixty feet on Railroad Avenue. We had to pitch in and help.

The Oregon Improvement Company with its Columbia & Puget Sound Railroad refused to give up its franchise and denied Hill the right to cross its tracks to his terminals on the tideflats south of the city. Burke took Oregon Improvement to the lower court and won. In 1892, J. T. Ronald, the Establishment's Mayor, ordered the Columbia & Puget Sound tracks along Western Avenue torn up.

Oregon Improvement, which had appealed the case, tried to run a locomotive through an intersection to keep the track where it was. It not only encountered the dedication with which the Establishment would fight, it encountered Mayor Ronald.

Ronald, with his police force behind him, stood directly in the path of the locomotive. The engineer, who had been instructed to plant the engine in the middle of the intersection, accidentally touched Ronald with his locomotive.

"They even hit our Mayor with one of their locomotives!" the Establishment screamed.

This made even the hostile Oregon Improvement Company back off for awhile and on January 7, 1893, the first Great Northern train on transcontinental track rolled into the depot at the foot of Columbia Street, carrying the construction superintendent's car and one passenger car. The final spike on the Great Northern was made of iron and driven in the presence of only the construction crew. The company had built a prodigious 556 miles of track in 1892 and hadn't time for any fancy gold spike ceremonies.

This was typical of Hill—get the job done first. Never mind the amenities.

Hill himself arrived two weeks later and said that in early June he would have a formal ceremony in Seattle and bring with him three hundred men worth "a thousand million dollars" to see the great virgin territory in which investments would be so very worthwhile.

But before that could happen, Baring Brothers, the principal backers of the Great Northern and most of the rest of the enterprises in the world, took its temporary nose-dive and Hill neglected to bring his party west. "That's all I'd need," Hill was quoted as saying, "a bunch of nervous millionaires on my hands."

Hill, who had planned wisely, didn't go under . . . but the Northern Pacific *Railroad* did. It was reorganized later as the Northern Pacific *Railway*—which it is today.

Final Wright's

All during the 1890's when Seattle really fancied herself a major metropolis, it was wormwood in the hearts of the folks that we operated out of a crummy little wooden depot on Western Avenue at the foot of Columbia Street. We longed for one of those mammoth mausoleums where the station master's voice reverberated with the busi-

ness about the train leaving for "Ev-er-ett . . . Mon-roe . . . Gold-bar
. . . Wen-at-chee . . . Spok-ane . . . and all points east . . ."

James J. Hill, who was the boss man of railroading in those days,
said: "He is a wise farmer who develops his farm before he builds a
palace on it. It is more important to Seattle to have goods delivered
to it cheaply than to have a fancy depot and I'm devoting my attention to the more important thing."

And he was.

When Hill came into the picture, eastbound lumber was costing 90¢ a
hundredweight, but there was no lumber going east . . . just empty
freight cars. When asked, the lumbermen opined they might be able
to compete at 60¢ a hundredweight. Hill snorted they couldn't possibly compete with southern pine at more than 40¢ a hundredweight . . .
and dropped his rates to that. Everybody in the railroad business predicted he would go broke. But he didn't. With this rate, lumber mills
sprang up all over the place and the competing roads had to meet his
price.

But, taking advantage of public sentiment, Charles S. Mellen, president of the Northern Pacific Railway, quietly bought up the property between Washington and University Streets along the waterfront
in 1898. And in 1899, he announced that he was going to spend half
a million dollars building a a gigantic terminal facility and grand
depot covering Seattle's waterfront.

An equally gigantic public campaign was launched with appropriate
drawings and presentations draped in blue velvet to sell the ladies'
clubs and all like that. The newspapers gave it a huge play. The
public went for it like chickens at feeding time. Now, if the City
Council would only vacate a few little street ends . . .

The few little street ends included Western Avenue for its full
length from University Street south to Yesler Way . . . a mere dozen
street ends along Western . . . and the obliteration of the waterfront.
An 850-ft. shed would run from University to Madison Street. The
station itself would occupy a whole block between Marion and Madison Streets, the waterfront and Western Avenue.

On December 31, 1899, the *Post-Intelligencer* devoted two full pages to the voice of the people on the matter. Interviews with prominent citizens were run on an alternating basis, "for" and "against" . . . and why they favored which. This worked out fine on the first of the two pages . . . but by the time the paper got to the second page of interviews, it had run out of "againsts" and only the opinions of the "fors" were represented.

It looked like a landslide for the new facility . . . and that was the kind of landslide that meant that after all of the struggle, the Northern Pacific would own and operate Seattle's waterfront to its own particular specifications. But among the "againsts" were some people yet to be reckoned with. They were McGilvra, Colman, George Kinnear, N. H. Latimer, Dexter Horton . . . and the old warhorse, Thomas Burke.

Advance polls taken before Burke got up before the City Council early in 1900 to speak his piece showed that the council was about 12 to 1 against him.

He said in effect that twenty-seven years ago when the Northern Pacific made its terminus at Tacoma—even though Seattle was the biggest town and offered the biggest subsidy—there was a man in a key capacity in the Northern Pacific Railroad who flatly stated that he would live to see the day when grass grew in Seattle's streets . . . that no locomotive would ever turn its wheels in our city . . . that for twenty years the city of Seattle fought for its life against that man, who not only tried to put Seattle out of existence but change the name of our great state from Washington to Tacoma.

That's the way Burke handled it.

And once more he fired up the old antagonism. When he thundered to a conclusion—demanding to know why we should hand over our waterfront to people like that—the Council voted 12 to 1 against the Northern Pacific's proposal. And the dissenter came in later to make it unanimous.

Ah, the Resurrection and the Life. In his own peculiar way, Mr. C.

B. Wright had served the City of Seattle for the last time at that meeting ...

And he had been in his grave for two years.

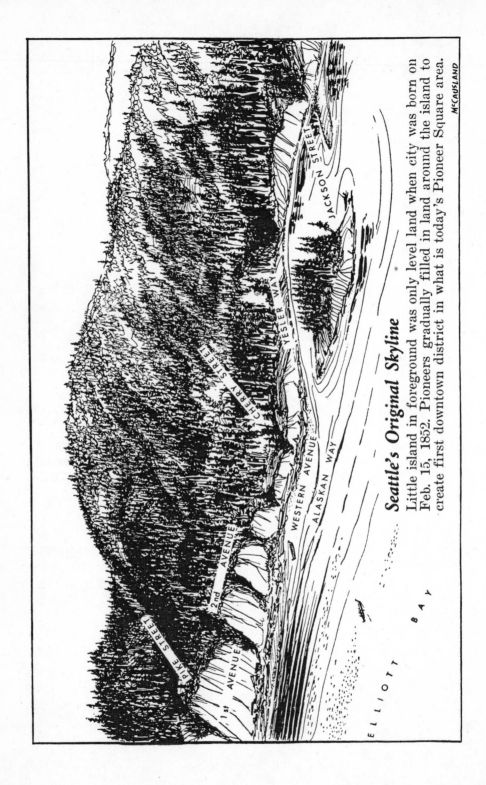

Seattle's Original Skyline

Little island in foreground was only level land when city was born on Feb. 15, 1852. Pioneers gradually filled in land around the island to create first downtown district in what is today's Pioneer Square area.

McCAUSLAND

PIKE STREET

1st AVENUE

2nd AVENUE

CHERRY STREET

WESTERN AVENUE

ALASKAN WAY

YESLER WAY

JACKSON STREET

ELLIOTT BAY

VIII

Archaeology of the Skid Road

The "ruins" of Seattle are not as old or as famous as those of Pompeii, but they're the only ones we've got. They have the further advantage of being here and not off across an ocean some place.

The Pompeiians couldn't have buried their city without a considerable contribution from Mt. Vesuvius.

Ours was a do-it-yourself project.

Pompeii is about two miles in circumference and some twenty feet deep. Our buried "city" is about a mile and a half in circumference and varies in depth from ten to thirty feet. So you can see we have a fair to middling underground area. It covers about twenty square blocks down in the Skid Road area of town. Ours has an edge on Pompeii in that we built another city right on top of it. That's more than they did. Most of the artifacts that were small enough to carry have been stolen from ours over the past seventy-five years, mostly by architects and interior decorators. However, the sidewalks and the store fronts of our buried city still are there for today's tourists to enjoy.

A lot of people are interested in Seattle's underground. But this group doesn't include the people living on top of it today. The best description of the present-day Skid Road habitue's attitude on this great historical phenomenon came from one drunk who asked me in dead seriousness, "What the hell do all these people see in our dirty basements?"

I didn't pause long enough to answer him, but the truth is it's been a long time since I have seen the underground in terms of dirty basements. I see Seattle's birthplace down there. I see the ghosts of the past . . . the craftsmen who put the underground buildings together in the first place . . . the people for whom the present-day buildings, streets, banks, schools and parks are named . . . the tough characters who took a wilderness and carved a city out of it—for profit and prestige. I see the carriages and the candles and the gas lights and the fights . . . yes, mostly the fights. They were the sparks that make the city's history unique . . . the cutting edge that created the city.

I see the big fire that made the underground possible in the first place . . . not in terms of the flames licking away at the buildings— that kind of thing has been written ad infinitum, ad nauseum in existing histories—but in terms of the human emotions and the greed and the derring-do which the fire invoked . . .

And most of all the lovely irony so well-expressed by William Makepeace Thackeray in *Vanity Fair: "Ah Vanitas, Vanitatum!* Which of us is happy in this world? Which of us has his desire? Or having it, is satisfied?"

In the beginning there was this island

As you will recall, Arthur Denny selected Seattle as the site for a city because it was the least worst spot he could find in the general vicinity. It was made up of eight acres of partially dry land at one corner of fifteen hundred acres of mud flats. All around it were cliffs about two hundred feet high that wet all over it every winter—and sometimes in July and August too. These cliffs have so many natural springs in them that it takes a labyrinth of pipes to drain them even today.

Going from north to south, here was the general layout of the land. At First Avenue and Cherry Street there was a little knoll about twenty-five feet high. It dropped off to the beach which came up to First Avenue. There was a small inlet between Cherry Street and Yesler Way that presently is occupied by the Mutual Life Building. In the early days, it was the log pond for Henry Yesler's mill, which gets a great play in our history books. The mill itself was on a small peninsula about three feet above high tide. The beach then cut back to what is about First and Washington, where it encountered a salt-water stream that created an island south of Washington Street.

This stream was fed by a lagoon, which lay mainly between Occidental Avenue and Fourth Avenue South. One arm went as far north as Yesler Way between First Avenue South and Occidental Avenue. At Jackson Street on the north side of today's railroad stations, there was a sand bar created by part of the Duwamish River. The sand bar extended from about Fifth or Sixth Avenue and Jackson down to Occidental Avenue, leaving a gap of about twenty feet between the mainland and the island.

The beach then curved east to the foot of Beacon Hill and followed the general line of Airport Way, which was known as the Beach Road back in the early days. Everything between the Beach Road and West Seattle a mile or so away and everything south of King Street was tide land and the delta of the Duwamish.

The high point of the island was between Jackson and King Streets on First Avenue where a bluff sixteen feet above high tide was used by the Indians as a campground and for smoking salmon. It tapered gradually to tide level at Washington Street on the north and somewhere between Occidental and Second Avenue South on the east.

As you look at it today, the whole area is somewhere between eighteen and twenty-four feet above high tide. The island is not only completely buried but the water around it has been replaced by fill land. Most of the fifteen hundred acres of tideland has been filled to a height of twelve feet above high tide.

Unlike Pompeii, which got filled up with one big blast from one big volcano, our forefathers worked at the job for nearly forty years. And even then they had to have an assist from the biggest fire this city ever saw—either before or since—to complete it.

While the fellows were busy burying the island, they also were busy building the biggest city in the Northwest. The two projects interacted closely on one another. And when you read about the fights that went on while the island was being obliterated, you also gain an insight into the kinds of characters it took to build the city.

It took vision—double vision

To all practical purposes, Maynard and Denny owned and operated the original townsite. In their mind's eyes they each had a vision of what their city would look like someday, and on paper it looked fine—even if they saw two different things.

Only Christ could have walked on half of Maynard's streets. They were under water. And what a headache his City Hall would have been for the engineers! It was on a solid foundation of slippery blue clay on the side of a cliff. The Civic Center he visualized would have been built on a slope of about sixty degrees.

Denny's vision was interesting, too. His dreamed-of "broad highway" of northwest-southeast streets went from three feet above high tide to a hundred and forty above, with a corresponding ninety-degree drop to the beach and seven ravines in twelve blocks. Only a mountain goat could have enjoyed the fifty-degree angle of his east-west streets. Historian Welford Beaton had some comments on their topographical raw material in his book, *The City That Made Itself:*

> Nature apparently grew tired before she finished Seattle. She made a wonderful harbor, produced an empire of timber . . . made a pass through the mountains that was a natural avenue of ingress . . . hung picture windows on the horizons . . . gave her a climate that blended with her physical charms—and then left the townsite itself like a tousled, unmade bed.

Where there wasn't water or cliffs there was swamp, driftwood, and trees that were ten feet in diameter at the base, and, of course, a great collection of impenetrable underbrush. Much of what we know as Pioneer Square today was pretty swampy stuff when the folks first showed up. There was no such thing as the present gradual slope of Yesler Way up from the waterfront. It consisted of crossgrained hills and hollows all the way.

You can't see any of this sort of thing on the surface of today's streets, but when you get underground, you still find the humps and hollows that weren't erased in a general levelling process. One basement level may well be three to six feet above or below the location next door. Some of the sub basements are still flooded either on a year-round basis or at high tide.

So it's obvious that from a topographical standpoint, this island looked like a pretty punk location for a city. After his reference to the lousy job the Lord had done, Mr. Beaton creates a happy ending to his little homily by adding, "then Man stepped in, completed the work which Nature had left undone . . .".

Let's see how Man handled it.

Manhandled it?

Yes.

On May 23, 1853 when Denny and Maynard filed what since has been referred to as the Plat of the Town of Seattle it became obvious they had not followed the same script. In one of his rare attempts at humor, Denny reported later that: "the doctor who occasionally stimulated a little, had that day taken enough to feel that he not only was monarch of all he surveyed but what Boren and I had surveyed as well . . ."

It was his way of saying that Doc Maynard was drunk on the day they laid out the town. Denny, who was not drunk—who never was drunk once in his whole life, not once—filed the plat on his claim during the day. That evening, when the good doctor sobered up, he filed his plat. But when they tried to match up the two plats, there was a problem.

The main streets didn't meet.

Denny's streets, heading southeast, encountered the middle of Maynard's blocks. Doc's streets, heading due north found themselves at a dead end against the middle of Denny's blocks. It doesn't matter much now because the north-south streets bend at Yesler Way so they do meet.

But between 1853 and 1889 they didn't—and did that ever create confusion!

There was a jog of about thirty feet along Yesler Way between Maynard's First Avenue and Denny's First Avenue. The jog was called the "throat" of the city because it was the passage that connected the north end of the city to the south, and all north or south bound traffic had to make right-angle turns at the jog.

The redoubtable Henry Yesler had a solid row of buildings from the waterfront right up to the east side of the little triangle that today is called "Pioneer Square." The eastern end of this row of buildings created the historically famous "Yesler Corner".

The fight over the Yesler Corner perched the city on the brink of bankruptcy. It forced on Seattle the most costly piece of real estate in her history. It nearly killed a City Councilman and generated the most virulent concentration of ill-will the folks ever cooked up. Arthur Denny was around to wring his hands about the sadness of it all, but I'll bet a cookie it never occurred to him he was responsible for it.

Arthur never had any trouble convincing himself that he was right about things . . . and he certainly thought he was right about the way he laid out the downtown streets. His little quip about Maynard's drinking habits has handed old Doc the blame for the cock-eyed system of streets we have downtown today.

Yet the truth is that, drunk or sober, Maynard was right.

And Denny was a surveyor. He should have known better. When he laid out his streets the way he did, he was violating the Donation Land Law under which he got his claim in the first place. He was supposed to have laid his streets in a north-south direction like Maynard did.

Three quarters of a century too late to do anything about it, a member of the American Society of Civil Engineers was called in by the city to tell us what was the matter with our street system. He said quite candidly that Seattle wouldn't be in such awful shape if some idiot back in the beginning hadn't got the bright idea of laying some of our downtown streets in a north-west, south-east direction instead of north-south like the law called for and as they were laid out south of Yesler Way.

We've had a lot of fights over our streets since that first disagreement. But it was the one responsible for a lot of the rest of them. Denny and Maynard might have gotten together if the two of them could have talked it over, but Denny had no patience with the latter when he was drinking. They were two stubborn men who wouldn't give an inch. And so, although it was Doc who had been drinking . . .

It was Denny's vision that was impaired.

Ohm Sweet Ohm

Although he was not a member of the American Society of Civil Engineers, the first project engineer for the regrading of Seattle was Nels Jacob Ohm, better known in the community as "Dutch Ned". His contribution to confusion consisted of removing the sawdust and waste products from Henry Yesler's mill and depositing it in the nearest holes.

When Dutch Ned first went to work, he faced a pretty sloppy mess every day. He had water on three sides of himself and even Pioneer Square leaked a lot at high tide. There was about three times as much water around as there was dry land. The instructions from Henry were, "fill her up".

And all he had was one lousy wheelbarrow.

Although Mr. Ohm was not a man of high voltage, he was a persistent cuss and spent the next thirty years laying the foundation for what is today's underground. And while his intentions were honorable some of today's sidewalks in the Skid Road should be marked "tilt" because the sawdust settled capriciously when concrete was laid in later, and you don't have to be drunk to feel like you're on a canting deck in a heavy sea. This condition is even more noticeable in Seattle's underground sidewalks.

The kids used to play football on what is now Pioneer Square, but the field got pretty muddy sometimes and Dutch Ned obligingly spread a fresh layer of his best sawdust over the square every day during the rainy season.

Dutch Ned's efforts also extended Henry Yesler's Pier to the west, and helped raise First Avenue South where the retail shopping district was attempting to lift itself out of the tideflats. Additional fill was needed to eliminate the little saltwater stream at Washington Street so there wouldn't be so much of a hill as the folks travelled up to the high point at Jackson Street. "One day," the early residents predicted, "we will be able to drive a wagon all the way from Yesler Way to Jackson Street!" Three whole blocks.

But by 1880, it dawned on Ned that he would not complete his re-grading assignment all by himself so he gave up and got a more lucrative job hauling the United States mail. Ned was a superstitious soul and it concerned him that the residents of Seattle's first grave-yard near Fifth Avenue and Jackson Street were afloat during high tide. He determined during his close association with the mud in the lower part of town that he was not going to float through eternity at high tide.

The settlers failed to reassure him when they moved the cemetery to Denny Hill 'and replaced the original cemetery with the gas works, so in 1880 he bought himself a plot as high on the hill as he could get in the new Lakeview Cemetery. He built his own mausoleum out of sandstone and had many pictures taken of himself standing beside his prize possession.

On April 18, 1898 at the age of sixty-nine years, the "father" of Seattle's underground was placed inside his permanent establishment.

Fate being what it is, however, not even Ned could guard against the 1949 earthquake . . . and his mausoleum as well as the Skid Road streets, is marked "tilt" and one of these days must come down unless some historically-minded organization with a little money in the kitty chooses to restore it to its original glory.

So we had an Indian war

I am not overcome with nostalgia every time I think of Seattle's one-day war with the Indians who got mad because the whites were stealing their land. In the first place there already are too many million words about every detail and about every biscuit that got burned . . . and who gets the credit for warning about the impending attack . . . and whether or not Arthur Denny should have defied some General in the Militia.

Some sketches made during the Indian war era did point up some archaeological facts that give us a picture of the early topography of the Skid Road. For instance, when the Indians tried to repossess their land on January 25, 1856, we still had that knoll at the foot of Cherry Street.

A north blockhouse built at that location provided a commanding view of the entire town which lay to the south . . . a clear indication that the low part of town was very low indeed. We also constructed the south blockhouse at what is now the corner of Occidental Avenue and Main Street. We then ran a breastworks between the block-houses.

The fortifications went down the hill to Yesler's mill, across the stream at Washington Street and then slightly above the water level on the shore of the lagoon on the east side of Denny's Island to the south blockhouse. Most of the population of the town lived on the Island west of the south blockhouse.

At high tide, there was a hundred yards of water between Denny's Island and the mainland to the east . . . and at low tide the water was replaced by mud a couple of feet deep. The settlers only needed to devote a limited amount of attention to fortifying this area. To attack from that angle, the Indians would have to get their mocca-sins all muddy.

They wanted their land back . . .

But they didn't want it back *that* badly.

There also was a possibility of Indian attack from the north through the woods near the shore. But there were those seven ravines all loaded with prickly blackberry vines which would wreak havoc with the half-nude Indians' buckskin clothing . . . and the "Decatur" was right down there in the water firing those boom boom bullets that Horton found out about later on.

No, the way to attack the town was down the paths from the hills to the east and especially down the trail criss-crossing what today is Yesler Way. It was handy, it was close and it was easy travelling.

It also was defended by marines.

The following story about the marines may or may not be true, but it illustrates a point and I like it. According to the story, the military men wore several suits of underwear and heavy overcoats. The In-dians were short of powder and also had to make their bullets out of the foil that came wrapped around tobacco.

The marines came out of the fray with their clothes looking like the moths had been after them, but without any more serious damage to their persons. The phoney bullets didn't do much damage, but 4,000 more Indians—with or without bullets—sure could have. And that's the number our friend, Chief Seattle, had under control and kept from joining the thousand or so who did go after us.

When the boys returned home after the war . . . that is, when they went the five or six hundred yards from the blockhouse to their cabins . . . Henry Yesler's mill started right up again and continued making sawdust for Dutch Ned to empty and after this slight interlude the preparations for today's underground were continued with no further interruption.

There's a story I like about the aftermath of the Indian war. It's the tale of Dexter Horton and the unexploded shell in the stump, and it does serve to remind us that clearing the land of huge tree stumps was one of the toughest grooming jobs we had in making our site more livable. The Indian war did help a bit.

Dexter Horton was the town's first banker, and one day he backed up to warm his rear end at a stump that was being burned in a land-clearing project. A shell had been deposited in the stump some years earlier by the Ship of War "Decatur". The "Decatur's" gun was known to the Indians as a "boom boom", because it went "boom" when a shell left the ship and "boom" again when the shell landed in the middle of one of their strategy meetings.

Well, the one that landed in Horton's stump had only gone "boom" once during the Indian war.

It boomed the second time for the benefit of the banker's backside . . . sending him sprawling and causing Seattle's banking business to be conducted from a standing position for the next few days.

The hallowed humps and hollows

As the Indian war strategy indicates, the topography from Denny's Island south was pretty unprepossessing, but the land to the north and east also had little to recommend it.

At the present time, the waterfront pretty much parallels First Avenue from Yesler Way to the Pike Place Market, but in those days Yesler Way and Pike Street were points of land with a crescent-shaped beach in between. The easy way to get between the two points was via rowboat. A man could step into his boat at First Avenue and Yesler Way and row the mile north to Pike—if the weather was disposed and the water calm. Then it was a mere climb up a bluff the height of a sixteen-story building—and there he was!

First Avenue was an entirely different proposition. It looked nice on Denny's map, but for most of the distance it ran along the top of a bluff that was cut up by ravines as deep as seventy-five feet—no problem to navigate if you had a long ladder. Also, parts of the bluff had a tendency to slide off into the bay during the rainy season.

The other choice was a walk around the ravines. This involved negotiating a hill which at Sixth and Cherry was about as far above First and Cherry as the Northern Life Tower—and still is, except that we've taken out the humps and filled in the hollows to make it a gradually ascending grade. That just shows the decadence of our modern civilization. We can drive from down to up. In those days most of the journey could be compared to climbing the Northern Life Tower . . .

On the outside.

And then there was the Jackson Street Hill. An eight-story building could be put on top of our present Freeway and not reach as high as what once was the top of that hill. In the good old Denny Days, it was possible to row southeast from Pioneer Square to Seventh Avenue. But then a man had to climb a 178-foot cliff if he wanted to go over the hill to Lake Washington.

Yesler Way is another case in point. Today it has a fifteen per cent grade. When Arthur Denny first looked up at that hill with his arms akimbo and opined, "that's a purty steep hill," he wasn't kidding. The grade was forty-nine per cent . . . another cliff.

But Denny wasn't thinking how hard it would be to get a man up Yesler Way. He was thinking how easy it would be to get logs down. All you had to do was to cut a bunch of saplings, place them crosswise on the downhill pull, and keep them well lubricated with dogfish oil. All that remained was to contemplate the lovely profits that would evolve when those big logs came thundering down the skid road to Yesler's Mill.

The Skid Road?

Yep. That's how that area of town got its name—from the skid road
that went from the forests at the top of Yesler Way down to the tide-
line.

The cliff hangers

City records show no indication of any concerted community effort
toward lessening the differences of elevations between the humps
and hollows in the twenty years that followed the Indian war, although individuals dumped garbage, dirt, sawdust or anything else
they could lay their hands on to make usable the particular hollows
to which they had title.

To a limited extent—and by that I mean *real* limited—they hauled
in dirt from the surrounding hills. For instance, they took some of
their dirt from that sixteen foot hill at the high end of Denny's Island and hauled it north to the low end.

Nobody was trying to fulfill the dreams of Denny and Maynard.
When each guy thought he had enough dirt to keep the customers'
feet dry in his store at high tide, he quit bringing in fill material and
built a building that would bring in some money.

Add to that the fact that the whole place was full of lumps anyway
and you find out why there is a hodgepodge of ground elevations
under the buildings today. Any given building constructed at the
levels created during this twenty-year period might well be three to
six feet above or below the building immediately next to it.

They didn't have the continuity of sidewalks that we have today.
Those came in when the streets were officially raised after the fire of
1889. Prior to that time a walk along First Avenue included several
flights of steps built right into the wooden sidewalks to accommo-
date the different levels at which the merchants operated.

Frequently the sidewalks were substantially higher than the streets
and the owners of the fancy phaetons were no little distressed by the
fun-loving dandies who stood on the high sidewalks and spit tobacco
juice on the passengers in the carriages.

A cryptic editorial in the *Intelligencer* on July 28, 1876 pointed out that the sidewalk on the south side of Mill Street (Yesler Way) had been raised ten feet, but had no fence or railing. "The walk," the paper said, "unless railed in will give an item in the shape of somebody being injured there, and then somebody will have a bill to pay . . ."

Not only were the streets at different levels than the sidewalks but there was plenty of mud in them . . . and from time to time the newspapers would run editorials stating that each wagon should carry a life raft so the driver could escape in the event the wagon sank out of sight.

This was tongue-in-cheek stuff—but not very much.

Until 1869 they didn't really have a city government to do anything about the streets. The governing body which exercised jurisdiction over the town was the County . . . and the County was much more interested in maintaining the Beach Road that led to the hinterland along the foot of Beacon Hill. They spent most of the road money on that road . . . building it up during the summer and watching it wash out during the winter.

The truth is that prior to 1876 there wasn't enough population in the town to warrant much road improvement. Oh, there were lots of grading ordinances passed. But if they called for expensive work, nothing came of them. Most people could get to most places in a rowboat.

The Spirit of '76

The year 1876 was big in Seattle history.

It was just a quarter of a century since the town of New York-Alki had faced a brave new world and found that the new world was a lot too brave for the little town.

John Pinnell's garbage dump, in cooperation with Schwabacher Brothers, was bringing the major trade on Puget Sound to Seattle's door.

J. M. Colman's railroad was the biggest industry in town.

Seattle's second incorporation—the one in 1869—seemed to be working fine. At least no new dis-incorporation had been attempted. The Northern Pacific, still groggy from the knockdown of 1873, was busy trying to get back up off the canvas and was feeling too ill itself to lend a heavy hand to Tacoma. The plan to eliminate Seattle had not succeeded. The railroad could tell this by the way our citizens were yapping at its heels and snapping at its shanks.

The Town Council made its first critical road decision: Henceforth when the word "regrade" was used it would no longer mean, "should we go around the left side of that stump in the middle of First Avenue or should we go around the right side?" It would mean, "We will go right *through* that stump!"

On June 8, 1876, the council passed an ordinance based on that new concept which created a "super highway" from James Street to Pike Street on First Avenue. The action tripled the length of that most major street in town. It would be possible to drive all the way from Jackson Street north to Pike—twelve whole blocks!

Instead of sloping the new street with the contours of the hill, they would gouge out dirt on the east side and use it to backfill a log bulkhead that would be built between the street and the beach on the west. The ravines would be filled in or bridged. Dirt would be brought in from as far east as Eighth Avenue to fill the hollows that couldn't be filled with dirt from the humps. There would be no grade steeper than 7 per cent in the whole length of the new street. The contractor who got the job would have to round up all of the horses and earthmoving equipment on Puget Sound to fill his contract.

In its wild, wild enthusiasm, the council even went so far as to propose they cut off the Yesler Corner with a diagonal street that started bending at Cherry and curved to meet First Avenue South at Yesler Way ...

Foolish fellows!

Henry Yesler allowed as how he could let his property go if the town would pay him $8,000, pay for moving the buildings he had on the property, give him relief from taxes while the work was going on . . . and not assess him for any share of the work being done.

And while Henry had his mind on the subject he pointed out that this fancy new version of First Avenue would open up the property to the north which Arthur Denny was developing into town lots. If the city was going to help Arthur, then by Jehosephat, it would regrade Yesler Way to the property on top of the hill that Henry was developing into town lots.

Cost of the total First Avenue project—exclusive of buying Henry's corner for the cutoff—was estimated at $15,000. That expenditure was really stretching things as far as the Council was concerned. The total city budget for that year was only $13,000. They figured that Henry's offer not only was no bargain . . . it would bankrupt the town.

However, they did agree that he had a reasonable point in asking for the Yesler regrade . . . especially in view of the fact he promised to kill the whole project if they didn't include it in the total regrade package. They knew that when Henry made promises like that, he was rich enough to keep them.

So before they got started on First Avenue they had to pass another ordinance calling for the regrading of Yesler Way between Fifth and Eighth Avenues.

The big spenders

Acting with an abandon that may have been equalled but never was excelled by the last of the big spenders, the council decided not only to regrade First Avenue and Yesler Way, it pulled all stops and ordered a resurvey of the entire town as far east as Eighth Avenue and north to Pike St. They even hired Eastwick, Morris & Co., the biggest engineering firm in the Pacific Northwest, to do the engineering work.

P. G. Eastwick had just completed a survey of Tacoma and we ordered him to make our survey bigger and better than Tacoma's survey. T. B. Morris, the other partner, had been chief engineer under Milnor Roberts in the construction of the Union Pacific Railroad. The "& Co." was F. H. Whitworth, son of the minister who'd played such a role in the development of coal in King County. Whitworth was just out of college.

Morris, however, failed to find time to leave his San Francisco home to participate in the survey. Eastwick was winding up loose ends in Tacoma. So young "& Co." surveyed Seattle.

However, we expected and got "big city" prices for the job.

The complete reconstruction design for First Avenue was $119.50.

The Council gulped a little at the $119.50, but after getting its feet wet in the big money, it carelessly wrote out a check for the engineering redesign of the whole city. That one was the biggest check ever written in the history of Seattle to that date for any kind of engineering work.

It came to $512.90!

Eastwick, Morris & Co. found out a few little discrepancies in the survey that Arthur Denny and his younger brother had made twenty-five years before. The Dennys had been a bit casual in their survey work and some of the buildings along First Avenue stuck out nine feet and more into the newly surveyed street. The people who found it necessary to move their structures were a little upset, but David Denny passed it off with a shrug. He informed Whitworth that every once in awhile the surveying chain had broken. They repaired it with bale rope which may have contributed to the fact that things went a little haywire. "But," Denny added, "we were intending to give good measure . . . and there was plenty of land . . ."

Anyway, Eastwick, Morris & Co. got the town on straight and everybody thought it was worth the memorable expenditure.

They learned a lot of things about their town. For instance, prior to that survey, nobody knew how high was up. There was no such thing as a "datum point" . . . and for the benefit of the uninitiate, the datum point is a thing chiselled into a piece of stone that says how high it is above (in Seattle's case) mean high spring tide. And it's from that point that the elevations of all the streets in town are measured. F. H. Whitworth, who did the taking of the measurements, had this comment on the operation: "At the time the U.S. Geodetic Department had no fixed datum on Elliott Bay for elevation, therefore it devolved upon us to fix some point as reference to datum. We took the average of the high tides for that month (June, 1875) and called the average 'average mean high tide' . . . we took the high tide observations because we could more accurately observe the high tide than the low . . ."

At that time they put the datum on a marker in the middle of Yesler Way. It was established at seven feet above the tide. Today as a result of subsequent fills the datum is on the bottom step of the Pioneer Building and is 18.79 feet above the average mean high tide.

In other words, sometime between 1876 and today, the land on Pioneer Square has been raised 11.79 feet. Right under that datum point, which is at the corner of First Avenue and James Street is the pre-1889 sidewalk 11.79 feet below today's sidewalk. Just across the street at the corner of Yesler Way and Occidental, the sidewalk of yesteryear is about 18 feet below today's sidewalk. There are other sidewalks in lower areas of the Skid Road that are as much as thirty-five feet above the pre-fire sidewalks.

The Eastwick, Morris surveys provide us with the clearest understanding of how the city's underground came into existence because theirs was the first authentic survey of the topography. It is to be remembered, however, that for a quarter of a century Dutch Ned had been dumping the waste products of Yesler's mill in the area. For instance, we know from early descriptions about that stream at First Avenue South and Washington Street. Yet the Eastwick, Morris survey shows that spot had an elevation of seven feet in 1876. Today's elevation in the same place is nearly seventeen feet.

The elevations prior to 1876 bear no resemblance to those of today. For example, Main Street just a block south of Washington Street, had a zero elevation in 1876 compared to just over sixteen feet today . . . while a block further south on First and Jackson shows an elevation of fifteen feet in 1876. Jackson Street went to minus seven feet at Second Avenue South and minus eight feet at Third Avenue South as compared to elevations of nineteen and twenty-one feet today.

Yesler Way, on the other hand, shows a reverse grading operation. It rose thirty-two feet between Occidental and Second Avenue South— from eight at Occidental to forty at Second Avenue South while the difference in the same area today is only twelve feet—indicating that the east part of Yesler was graded down and the west filled, in this location.

The city's underground area clearly reflects the differences in elevations between 1876 and today. Today's streets are more or less uniform. They probably don't vary more than four feet at the most in the whole area. On the other hand sidewalks in the underground area will vary from ten feet below today's surface directly above them to a depth of thirty feet.

What does all this have to do with the creation of today's underground?

Seattle's underground may seem like a musty dusty place today, but I suggest that the information of the following pages will explain why it is far from that in the historically filtered light in which I view it.

Citizen Yesler saddles and rides

By the start of 1877, the citizens of Seattle stood at First Avenue and Yesler Way and saw their broad highway magnificently mounting the hill clear to Pike Street. Arthur Denny viewed it with particular pride. By way of his minor share of the $15,000 assessment that would be levied, his excellent view real estate was wide open for public settlement at little cost to himself.

People would pay money to populate his donation claim with their little gray homes in the west. He had waited twenty-five long years for this moment. As a newly elected member of the Town Council, he knew that his investment of a few hundred dollars in the assessment that would be levied would bring great return in the real estate sold.

The residents would be less than twenty minutes from the central business district.

Henry Yesler viewed the project with equal admiration. The west side of First Avenue just north of the mill had been filled to a depth that would make it possible for him to sell property at the ever-increasing rate that it was commanding . . . or build skyscrapers on it and be repaid handsomely in rentals. The improvement was worth about $500,000 to him.

The other property-owners along First Avenue must have looked at the new street through rose-colored dollar signs.

Dutch Ned probably thought, "I wish I'd done that!"

When the assessment rolls were published a year later they revealed the entire project had cost $15,599.11. A dozen or two other property owners shared in $10,000 of that money . . . Henry's assessment was $5,000 or one third of the total cost of the project.

Now, Henry was not the kind of a fellow who would measure the $5,000 assessment against the $500,000 potential improvement it made in his property. Unlike his habit of looking through the small end of the telescope when he was selling something, he looked at the assessment charged to the rest of the Sons through the large end. If the city had been a little luckier he might have had a fatal apoplectic stroke.

Instead, he turned to his personal attorney, J. R. Lewis, who recently had retired from the Territorial Supreme Court bench, and demanded some kind of legal hocus pocus that would enable him to duck the whole bill. Lewis tried to reason with Henry, pointing out that money wasn't everything. But Henry thought it was, so Lewis looked around in his law books and they went to court.

Court was held on the second floor of Yesler's Pavilion on the southeast corner of First and Cherry. The Pavilion was perched precariously because the regrade had lowered the street at that particular junction some ten feet, and the upper floors of the building were supported by temporary posts. Henry planned to use the level to his advantage by excavating under his building and adding a new street-level floor. The Court could look out the window and see the brand new regrade work that had been done, including the fill that had added depth to Yesler's property on the west side of First Avenue.

As his opening remarks, Lewis said, "There is no evidence whatever that said Front Street (First Avenue) has ever been graded in pursuance of any duly-passed ordinance—*or graded at all!*" (Ed. note: Italics and exclamation point mine.)

While a combination of indignation and consternation choked up the city attorneys, Lewis then pointed out the city had acted illegally in assessing the individual instead of the property—that individuals who had hills or hollows in front of their property were charged more than those who happened to be level with the new grade . . . that assessments ran from $5 to $5,000 when assessments should have been equal and, finally, that the Legislature under the Organic Act that created the Territory in the first place was not authorized to pass a law permitting the incorporation of a city.

Therefore, Seattle did not exist.

If Seattle did not exist, there couldn't be a City Council . . . or assessments, taxes, licenses, or policemen, firemen and all of those other items that occupy the attention of a City Council.

The lower court upheld Henry and threw out the assessment.

That was the first time Henry Yesler brought his city to the brink of bankruptcy.

City? what city?

With the city's legality under question, its authority to pursue public works and to levy assessments was pretty cloudy and its government found its hands pretty well tied when it came to financial matters.

The clearest indication of the way the bets were going was shown by the discounts the banks made on city warrants or checks. They were discounted sixty-five per cent which meant that a policeman's paycheck was only worth thirty-five cents on the dollar.

The city fathers immediately appealed the decision to the Supreme Court . . . a move that gave them a year to solve their dilemma. The immediate solution involved establishing a system of licenses and fines for dispensing liquor, gambling, and sex. The distributors of such specialty items might have disputed the legality of the licenses and fines on the ground that the city didn't exist. But the gun of the policeman who collected the money did exist. And so did the public opinion which backed it up.

They paid.

So, thanks to Henry, a delightful new system of acquiring funds to run the city was developed—the wages of sin.

Later on the people specializing in the above commodities realized that if they were paying the piper then they could call the tune. They called a tune entitled "Wide Open Town." This was to cause some difficult problems in the next quarter of a century because the businessmen and owners of real estate in town found they had no taxes to pay under this system. It became a pleasant habit which they were loath to break when the time came.

The fathers then went to Washington D.C., where the representatives had some conversations with some congressmen who recognized that a problem did indeed exist. So Congress passed a special law retroactive to 1869 giving the Legislature the authority to grant Seattle its incorporation.

This put Seattle back in business on all fronts, but it left Henry's case still pending.

The Supreme Court held that the city was not in existence at the time Henry won his case in the lower court. Therefore he did not have to pay his assessment. If the others also had gone to court, they would not have had to pay theirs. The retroactive act of Congress did not apply to Henry. But it did apply to the others.

Henry never did pay the $5,000.

Arthur Denny never spoke to Henry again as long as he lived . . . which turned out to be sixteen more years.

And from Henry's peculiar outlook on life, Arthur would have had to do some tall talking to come up with a conversation worth $5,000.

A toast to the whore of the central core

The people of Seattle who presently are struggling for the preservation of the central core of the city think they've got something new, but the Supreme Court Decision on Yesler's assessment handed the city the same problem nearly 100 years ago. The solution to the problem then might well come up for consideration today.

Henry of course viewed the shambles of the city's finances with the same aloof detachment of a cat sitting on a drainboard viewing the wreckage of the family's best crockery which it had just knocked to the floor.

For instance, Henry was not about to assume any responsibility for the death of ten-year-old Joseph Bufonchio who drowned in a chuckhole at Third Avenue South and Jackson Street. For that matter, neither did anyone else and in his hilarious book, *Totem Tales of Old Seattle,* Gordon Newell makes the point:

> The reporter who covered the incident seemed to consider accidental drownings in Seattle's city streets as more or less routine tragedies although he did comment on the unusually large crowd which gathered to watch policemen and a few volunteers probe in the mud for the boy's body. He estimated the crowd at two thousand, give or take a dozen or so and everyone was vastly entertained when the boy's father arrived on the scene, and, in his grief and anxiety, fell into the mudhole that had killed his son.

> "Several other laughable incidents happened," the reporter added whimsically. "A local pugilist named 'Chicago Ed' hooked a snag which he thought was the body, and in his struggle to lift it from the murky depths, he, too, fell in the water to the further delight of the crowd."

Henry did get upset, however, when the jog on Mill Street (Yesler Way) in front of the Yesler-Leary building got so choked with mud one winter that traffic came to a complete standstill. This jog—the one they called "the throat"—was the busiest thirty feet of street in the entire city.

At Henry's insistence, an emergency session of the City Council was called. There was no money in the till and in their desperation, that august body hit upon a unique solution that pleased all concerned.

Like all organized groups, the professional and business women of the community had felt for some time that the efforts of their group on behalf of the city's welfare lacked the public approbation that they deserved. They were lobbying before the City Council for a position of greater prestige at the same time that the problem of repairing this important segment of the street system came up for deliberation.

The ladies pointed out that they made a major contribution to the town coffers in the $10-per-month fines that were voluntarily collected and turned over to the City Treasurer. They diffidently mentioned that several thousand dollars a year accrued to the city coffers through their efforts.

One of the Councilmen had an electrifying thought that has remained unmatched to this day. "On a short term basis," he wondered, "would the ladies make an additional effort—in keeping with the Seattle Spirit?"

Indeed they would!

So the fines on the ladies were increased 50 per cent, an increase to be in effect until the city's sore throat could be cured with planking. Today, it probably would be necessary to conduct an unusual enterprise like this on sort of an under-the-table basis. But not then. They handled it like a United Good Neighbor Campaign. The bid for the planking job came to $2,150. The Council made an announcement that appeared on the front pages of the newspapers stating the problem, the financial goal and the method of achieving it.

Each day the amount of money set aside in the City Treasury for this project was announced in the papers as an enthusiastic citizenry cheered from the sidelines and loggers from all over Puget Sound came to town to do their part.

The money for the planking project was raised in three days. The fines were dropped back to normal, and the work went ahead.

There is no way of gauging the herculean effort that went into this fund raising campaign nor the number of man-hours involved. But when I build my historical park in the Skid Road, there'll be a monument to these enterprising women who gave so unstintingly of their time to meet a major crisis in Seattle's history.

Flight to suburbia

The flight to suburbia is considered one of the great tragedies of our time and yet it's just another case of history repeating itself, because in the 1880's the downtown core suffered from the same ailment that it does today.

And in my book this is another one that has to be chalked up to good old Henry . . . well, maybe part of it should be chalked up to Henry.

Some of the more notable suburbs which were born in the 1880's include Ballard . . . the Town of Yesler, better known today as Union Bay Village . . . West Seattle, Woodland Park—the present site of our Zoo—Ravenna . . . Green Lake . . . Kirkland . . . East Seattle on Mercer Island . . . Wallingford . . . Georgetown. An enterprising Son of the Profits by the name of T. I. McKenney sold out a complete plat on Queen Anne Hill in 1883, but the courts found in 1905 the land hadn't belonged to him so the buyers either had to buy it all over again from somebody else or abandon their land.

Altogether there were eighty-three major subdivisions around the perimeter of the city. In the first five years, there was one for every two hundred people that showed up—and that's a lot of subdivisions for that many people. Seattle was a boom town, to be sure, and the quick money was to be made in real estate. But they shied away from the central core, thanks to the Supreme Court decision in the Yesler case.

True, the condition causing the original court decision was corrected by Congress when the latter passed the law making the city an entity. But this didn't change the attitude of the course on the city's power to levy assessments. As Judge Hanford, our legally-oriented historian, put it: "For a long time, property owners desirous of having streets improved for practical use, voluntarily paid whatever assessments were levied, but in contested cases, the courts were able to find fatal objections to the different modes of making local assessments."

Here's an illustration of what Hanford was talking about. If the city wanted to replace a boardwalk on First Avenue and it had the money in the general fund to do so, there was no problem. If all of the property owners along the way agreed to pay an assesssment, it had no problems. But if one stinker took the city to court, the courts invariably found against the city on the ground it did not have the authority to levy that assessment.

On the other hand, when David Denny subdivided his farm out near Lake Union, his best bet for selling lots lay in putting in streets, water mains and sewers. This was no problem to Denny because he just added these costs to the price of the lots and the people who bought the lots cheerfully paid. The problem never got to court.

So from January 26, 1880, when the Supreme Court handed down its decision on the Yesler case until the fire of 1889 solved the whole thing for everybody, the central core was a pretty crummy place indeed. The only source of revenue for doing anything about the downtown streets came from fines and licenses, which in turn came from the professional and business women, the gamblers and the saloons.

Yet, here property values went as high as $1,250 per foot. Everything that made the city tick was concentrated in half a dozen blocks on First Avenue and First Avenue South . . . every bank, every retail store, every newspaper, every major pier, every wholesale house, every sawmill, every department store, every hotel, every restaurant, every bawdy house, every saloon and major office building. All were jammed together in one hodge-podge mess.

A matter of gravity

Buried in the files of the City Engineer's office today is a little-known and even less publicized drawing which shows the real reason why Seattle's streets in the Skid Road were raised after the fire. There were a lot of towns around the country that got themselves burned to the ground in those days.

But they did what any normal town would do under the same set of circumstances. They rebuilt right where they were. Oh, yes, maybe they added a few frills here and there to make the costs of rebuilding more palatable to the folks, but the massive effort we went to of rebuilding one to three flights up . . .

There had to be a reason.

The reason was not one of the major pieces of publicity put out by the Chamber of Commerce . . .

But about the drawing in the City Engineer's Office. Well, it shows a sewer sloping diagonally past the front window of one of the major saloons that existed in the lower end of town before the fire. Other mute testimony to the need for raising the streets lies in the toilet facilities that exist in Seattle's underground today.

The blunt truth is that before the fire, you had to climb a ladder to use the plumbing facilities in the heart of Seattle's main business district.

This was a little detail that Arthur Denny & Co. overlooked when they planned their splendid city in this location. They didn't allow for the cliffs . . . and they didn't allow for the bottom part of town.

Prior to 1882, when there weren't many folks around, it didn't matter very much, but as the population increased, the City Health Department started hollering about sanitary conditions. In 1882, Dr. Edward Loomis Smith, the health officer, reported that our sewers were worthless, when it came to serving a town of 4,000 people. The situation deteriorated rapidly in a town where the population increased ten times in the next seven years.

Smith reported that our sewers flushed in reverse twice a day when the tide came in. Being as most of the city's sewers zeroed in on the so-called "pocket" of town, the folks doing business downtown needed no printed reminder of the problem. They just somehow seemed to sense it—and they didn't need a sixth sense to do it.

Everybody was ready for a nice fire.

Having wonderful fire. Wish you were here!

On June 6, 1889, Seattle had what has been known in our historical cultural circles ever since as "The Fire."

It didn't compare to the London Fire . . . or the Chicago Fire . . . or the San Francisco Fire or any of the other really *big* fires in history. And I must confess that having been brought up on the Seattle Fire I was somewhat astonished to find it didn't even make the World Almanac for 1889. For that matter the Almanac people didn't think there was a fire anywhere in the world worthy of being listed for that year and I think we ought to get together a committee to protest . . .

Oh, well, it was the biggest fire we ever had. It was the biggest fire any city in the Pacific Northwest ever had. And the timing was right. No fire in the Pacific Northwest ever had such good timing . . . and in a fire, timing is everything. Take the Chicago fire for an example. There were only 250 people killed but with Mrs. O'Leary's cow and all there was drama to it, and between that and a lull in world news, it got a big play.

Then consider the Peshtigo, Wisconsin fire. Fifteen hundred people died. It killed off two or three times as many people as any other fire we ever had in the United States—but it didn't even rate one word on the wire services. Why? Poor timing. It took place on October 9, 1871—the day after the Chicago fire and the Chicago fire was hogging all the newspaper space.

If Tacoma had had a fire, they'd probably have goofed up the timing like Peshtigo did.

Ellensburg, Vancouver and Spokane had fires in 1889, but by the time they got around to their fires we'd skimmed the cream off the top of the publicity. Vancouver's was a couple of weeks after ours—on June 22. And Spokane's didn't come off until August 4. Spokane really should have gotten a better play on theirs than they did. The reason their fire got out of hand was that the only guy who knew how to run their brand new water system was away on a picnic.

And our fire . . . it could have been on June 1, instead of June 6, and we'd have been no place. They drowned 2,200 people in the Johnstown Flood just the day before. Or we could have had ours in 1887 the day after a flood knocked off 900,000 people in China.

As it was, ours was just right.

It was big news all over the world. It brought in about $120,000 in relief money and credit because we were a brave little frontier town that had been wiped out and was manfully trying to rebuild itself. We softened a lot of hearts by our stand on Johnstown, too. We had made a pledge for the relief of the flood victims back there . . . and we stuck to our pledge even though we, ourselves, had been burned out.

"What," a reasonable person might well ask, "was so hot about your fire?"

For one thing it didn't kill anybody off, which would have marred the pleasure of the occasion. For another thing it did about $15,000,000 worth of damage, which makes it at least presentable in the company of other fires. If we had a $15,000,000 fire even today it would make some headlines around and about. I could throw in the fact that an estimated 1,000,000 rats were killed, which was an indication that we were a growing city. They didn't even have rats on the West Coast until 1851, just 28 years before, so even our rats made news.

And we have other reasons for rejoicing. For a decade we had been trying to pass up Tacoma on the population front . . . and in the six months following the fire, our population went from about 23,000 to about 43,000. Tacoma, which had been leading us by 10,000 citizens before the fire, wound up 6,000 behind us when Uncle Sam counted noses during the census the next year.

There might have been detractors who would point out that our increased population was made up of scalawags . . . burglars . . . pickpockets . . . pimps . . . prostitutes . . . confidence men and like that. But I, in turn, would point out that our city had to have the people you could issue liquor licenses to or fine in police court in order to meet our increased expenses.

I'll admit there were one or two isolated incidents where the persons involved were not entirely pleasured. There was the fellow who had paid $1,000 to buy a store earlier the same day and it promptly burned to the ground. Then there were the three looters who stole a barrel of whiskey and towed it to Alki Point where they sampled the contents. One of the trio fell in head first and was almost dead drunk when somebody pulled him out. A lady looter stole a barrel of flour and didn't discover it was plaster of paris until *after* she'd baked a batch of bread with it.

Also the misery of another man was understandable. The restaurant he owned a block away from First and Madison burned in the first hour. He knew there was a fortune to be made after the fire by anybody in the restaurant business so he ran four blocks down the street and bought a brand new restaurant from the owner because the latter feared he was going to be burned out!

A couple of hours later the new owner learned that the old owner of the restaurant had been right.

But outside of a few incidents like this, it was a dandy fire.

Joy to the world!

The next day Seattle woke up, shook itself, found there were no broken bones and whooped enthusiastically into the most important three weeks in its history. It was a little warm underfoot, but that pile of junk that had been known as the city center the day before was gone.

Sixty-six blocks of the town's prime business district lay in smouldering ruins.

Every pier on the waterfront from University Street south to Lane Street twelve blocks away had been burned out. Only the Oregon Improvement Company dock remained intact, and it was isolated by burned out plank on piling from the nearest solid ground three blocks away. The fire had wiped out everything west of Second Avenue, north of Yesler Way and as far as Fourth Avenue on the south side of Yesler Way.

There were a few snaggle-toothed remnants of masonry buildings and some low ridges created by the engineering genius of Dutch Ned and the philanthropy of people like John Pinnell, but other than that the landscape bore a strong resemblance to the sight that had greeted Arthur Denny thirty-eight years earlier.

But it was a gorgeous, sunshiny day. As the smoke began to clear, the folks could even see Mt. Rainier from down in "the pocket". The sleazy wooden buildings in the lower end of town were gone. The rats and fleas had been incinerated. And all those buildings which had prevented widening or raising the downtown streets were heaps of rubble.

Like Denny, they thought, what a wonderful place for a city!

And this time, they meant City.

On June 7, 1889—the day after the fire—the most remarkable meeting ever held in Seattle took place at eleven o'clock in the morning in the Armory on Union Street between Third and Fourth Avenues. There were about six hundred people there: a lot of average citizens, all of the Sons of the Profits, and the Mayor and Town Council, who were on hand to hold their fingers up and see which way the political winds were blowing. It was prophetic that this was the first major meeting in the city's history that had not been held in the *Yesler* Cookhouse, the *Yesler* Hall or the *Yesler* Pavilion. But that isn't what made it unique.

There was an electric feeling of optimism in the air—like the one that seizes the crowd at a football game when it senses that the home team is going to win the championship. It was one of the few times in the city's history—perhaps the only time—when everybody was pulling together.

Nobody was mad at anybody else.

The jubilant crowd vociferously rejected the base suggestion that we renege on the $585 that had been collected by the Board of Trade for the relief of the Johnstown Flood victims. "To Johnstown," the crowd howled. "Let it go to Johnstown!"

By a unanimous vote, the crowd resolved that it would "prohibit forever" the erection of any wooden buildings in the burned district but that permits would be granted for the erection of tents for the temporary transaction of business. Angus MacIntosh and Jacob Furth pledged that their banks would be of all assistance possible and would not attempt to make any profit at all from the fire. Watson C. Squire, former Territorial Governor, echoed the sentiments of the businessmen by announcing he was only waiting for the bricks of his building to cool before he started building again, and somebody topped that by announcing he had a hose cooling his bricks so he could get started that much sooner. It was announced that Tacoma had pledged $10,000 for Seattle's reconstruction. San Francisco had pledged an equal amount and telegrams from all over the country were coming in with pledges. A relief committee was formed for dispensing these goodies and there was every evidence the city would reach the highest pinnacle of employment in its history.

There was even a totally new concept introduced in the thinking of the Seattle folks. Perhaps it had arrived with those wayout creatures which the folks called "archytecks," who had been gradually drifting into town. Perhaps the city was maturing. Whatever the cause, beauty became a factor in the city's plans for the first time. It was pointed out that buildings could do more than keep out the rain.

And, of all things, the women wanted trees planted in the streets. Trees?

Good God! Trees were for cutting down . . . and then up . . . and then sold.

The ladies' idea was slow in materializing. It was to take three years, but the women were persistent, and before they were through, 3,000 trees were planted in the city's downtown streets. They were later to be removed in the name of progress, and the idea was not to be revived until sixty-two years later when we were getting ready for a World's Fair in Seattle.

All of this was great, but there were some basics to be considered. It was obvious that Seattle would be a bigger city than the one anticipated when Arthur Denny and Doc Maynard originally laid out the streets. Most of the main downtown streets, especially First Avenue, had to be widened. The streets in the lower end of town had to be raised so sewers could be given steeper outfalls and sewage would get a one way ticket to the bay.

This was fine in theory, but there were practical details like the cooperation of the property owners to be considered before the new idea became an actuality. Of these, Henry Yesler was the biggest and most important. Only with his cooperation could the "throat" of the city be cut and that maddening jog at the Yesler Corner eliminated.

It was with these things in mind that the crowd fell silent when J. R. Lewis arose to speak. He not only was a member of the Establishment, he was Henry Yesler's personal attorney. His remarks got the biggest play of all the front page stories the next day.

"Now," Lewis said, "let the Council get a little more backbone. It has it if it will use it. Let it make a street eighty-four feet wide from Stetson & Post's Mill all the way to Belltown."

A mighty roar greeted this announcement.

The translation of that remark reads: "Let the City Council have the guts to cut Yesler Corner"—and this from Yesler's own attorney.

It read even more than that. In the back of everybody's mind was the image of Henry Yesler as the great obstructionist. Henry could throw more monkey wrenches than a mad mechanic, but in this most critical moment in the city's history he was apparently going to go along.

It was the high point of the meeting. Immediately a planning committee of leading citizens was named to put all of the recommended changes on paper so the Council could enact the ordinances necessary to create the most beautiful . . . the most modern . . . the cleanest . . . the best city in the world.

Seattle would rise again, like the Phoenix out of the ashes.

The Seattle Spirit rides again

Three days later, the real Seattle Spirit was back in the saddle again. The Citizen's Planning Committee appeared before an evening meeting of the City Council to make its recommendations. It was perhaps symbolic that the lighting system had failed and the county courthouse in which the Council met was lit by only four candles.

The noble six hundred citizens were back, too—or most of them— but not to cheer the Council on. They were there to object. On motion of somebody in the crowd, all of the clauses and all of the sub clauses were read seriatum. And every single recommendation made by the planning committee was objected to by the property owners involved.

Hours later, when the Council adjourned, everything that had been approved unanimously at the first meeting was rejected individually at the second meeting.

The *P.-I.* said: "Several of the property owners appear willing to have the property of others condemned for the public good, but object to any interference with their metes and bounds. Mr. J. M. Colman expresses it aptly when he says, 'I am willing to cut as much off Mr. Yesler's property as he is willing to cut off of mine."

Normalcy had returned to Seattle.

No action was taken by the Council. Yesler's reaction to the idea of cutting his corner had not yet been made public and until the Council knew where it was on that front there was no point in doing anything.

On June 11, the *P.-I.* ran an editorial supporting the proposed re-plat of the city presented by the Citizens' Committee, stating that the problem of the streets long had been recognized . . . that Chicago and Boston both had taken advantage of similar fires to improve their street layouts. "Opposition to the re-plat has and can have no other basis than selfish interests", the paper said. "We believe that the sentiment of the city is overwhelmingly favorable to the proposed improvements and we believe the council will have the integrity to be guided by this sentiment . . ."

On June 21, a hot summer evening, the Clerk of the Council droned through four hours of detailed street changes involving about thirty-three blocks of the city from Jackson Street to Union Street and from the waterfront to Eighth Avenue.

Most of the Councilmen went to sleep.

But they woke up long enough to pass the ordinance, which included widening all of the north-south streets from sixty-six to either eighty-four or ninety feet. And they put some teeth in the part of the ordinance involving the burned area. They made a provision that anyone who left so much as a fence post at the original width would be fined three hundred dollars a day for every day it remained there after thirty days. This section was of critical importance because nine feet was taken from each side of the major burned area streets. The penalty insured a setback of all construction. However, the city had attempted to raise the streets many times in the past and had not succeeded. There was no guarantee the city could get the streets raised this time. So construction was begun at the lower level . . . which is why the first floors of many buildings in the area are underground—but set back the nine feet. There was no penalty for initiating construction at the original and lower level of the streets.

They also included in the ordinance a section which stated that a diagonal street would be cut across the Yesler Corner. If that corner wasn't cut, the streets couldn't be raised, and new sewers could not be installed in the lower end of town. The corner couldn't be left as an island untouched in the rest of the replatting of the city.

The Mayor didn't sign that ordinance. He was waiting to see what Henry's reaction would be.

The *P.-I.*, however, quickly inserted a rumor story that Henry Yesler was going to go along with the gag. Accompanying it was the following editorial:

> Those who in the past years have had knowledge of the liberality of Mr. Henry L. Yesler will not be surprised to hear that he now proposes to make the city a free gift of a considerable part of the "Yesler Corner," concerning which there recently has been so much talk. Just what proportion of this corner Mr. Yesler proposes to dedicate to the public use we are not authorized to say, but it may be safely assumed that whatever he does he will do handsomely and generously. Any other policy would be out of keeping with the spirit of his gift.

> It would be an extremely gracious act for Mr. Yesler to give way on the whole proposition, subordinating his own personal interests to that of the city by whose development his great fortune has been made.

Christmas comes but once a year . . . and not in June

On June 24, in a choleric, stamping rage, a seventy-nine-year old Henry with a shaking beard stood in the middle of the ruins of his city and tore up a will he said had bequeathed a million dollars to Seattle.

He made the announcement that should the city so much as touch one foot of his property he would take the city to court and drive it into bankruptcy. He said, "I could not be paid enough for the property to make up for the income for the buildings I had planned to erect there."

He said that had the council not taken its action, he had planned to encircle the Yesler Corner square with huge, modern structures. As it was, he would leave the buildings on his property around the square in ruins and would erect a ten foot board fence which would in effect enclose the heart of the city and ruin it. His last kindly thought was:

> I will build corrugated buildings on the property extending down Yesler Way on both sides to my wharf to bring in enough income to pay the interest on what I owe and I will live on the income from the other property that I own. The city will have the biggest lawsuit it has ever seen ..."

The newspapers sent reporters out to interview the average man on the street and found that he was overwhelmingly in favor of cutting the Yesler Corner.

In a Page 1 story headed "That Yesler Corner," the *Daily Times* quoted an "old timer" as saying: "Old timer recalls how Yesler acquired the land through a gift, and at one time intended to relinquish the corner so that Front (First Ave.) and Commercial Streets could join. The corner cost the owner not a cent." On the second page was a story headlined " 'Boss' Yesler Stands in Way of Queen City's Beautification and Progress." An earlier story stated that "Nineteen out of twenty property owners are behind the Council on the replat action. A hundred prominent citizens say that the city's future means more than the few individuals' complaints ..."

Yesler offered to cut off nine feet instead of the eighty four feet that was being sought . . . giving the people the notion that he was opposed to condemnation. And on June 25, the *P.-I.* said:

> Mr. Yesler says this is the best he will do. By it he virtually makes a threat to the city, and says: "Accept this or be involved in litigation with me as long as I live, and see the Yesler-Leary, 'Pioneer' and Kellogg Drugstore corners stand marked only by shapeless ruins and surrounded by high board fences." He says he is in a condition to do all this and those who know him best say he will not hesitate or fail to carry his threat into execution. That is the way the matter now stands.

The Establishment was on a real interesting spot on this one. They were baking a cake called "money." They had arranged for more money at a lower interest from both San Francisco and eastern capitalists than the city had ever seen before. Already the town was booming. Real estate was commanding a higher price than ever before. Two weeks after the fire, 138 new buildings already were under construction, but the Yesler fight would jeopardize chances to get money. The big three at that time, Jacob Furth, Bailey Gatzert and Angus MacIntosh, all made public statements urging acceptance of the so-called Yesler Compromise.

MacIntosh summed it up best. He said:

> I am firmly convinced that entering into litigation with Mr. Yesler will have a serious effect upon securing capital. Heretofore one of the greatest points in our prestige has been the harmony of our citizens on matters of public moment. Litigation would destroy this confidence. I have known Mr. Yesler for seventeen years and I am sure he would contest this point with the city as long as he lives. While I don't believe the city should take into consideration the wishes of any one individual, I am convinced that litigation with Mr. Yesler would seriously impair the interests of the city and would retard its rebuilding.

Furth said, "San Francisco capital which was freely offered us a few days ago is now holding off for this reason . . ."

But Yesler's attitude was too much for Burke. He jumped into the fray against the rest of the members of the Establishment. Referring to Yesler's compromise as a palpable absurdity, he pointed out that only a tiny portion would be pared out of the Yesler property . . . and that the rate of damage asked by Henry, if paid, "would establish a measurement which would bankrupt the city if it were applied to all of the others whose property would be taken away from them for the proposed replatting . . . There is no reason shown and none can be shown why one rule of damages should be applied for the benefit of one man and a different rule for all the rest."

The public was confused. The men they normally looked to for leadership were split wide open. And if you think the public was confused, the members of the City Council who knew who was who in the Establishment were really confused. It was evident that the general public was in favor of cutting the corner. But it wasn't that organized. Yesler, on the other hand was very much organized. He had tentacles into most of the pocket books of the town. He could hurt them. Burke could hurt them, too.

The Council met on the afternoon of June 26th as a Committee of the Whole and agreed to cut the Yesler Corner. That night the matter came up before the regular meeting of the Council. The pressure they were under is indicated by the fact that one of the Councilmen had a heart attack and nearly died while they were waiting for the meeting to open . . . reducing the number of City Councilmen to seven. There had to be seven votes in favor of cutting the Corner. That meant the vote had to be unanimous.

In an atmosphere of breathless suspense six of the Councilmen voted in favor of cutting the Yesler Corner.

And then Councilman Burns voted no.

He'd been reached by the Yesler people after the meeting of the Committee of the Whole. The Yesler Corner was left standing and everybody went home. The decision was reached. That was the end of it . . .

Except for the public reaction.

The masses . . . blew their collective cork. It took just three days of public reaction for the councilmen to realize that with the Yesler Corner left standing their political future had just become their past. On June 30, 1889 there was a front page story in the *P.-I.* that started out in the following manner:

> In obedience to the almost unanimous wish of the people of Seattle, and to the dictates of their best judgment of its members, the city council last night enacted an ordinance cutting off the Yesler corner in accordance with the plan originally proposed by the citizen's committee. There was no dickering over compromises, no consideration of private and personal as opposed to public interests, and the result was the "straight cut" by which the west line of Commercial street will be extended through to Front Street, striking the latter at a point a few feet south of the intersection with Cherry . . .

And what did Henry do?

Well, he was a man of his word. He did just exactly what he said he'd do. When the land was condemned, he took the city to court. He demanded damages for the 13,000 square feet of land the city had taken away from him to provide the bend in the road and the new public square. Both of them are there today and form what we call Pioneer Square. That was the piece of property Henry had offered to sell the city in 1876 for $8,000.

And when Henry took the city to court, he really "took" it.

He got $156,000 for that 13,000 square feet, or $12.00 a square foot.

But the replat of the city called for removing nine feet from each side of the thirty three blocks between Jackson and Union Streets. In order to keep peace with the San Francisco bankers and rebuild the city, every other property owner in blocks which were widened had to take proportionately less money to keep the total down. These people had 250,000 square feet. The total amount they received was $144,000.

Which averaged out at 66¢ a square foot.

Hell bent for erection

It took time, of course, for that lawsuit to be processed through the

Drawing of reconstruction done for WEST SHORE MAGAZINE *a few days after the fire.*

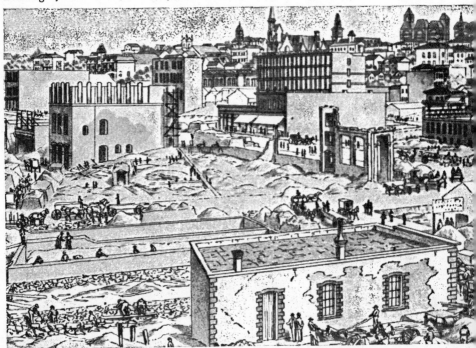

courts. But, happily for the town, neither Henry nor the lawyers were running things immediately after the fire. If people had waited for the due processes of law, we wouldn't be in the process of restoring those beautiful old buildings in the area today . . . we'd just be starting to build them.

So we did it by Guess and by God . . . and we did it fast.

Word was around that the Great Northern was coming in to release us from the bondage of the Northern Pacific. Money was coming in from all over the country. People were arriving in droves—enough to almost double the population in six months. The business that was being done in tents was intense. And the businessmen weren't about to wait until the regrading was finished to begin their construction.

Building had started so soon after the fire that the building areas had to be kept flooded so the workmen wouldn't burn their feet. And if Henry Yesler or anybody else had gotten in the way, somebody would have hit him with a brick. As it was, the City Engineer

Arched building in foreground still stands at First Ave. South and South Washington St.

and the private builders came to blows a number of times. The City Council was repeatedly called upon to determine whether the City Engineer could shove debris from the streets on private property so he could get the streets raised or whether the private builders could shove their debris on public property so the buildings could be constructed first.

If the whole area were to be laid bare today, it would look like a big waffle, with the streets forming the ridges and the land in between them the depressions. The streets were raised from curb to curb, using as fill dirt from the surrounding hills and any kind of debris the town fathers could lay their hands on.

We got a lovely example of what's under there in the 1950's when a flood from a broken watermain undermined the center of First Avenue and an old rowboat floated out.

Later on, some of the fill material proved to be quite unstable. After automobiles arrived on the scene and a gas station was established at Yesler Way and Western Avenue, a tank truck driver stuck the nozzle of his hose in the aperture at street level and started filling a buried gas tank with gasoline. After he had put eight hundred gallons in what was supposed to be a four hundred gallon tank, it occurred to him something might be wrong. Investigation showed the tank had departed with an outgoing tide.

The raised streets were neatly separated from the hollows by bulkheads built to the desired new grades at each curb. These walls were built either of quarry stone brought in by the Northern Pacific from nearby Wilkeson or of logs brought in by the Seattle, Lake Shore & Eastern.

This left the original sidewalks anywhere from ten to thirty-two feet below the new level of the street. Since most of the businessmen were not inclined to wait until the streets were regraded to get out of their tents and into permanent buildings, a lot of the buildings were constructed at the old street grade. (Their judgment was quite correct; the city turned out to be pretty slow at completing many of the streets—in some cases, not until forty years later.)

It didn't take too long for them to figure out that having their sidewalks and store fronts way down there was not at all satisfactory. For one thing, teamsters found the edge of the street a mental hazard and every now and again a team load of supplies would be backed over the edge of the street and end up in somebody's show window.

They solved the problem in a number of ways. Wooden sidewalks were constructed from the level of the curb to the second floor—in some cases third floor—of the buildings. Many of the building owners moved their first floor operations up to the level of the street, leaving the original first floor as a basement. Others who weren't very far below the surface of the street built stairs going down right in their buildings. There were some who had a little pull with the city and got steps going down through the sidewalks. In some of the niftier places, like the Pioneer Building, they had fancy iron steps leading down into a sky-lighted well.

All of these remedies were tried . . . and the vestiges of all of them may be found in Seattle's underground today.

The Phoenix

Early in the game, the *P.I.* waxed editorially rhapsodical with the notion that the fire not only destroyed the Seattle that was, but "At the same time, it prepared the way for the greater and more beautiful Seattle that is to be . . ."

Historian Prosch pointed out that "within two years of the fire Seattle's business quarter was finer, more convenient, more modern and better than that of any other place with like population in the world."

In that period some 3,500 buildings were constructed—most of them in the burned area. And most of them were designed by architects. E. H. Fisher, an Englishman who had designed most of the buildings in Victoria, B.C. and who was considered to be the dean of architects in the Pacific Northwest, just happened to be a Seattle resident at the time the town burned. The construction that took place downtown was heavily influenced by his style.

During the reconstruction, a reporter sent here by a New York newspaper was interviewing the folks and encountered Fisher. "And which building are you designing, sir?" he asked. With no little astonishment he noted for the benefit of his readers that Fisher was

designing and supervising the construction of not one but fifty-four
downtown buildings.

It was the Fisher influence that gave homogeneity to the buildings
in the immediate vicinity of Pioneer Square and some still stand
there in testimony to the artistry and craftsmanship of stone, brick
and carpentry that have gone out of existence as a result of what we
laughingly refer to as progress.

Pioneer Square was made into a park by the city and became the
centerpiece for all civic celebrations. The ladies got their trees
planted and anybody who was anybody at all had his offices in the
immediate vicinity of the Square. Great hotels, restaurants and retail
stores joined them. The Pioneer Square area became the ne plus
ultra retail, business and commercial center of the Pacific Northwest.

By 1897, the dream of half a century had been fulfilled. The sewers
were behaving the way any properly raised sewers should behave.
Pioneer Square was the hub of electrified transportation from all
parts of the city. Streets and sidewalks were immaculate. Window
boxes of flowers abounded. Well-dressed men and women strolled
about and acknowledged one another with polite nods.

The birthplace of the city finally had come into its own . . .

We were as slick as Fifth Avenue in New York.

IX

Wry and Water

Sometimes Seattle has survived in spite of and not because of her Sons of the Profits. Most of the time the city has rocked along like a mother lode which was here to be mined if the boys didn't have some place else to make a buck. But once in a while in their ambivalent relationship, she's found them with their hands in the cookie jar and given them a good swipe that has sent them off yowling.

This happened not once but twice during her first fifty years—in connection with her water supply. The Sons couldn't believe that their mother, who had drinking water in such abundance, would abort their normal profit-taking proclivities. So when they got knocked down the first time, they proceeded to try, try again . . . got knocked down again and have been very good boys in this respect ever since.

It took an overturned pot of glue to do the trick the first time . . . and the defection of one—and only one—member of the Establishment the second time. As it was, the boys got away with a couple of handfuls of cookies each time . . . but at least they were deprived of a permanent pipeline into the city's most basic asset.

In the beginning, there was Henry Yesler

During Seattle's first couple of years, it was every man for himself when it came to getting a drink of water. There were enough springs on the sides of First and Beacon Hills to supply a sizeable number of people with all of the drinking water they needed. Those springs are still there today, and at great expense we try and route them under the city into Elliott Bay, but slides every now and then serve to remind us that if the network of pipes under the city ever got clogged Nature would take over and we'd be in a real mess.

Henry Yesler was the first fellow who figured out a way of making money out of those springs. He attached big wooden boxes to some of them at the top of First Hill and then ran the water in flumes down to a tannery and a brewery and his mill down on the waterfront. For a small charge anybody at the bottom of the hill who wanted to hook into the flume could do so.

The first flume ran down James Street and made a right turn past Henry's house on First Avenue. It was on stilts because he couldn't figure out a cheap way to put a V-shaped flume underground. The stilts were about ten feet high which put them just below the present level of the street.

But the folks got tired of having bugs in their beer. Henry wouldn't spend the money to cover the flume, of course, and a crisis developed. It was then that Yesler and Charlie Terry got the Legislature to give them the franchise for supplying the town with water and collecting the profits.

The logs were properly made and buried and the beer turned out okay. This was the system for some years until the increase in the downtown population made bigger mains necessary. These were made out of wooden slats wired together with hoops. By that time, Henry was in a position to make easier money faster than by peddling water, so the original log pipe system lay lost and ignored for about a hundred years . . . until the recent Freeway construction across First Hill brought it to light.

After the log pipe, there came a complete hodge-podge of systems. Some guy would have a good well and one by one new neighbors would tie into it. In other cases someone drove pipe deep into the hills to supply himself and those around him. Springs, wells, and underground streams were tapped with different sizes and lengths of pipe . . . none of which was registered in any central place like city hall.

The birth of Spring Hill

The first major attempt to capitalize on drinking water came on August 20, 1881 when one Louis R. Johns, aided and abetted by the ubiquitous Justice J. R. Lewis, put together the Spring Hill Water System—so called because of those numberless springs that existed

on the faces of First and Beacon Hills. In those days there was no
saddle between the two hills as there is today. It was a continuous
bluff about 100 feet high. Along the side of this bluff the new company built seven tanks capable of holding 200,000 gallons of water.
The tanks were about 125 feet above high tide. The Spring Hill
people also bought up the hodge-podge of private systems in the
town below and connected them to the new system.

The fellas bet $25,000 there was enough glacial water trapped in the
hills to service a population of almost infinite size.

They lost the bet and went broke.

But they kept fooling around with the deal for a couple of years
which gave a fellow named Jacob Furth time to arrive on the scene.
Born in Bohemia in 1840, Mr. Furth was 42 years old at the time of
his arrival in Seattle . . . and it wasn't with the usual ten bucks, either. He'd already done that part of it in San Francisco 26 years before.

Mr. Furth arrived in Seattle in 1882 with fifty thousand bucks.

Why, with that kind of money, a fellow could go into the banking
business in Seattle and overnight become the biggest banker in
town.

And that's what Furth did.

He was our first and probably last "instant" banker.

Nobody had any collateral so he had to loan money without it, using
just his own judgment of a man. He was a man of majestic appearance, with a long pointed beard and piercing eyes. Within ten years,
Furth's bank was the biggest in town . . . and at no time did he call
on the stockholders for further investment. It's an irony there's no
street, statue or park named after him—a situation we should correct by changing First Avenue to Furth Avenue, or teaching people
to lisp.

For the next quarter of a century or more, Furth and his bank, the
Puget Sound National, became the most important factor in the
city's financial development.

So, it's in no way startling to find that when the city faced the prospect of doing without water, Furth was the first man sought out. He

pulled in two veterans of the financial battles of Seattle, Bailey Gatzert and John Leary, and relieved the original Spring Hill incorporators of the white elephant they had on their hands.

By June 1, 1884, the people of Seattle began drinking Lake Washington water pumped into two 200,000-gallon tanks from a pumping
station in Lake Washington at the foot of Holgate Street. Then in
1886, a 4,500,000-gallon reservoir that occupied a full block between
13th and 14th Avenues and Plum and Holgate Streets became the
storage facility for the city's major water supply. The altitude was
312 feet. It was filled by a pump capable of delivering two million
gallons a day.

Let's lay it on the line. Seattle had a good water system—better than
that of any other city in the territory at the time.

The philanthropists

When the Big Three took over Spring Hill, it was more a matter of
public service than profit. The city, hamstrung by the court decision
in favor of Henry Yesler on the regrading of First Avenue, didn't
have a dime to invest in a water system . . . and it cost a lot of money
to build the pumping station and the reservoir at the top of Beacon
Hill.

F. H. Whitworth, the engineer who determined how high was "up"
for Seattle's streets, suggested at this time that ultimately the folks
should be thinking about getting their water from Cedar River, but
in his annual message to the council in 1883, Mayor H. G. Struve
put his finger on the problem by pointing out that legislative restric-
tions made it impossible to incur the indebtedness that such an improvement would necessitate.

The Big Three did not have to invest enough money to speak of in
the system to get it. The original incorporators were glad to get out
without losing even more money than they already had lost. When
they took over, the population was about 4,000 and the water rates
granted by the Council were based on long stretches of expensive
pipe with very few revenue-producing connections. As sort of a subsidy, the franchise granted Spring Hill a monthly payment of $7.50
per hydrant . . . and at the time they started, there weren't very

many hydrants. Spring Hill was a vast money loser. However, by the time that Spring Hill was forced to relinquish the reins, the population had jumped to 43,000.

The Big Three weren't just making money; they were carrying it to the bank in big water buckets.

Considering they hadn't paid anything for the system in the first place, they were doing rather well.

When the City Comptroller dug into their records after the City took over the system in 1891, he came up with an interesting announcement: they had been making a net profit of $91,000 per year . . .

A 91,000% return on their investment.

The bright young man

Nobody blew any bugles or shot off any skyrockets when a young man by the name of Robert Moran got off a ship from San Francisco and arrived in Seattle without even the proverbial dime in his pocket.

He was eighteen years old and ambitious.

Young Mr. Moran had been born in New York City on January 26, 1857. He was a born Son of the Profits, and handy with tools. His first seven years here he served as an engineer on boats plying between Seattle and Alaska—and he hung on to every penny he made, like the hero in a Horatio Alger story.

During that seven years, he watched a $100,000 fire wipe out Henry Yesler's wharf but that didn't deter him from opening a machine shop on the wharf after it was rebuilt. The wharf was a monstrosity of sheds, buildings and miscellaneous junk covering three square blocks . . . a fire waiting to happen all over again . . . but the rent was right and he sent back to New York for his mother and brothers so the family could work together and make a million dollars.

But there was a problem. He still had one wild oat left in his system that neither he nor anybody else knew about when the Big Three took him under their wing and groomed him for membership not only in the "Sons" but possibly even in the Establishment.

One lousy wild oat . . . and oh, how it grew. . . . He had to have a run at public office.

At this stage, Furth, Leary and Gatzert saw no harm in letting their young protege have a fling at politics. After all, Leary and Gatzert had served terms as Mayor and Furth had served on the City Council. Why shouldn't Moran get this public service kick out of his system while he was young and couldn't do any real harm?

Moran got started into the thing reasonably enough. In the five years since he had opened his machine shop, he had built it into a $40,000 a year business. There was no doubt in anybody's mind that he was on his way to becoming a real Son of the Profits . . . an asset to the business community. But he was more than a little concerned about the matter of fire protection for his machine shop. The whole downtown area, and particularly Yesler's Wharf, looked like a tinder box. It gave him hot and cold running chills.

He was elected to the City Council in 1887 and placed on the Fire and Water Committee, where he was exposed to the rabid public-ownership nuts who were trying to use public water as their entering wedge. The Big Three felt it would be a good thing for Moran to have close exposure to such people, because he soon would be making a lot of money and would be fighting them. Knowledge of their tactics could become a valuable tool to a Son of the Profits in the long haul fight between private and public enterprise.

Unfortunately, Moran was only 32 years old. He still was impressionable. And he had that machine shop down there in that fire trap. The public-ownership people were known as Populists in those days. And they were too smart for Moran. For the one and only time in his life—maybe a year or two—he fell for their propaganda line and favored public ownership.

For this one deviation in an otherwise perfect life as a Son of the Profits, Moran is known today as the Father of our municipally-owned water system.

The education of Bob Moran

Early in 1888, there began a series of events that probably couldn't be explained by anybody but Robert Moran, but I'll put them together in the order that they happened, draw my own conclusions and let the reader draw his.

First, Bailey Gatzert—together with Leary and Furth—put together for very little money an outfit called the Seattle Shipbuilding and Drydock Company, down about where Todd Shipyard is today—only there was no Harbor Island at the time. Gatzert was president of the company and hired Moran as the general manager. He also made arrangements for Moran to acquire the property next door for his machine shop—all of this neatly out of what turned out to be the fire zone in downtown Seattle.

I think that at this time, for a brief period, Moran was seriously in favor of public ownership of the city's water system. On the other hand, he must have known that public ownership might do his mentors out of a considerable amount of money. Nobody really took the advent of public water as a serious possibility for a very simple reason. At the time there was no way for the city to raise money for public works except through the issuance of general obligation bonds on property values. Such assessments were limited to 4 per cent of the total evaluation of the property—and that assessment long since had been reached.

So, in effect, it might have been a wonderful idea, but there was no way for the city to take over the Spring Hill system—or build a million dollar gravity-flow system down from Cedar River, which was the general idea of the public-ownership people. That, alone would have cost 10 per cent of the total assessed valuation in the city.

The Populists, a group that had originated in Russia, hollered for it anyway. They didn't care whether it was economically feasible or not. It was part of their propaganda for public ownership of everything.

Well, Moran got elected mayor at the July election that year and in the fall sent a message to the City Council asking for an ordinance that called for an election on public vs. private ownership of water. His attitude in the following was in direct opposition to the people who employed him in the shipyard. His message to the council asked that such an election be held

". . . to determine whether this city is to have an abundant supply of pure water at cost, or continue to pay tribute to private individuals on all water used in the future . . ."

To say that Moran was in an awkward situation in sending that message is the mildest kind of understatement. He was employed by the Big Three—Gatzert in particular—in the occupation that one day would make his fortune. At the same time he was proposing legislation that would cause the Big Three to lose a whopping $91,000 a year—give or take a few bucks. And as far as anybody knew at the time, Seattle had a perfectly good water system.

It was the sewage system that back-fired. That was the thing the city should do something about. There was a real, critical and immediate need.

It was also out of character—either before or afterward—for Moran to be in favor of public ownership of *anything*.

Well, the Council was delighted to provide Mr. Moran with the election he sought and immediately responded by setting an election date of November 19, 1888 giving the people a chance to vote on whether or not they would like to have a water supply obtained by gravity flow from the Cedar River Valley. In its message back to Moran, the council kicked in a few choice words of its own about having the "life blood" of the city subject to the "caprice or rapacity of any corporation . . . who will not scruple to exact from us all that the business will bear and their charters authorize . . . Should the public own its water system, there might rapidly be extended over the whole city a complete system of fire hydrants, which is impossible to do by our present rates, as such rates would almost lead the city to bankruptcy."

The Council took care, however, to say some nice words about the Spring Hill ownership . . . pointing out that nothing personal was meant. The city was only worried that someday somebody else might take over Spring Hill.

Let it suffice that a couple of weeks later, Moran vetoed the ordinance calling for the election . . . on the grounds that a bond issue could not be voted at a special election. It would have to go on the ballot at the next regular election, which was the following July 8, 1889.

At that point the whole subject was dropped. It wasn't mentioned by Moran . . . or the Council . . . or the newspapers . . . or even the public water people, any place that I can find. As the months went by and the General Election got nearer, no move was made to put it on the ballot and to all practical purposes, the issue of a publicly-owned water system was dead.

There isn't even any indication that Moran intended to run for re-election as Mayor.

I think he had reverted to form as a "Son of the Profits."

A case of irony—"cast iron" irony

But a funny thing happened on the way to the polls.

The town burned down.

It was an event that hadn't been scheduled on anybody's business or social calendar. For that matter, even when it started, the fire didn't appear to be anything beyond the capacity of Seattle's volunteer fire department, which had won a lot of contests with similar fire departments in the Pacific Northwest.

The worst fire in recent months had been the one at the Arlington Hotel on February 5, 1888. The fancy, three-story structure at First Avenue South and South Main Street was "in-the-red," in the firemen's vernacular, when the fire department arrived. Flames were shooting from the third story window and the roof. The firemen had the dexterity, know-how—and water—to put it out without too much trouble.

Sixteen months later—almost to the day—on June 6, 1889, an over-turned pot of glue started a comparable fire practically equi-distant from the fire headquarters at Second Avenue South and Yesler Way under almost identical conditions. Yet here's what the *P.-I.* had to say about the second fire on the front page the following day.

After pointing out that at the start the fire looked easy to conquer, the *P.-I.* said the one engine hooked up to the hydrant at the corner of First and Columbia and laid two lines of hose. The city's only other engine went to the rear of the building to pump salt water— but the tide was out. In comparison with the Arlington Hotel fire this doesn't count, because it was two lines of hose that subdued that fire. The hotel wasn't that close to salt water.

The paper continued with the following, which turned out to be the epitaph for the Spring Hill Water Company:

> A cheer arose from the crowd as the beat of Engine No. 1 was heard, and two streams of water were turned on to the fire, but the cheer of hope died away in a wail of despair when after a few minutes' pumping the streams became so weak that they did not reach the top of the building, showing that there was no water to fight the fiend of fire, which by this time had reached the center of the building . . .

As some wag said, "A horse could have done better."

Well, that was the beginning of the biggest fire we ever had in this town, before or since. And it was the beginning of the end for privately-owned water. Adding insult to injury, the fire also burned down the firehouse.

And here's the irony—there were 4½ million gallons of water sitting in the reservoir at the top of Beacon Hill. And at the foot of Holgate Street there were pumps capable of delivering an additional two million gallons a day.

That was the water reserve on hand at the time the flames first flickered . . . there was plenty of water at the time the fire started.

The pumping engine which first reached the fire was capable of supplying two 2½ inch streams—not big but adequate.

Three years before—against just such a contingency as this—the Spring Hill Company had laid a grid of eight-inch cast iron water mains in downtown Seattle . . . and I believe a number of them still are functioning.

Yet no water came out of the hydrant.

What happened? I don't know.

Neither does anybody else to my knowledge. There is a popular theory that the water was conducted to the fire in wooden pipes and that they burned . . . but it doesn't make any sense. There was no fire anywhere else in town but right there at First Avenue South and Madison Street where the big fire got her start.

No subsequent investigation has found the reason why that water didn't go down the hill out of the reservoir and up out of those nozzles.

Probably somebody way down below Gatzert, Leary and Furth in the water system made the kind of a mistake they haven't even yet made an eraser for. But the people were there. They *saw* the failure of the water system. And that remorseless, amorphous creature "The Public" went on a rampage that nothing could stop. They wanted the blood of Spring Hill.

Up to this point neither Moran nor the Council had taken any step to put the question of public power on the ballot. And even then, it was twenty days after the fire that a notice signed by Robert Moran, Mayor, and C. W. Ferris, Clerk, was published stating that the question of whether or not the city should spend a million dollars for a waterworks be submitted to the voters at the General Election July 8. The notice said:

> Every voter who shall vote for erecting the above-described waterworks and authorize the expenditure of a sum not to exceed one million dollars for such purpose will vote a ballot containing the words "Water Works, Yes." Every voter who shall vote against said water works will vote a ballot containing the words, "Water Works, No."

The vote was: "Water Works, Yes," 1,875; "Water Works, No," 51.

Fifty-one votes for Spring Hill. Well, that sure showed the Big Three where they stood. On that particular day they had seventeen friends apiece in town . . .

If they included themselves.

The man with the brief case

I can stomach a man with a brief case. I can even stomach a man from out of town carrying a brief case because that's the casual description of an expert.

But the guy who gets my guard up is the one from out of town with a brief case and a folding tripod—and a couple yards of blue velvet. When he unfolds that tripod and asks for a nice table for his blue velvet . . . and then starts spreading beautiful colored charts and maps around and clears his throat for a "presentation" . . .

That means you're going to get stung when he presents his bill.

Well, I wasn't there when the big hydraulics expert from Chicago, Benezette Williams, arrived in town shortly after the election. But from all I can read, I'll lay you odds he had the blue velvet with him. It was the first but by no means the last time the city of Seattle got the blue velvet cloth treatment from an out-of-town expert.

Anyway, by the time he was through with his spiel we had contracted to give him about 10 per cent of the total city budget for the years 1889-90 and he had agreed to tell us how much it would cost us to buy the Spring Hill Water System and what the tab would come to for bringing water by gravity from the Cedar River watershed.

When somebody complained that the price was a little steep, he pulled one out of the hat like an encyclopedia salesman with his final bonus offer. He agreed to tell us, without additional charge, what we could do with our backwards sewer system.

The upshot of it was, we agreed to pay Benezette Williams $35,000.

We pointed out, however, that there was some risk on his part. The election that had been held on July 8 to vote a million dollars worth of bonds had no legal status. Washington was still a Territory and until we gained statehood the July 8 election was just a means of sounding out the voters to see how they felt about water.

On the other hand, we also pointed out that a Constitutional Convention had been held on July 4—just four days before the election —and it looked like statehood was coming along nicely.

Mr. Williams agreed that for that kind of money, he'd take a chance that we really would become a state and be granted the power to pay him his bill. Meanwhile, he wasn't really busy elsewhere that summer and why didn't we just let him go to work right here.

We expressed the thought that that was very generous of Mr. Williams.

Now, I must confess there were some problems involved. When the Big Three bought the Spring Hill System they neglected to acquire with it any diagram of what pipes there were or where they went. For that matter it is extremely unlikely the original incorporators of that system had any notion about details like these themselves. And I suspect the truth is that none existed—ever.

Mr. Williams could look at the pumping plant on Lake Washington and figure out how much that was worth . . . likewise the reservoir on top of Beacon Hill and the various and sundry installations that had been made by Spring Hill. But for the most part the only thing that anybody knew for sure was that when he turned on the faucet in his home or his business he either did or did not get water.

If he got water, he paid Spring Hill for it.

If he didn't get water, he screamed for Pete Berquist.

Pete was the meter reader.

He was the only man in town who knew where the pipes were buried. And his system of reading meters consisted of notching a pine tree at one spot . . . looking for a mark on a big rock and going ten paces west in another place . . . or remembering a particular piece of broken plank in a board walk and heading three paces north.

With the aid of Pete, Mr. Williams reported to the City Council that the Spring Hill System was worth exactly $119,170.

But Mr. Furth, the spokesman for Spring Hill, also had read the notice that the people would pay a sum not to exceed $1,000,000 for a waterworks. The ballot didn't say anything about that monkey business of buying a gravity feed system from up in the woods. He was very happy that the folks had voted the million, because when he studied the value of Spring Hill, it somehow came to that exact amount.

However, he talked it over with the other members of the board of directors and they had agreed that inasmuch as they were loyal native sons, it was their duty to come down in price by taking in the deterioration of the system and its equipment over the years.

They would cut the price to $840,000.

Wasn't that nice.

Well, they negotiated back and forth in a not unfriendly fashion and thanks to Pete's comprehensive data on the system came up with an exact price that was agreeable to all concerned.

The exact price was $352,265.67 . . . which, of course, was just about $352,265.57 more than the Big Three had paid for the system in the first place.

But Mr. Williams failed to note, and Furth neglected to mention, that there was $50,000 in outstanding bonds that the company was pledged to pay . . . making the real purchase price $402,265.67.

Mr. Williams really didn't earn his $35,000 on that one.

Now let's take a look at his survey on the Cedar River Watershed.

Like Teddy Roosevelt at San Juan Hill, Williams charged off into the underbrush followed by his faithful cohorts. They hit trees with blazing axes from the Beacon Hill reservoir south to Black River Junction, east through the town of Renton and up over the Renton Hill and through the forest to Swan Lake.

Following his safari, Williams returned to Seattle and called together a collection of city engineers and councilmen and announced where the city of Seattle ought to get its water, should it be able to finance a gravity flow system. With no little showmanship, Mr. Williams dramatically stated that the city should not get its water from Cedar River, but rather that it should obtain its supply from Rock Creek where there presently was a daily flow of 10,000,000 gallons and that one day that flow would increase perhaps to 15,000,000.

It always has been a puzzlement to engineers how a stream would add 5,000,000 gallons a day to its capacity as time went along, but Mr. Whitworth, who first had suggested Cedar River, was perturbed as well as puzzled. He was doing some engineering work for a mine in Issaquah when the Williams report crossed his desk . . .

He read it and made a beeline for Benezette.

"Mr. Williams," Whitworth said, "You have your decimal point in the wrong place. There's only a flow of one million gallons a day."

Williams checked the figures in his published report again and said, "My word, so there is. So there is."

Williams and his loyal followers took off into the underbrush again, and when they returned Williams withdrew his first report and recommended the exact location that Whitworth had recommended without charge nearly a decade before.

Some years later, the then City Engineer, R. H. Thomson, rechecked the Williams report, concluded it was bad engineering from start to finish and did the engineering work all over again before building the first Cedar River pipeline.

Thomson sticks the last pin in Williams' public image by referring to the latter's advice on what we should do with our sewage—

"Dump it in Lake Washington."

After all, if Lake Washington water was worth drinking, why not dump our sewage there too?

The earthworm

R. H. Thomson belongs in this book not so much because he made a lot of dough himself—although he was "keerful" with his money— but because he gave the Sons of the Profits fits for forty years that can be proved . . . and another twenty that can be richly suspected.

Thomson showed up in Seattle thirty years to the day after Denny's advance party landed at Alki on September 25, 1851. He departed from this world on September 7, 1949 leaving general havoc behind him in Seattle—at least among the money men.

The city has never been the same since.

To think that the measly little Empire Way cut-off has been named the R. H. Thomson Expressway in his honor must leave R. H. writhing wherever he is. Even naming the main freeway through Seattle after him would be pretty puny. Why, they only moved 6,000,000 cubic yards of earth for the Freeway.

Thomson, all by himself, moved nearly nine times that much.

He was a wild-eyed earth surgeon who tried to flatten Seattle so it would look like Kansas City. When he was at the height of his demoniac works, he was quoted as saying "Seattle lies with gaping wounds like a patient on an operating table . . . but these are necessary if she is to survive and become a great city."

Thomson was really hell on hills.

He leveled everything he could lay his hands on . . . even tried to level Beacon Hill, but the folks wouldn't let him get hold of it. Knocking down a hundred-foot hill was nothing to Thomson. Sticking in a ninety-foot fill like the one on Westlake was mere child's play. He created such beautiful property as that less than desirable area down around Jackson Street where Chinatown holds its sway . . . and the Denny Regrade area which finally is coming into its own with a few skyscrapers.

He regraded most of Seattle's downtown streets.

His attitude on hills is found in his autobiography *That Man Thomson:* "Some people seem to think that just because there were hills in Seattle originally, some of them ought to be left there . . ."

He wasn't about to let Seattle fall into the trap of being as beautiful as San Francisco.

He had method in his madness. His objective was to create a connection between downtown Seattle and her hinterland. And during his term as city engineer—from 1892 to 1913—he succeeded in this endeavor. He also cut the city in half by cinching construction of the Lake Washington Ship Canal.

Talk about a man to match our mountains.

He knew how to hit a Son of the Profits where it hurt . . . not the kind of hurt that comes from the loss of a parent or wife or beloved friend, but one down deep inside the heart—of his pocket book.

Every time Thomson opened his mouth it cost the Sons of the Profits money. And it wasn't the kind of money they liked spending—it didn't follow their formula that for every dollar spent a hundred dollars should shower down from some place else. Thomson cost them real *money* money. The sewers that Thomson built had to be wider and deeper than anybody else's sewers . . . and he was always shoving bigger and more expensive water pipe at the town in the most unscrupulous manner. That's what he was—unscrupulous.

That boulevard business was a typical Thomson enterprise.

Neither the City Council nor the Sons of the Profits would go for the wild extravagance of creating boulevards. But bicycling was big in Thomson's day. Six hundred cyclists would gather in one spot on a Sunday morning, for instance, for a day's outing. So Thomson created what he called bicycle paths. When he got an okay for them, he just condemned right-of-ways wide enough for boulevards . . . and when nobody was looking, made the boulevards out of the bicycle paths.

Enter Mr. Ammidown

Well, statehood did arrive on November 11, 1889. We paid off Mr. Williams. The following February we made a down payment on the Spring Hill System and in June, 1890 the voters voted the money under the new state constitution to pay for the system.

Mayor Moran happily said, "The city has got to the stage when the question of whether we should control our own water supply or be under the power of a gigantic corporation has confronted us and been decided . . . *Happily this great question is now eliminated from the future . . .*" (Ed. note: Italics mine.)

Oh, boy Some prognosticator!

But then, Moran had never heard of Mr. E. H. Ammidown.

Ammidown was busy attempting to corner the United States wool market and never had heard of either Moran or the city of Seattle, for that matter. Both Ammidown and the city of Seattle were digging themselves into financial holes—at the bottom of which they would meet.

Henry Yesler really fixed the city's financial clock when the courts awarded him $156,000 for his famous corner, but the city continued on its "do-it-now, pay later" program of public works . . . only to learn a little too late that other property owners took a page from Yesler's book and refused to pay their improvement assessments. And in 1893, the temporary nose dive of Baring Brothers, the great financial house in London, cut off Seattle's financial legs and at the same time forced Ammidown to drop the ball in the wool market.

An agile man, despite his 63 years, Ammidown came west to promote some mines at Monte Cristo, near Everett, where he recouped his fallen fortunes, paid off his creditors and got himself back in good standing with the bankers. While he was in the Pacific Northwest, he did a little prospecting in the Seattle City Engineer's office and came up with a new kind of gold mine. It was Benezette Williams' $35,000 report on obtaining water from Cedar River. Forgotten by everybody, the report was just gathering dust.

Ammidown found Seattle's water system was a patchwork quilt with no lasting qualities at all . . . that there was a move to fill in the tidelands south of King Street . . . and there was a lot of talk about obtaining electric power for the city and that some ambitious fellows were planning to build a ship canal through Beacon Hill at Spokane Street.

Well, to a man knowledgeable enough to nearly corner wool, putting together a little deal for a small town away out west seemed like a simple proposition indeed.

Being a member in good standing of the New York Chapter of the Sons of the Profits, Ammidown kept sniffing and discovered the federal government recently had opened up the area which we now know as the Cedar River Watershed for homesteading. He decided that this would be a dandy time to build his little gray home in the West.

So, at the usual price of $1.25 per acre—or a total of $200, Mr. Ammidown staked out his claim and prepared to settle down. After all there comes a time in the life of every man when he wants to possess some land of his own. And everyone who lives here knows that this is God's Country.

Mr. Ammidown then made a further contribution to the economy of the region at a time when employment was low. He assigned a young hydraulic engineer to make a study of the work that Williams had done. R. H. Thomson refused to let the young man take his work home with him, but the Williams plans were a matter of public record and he couldn't refuse access to them to any bonafide citizen.

The young engineer had nothing better to do during the winter of 1893-94 than copy the Williams report verbatim.

In the meantime, Mr. Ammidown whiled away the hours by improving his homestead and visiting people like Governor Ferry, former Governor Semple, Arthur A. Denny, Moran, Colman, Furth, and J. D. Lowman. He became a member of the Seattle Chamber of Commerce and made friends of the fellows there. He became friends with the publishers of the newspapers and in general got acquainted on a first name basis with his fellow members of that great world fraternity, the Sons of the Profits.

Mr. Ammidown had interesting anecdotes about his previous life in Wall Street. He also made it known that he had an unlimited line of credit with some Boston bankers. Now, this was a subject near and dear to the hearts of Seattle's financial community. It had been the feeling for years that the development of Seattle had lagged for want of investments by eastern capitalists.

And Ammidown's proposal was fascinating.

He was primarily interested in developing privately owned power. On the other hand, there were the fellows who wanted to build a canal through Beacon Hill, create Harbor Island and fill in the tidelands south of King Street. The city water grid was a mess that needed to be modernized. And there was that matter of bringing in water from Cedar River.

Five million dollars would take care of providing all of these things for the city. On the other hand, Ammidown's group was prepared to invest in any part of them that seemed reasonable. The things that seemed reasonable to Ammidown were: first, he would provide power from the water at Cedar River. Secondly, he would build a water pipe from the source of power that could deliver water to Seattle cheaper than it had ever been delivered before. He would even make the pipeline bigger if the folks behind it were serious about sluicing out the canal through Beacon Hill.

Well, he worked it out with the business community that he would either buy the existing distribution system in Seattle and put in a brand new one, or he would deliver water to the outskirts of the city and let the city handle its own distribution.

In either circumstance, he was backed to the tune of $5,000,000, . . . and the men in Seattle could take any part of the package they felt like investing in.

It was one of those lovely deals so enticing to the Sons of the Profits. For an investment of $1 on their part they could get an additional $99 invested by someone from out-of-town increasing the value of their property and other enterprises.

In his quiet way, Mr. Ammidown became very popular in business circles.

By and by the word trickled down to City Hall that Ammidown had been taking right-of-way options on some land that ran from Cedar River through Swan Lake, Renton Hill, Renton Valley, Black River and over Beacon Hill into Seattle. The property descriptions sounded suspiciously like they might have been taken from the Benezette Williams report.

Could it be Ammidown was taking advantage of Williams' work?

Somebody said, oh no! But when they checked, it was, oh, yes! Mr. Ammidown's homestead . . . the place where he proposed to settle down for the rest of his life. It straddled Cedar River at the spot which the Williams survey designated as the intake for the pipeline. For two hundred bucks, Ammidown had swiped Seattle's proposed new water system!

The fun begins

This tale may come as something of a startlement to the folks who think that public ownership of Seattle's water supply was something that just happened. It happened all right, like a bar room brawl on St. Patrick's Day.

In mid-April of 1895 the Sons of the Profits rolled up a batch of heavy artillery and prepared to put the publicly owned water system back where it belonged—in private hands.

Ammidown was the front man.

In his first proposal, he said that if he was given the contract to supply water to Seattle for fifty years, he would deed all the land to the city with the improvements made on it in return for the fees paid for the water bought during that period. He could make a low price because his primary need of the water was for power. The same water could be used for drinking.

The city was to buy the water for two cents a gallon.

This was less money than the city was paying at that time just for pumping the water out of Lake Washington, let alone distributing it to its customers. It could get clean, fresh Cedar River water right now at a guaranteed cost for the next fifty years. Everybody knew that every year it would cost more money to pump water out of Lake Washington, and that every year the water in Lake Washington would become more polluted.

The estimated cost of putting in the system was $1,250,000.

The city didn't have a Chinaman's chance of raising that kind of money. It had been thoroughly stuck with the purchase of Henry Yesler's property, and the other costs that followed the fire. The depression of 1893 had depreciated land values and the city already was away over its bonded debt limitations.

Ammidown owned the intake system, and he had options on the land for the pipeline. The city figured it had no alternative to dumping the Spring Hill system and accepting Ammidown's offer.

Then somebody got greedy.

Ammidown reported a second proposal to the City Council. The Boston bankers insisted that the clause which gave the City title to the land after fifty years be removed. In its place they wanted a clause inserted stating that the city would appoint an appraiser, the Ammidown Company would appoint an appraiser and the two appraisers would appoint a third man, and these three men would then determine the price the city would pay the company for the system after the half-century expired.

The City Council would have gone along with the first proposition, ... but it balked at the second and decided it would see if it couldn't find a contractor who would spend the million and a quarter and accept his payments over a long period of time.

This was proving a difficult matter in light of the fact that the City Treasurer recently had absconded with a bunch of money and the integrity of the city government was at a new low—which made it really quite low.

Freshet as a sweet breeze

While the folks in Seattle were jockeying for positions, the future of our water system was being determined in Spokane.

In the early nineties, the Spokane water system had become such a hopeless mess that the city shoved all of its chips on a new intake system in the Spokane River. It spent all the money it could get, up to its debt limitation, and shortly after a fancy new system had been completed, a spring freshet wiped it out again.

The Chicago firm which had bought Spokane's bonds in the first place came up with a proposition that never before had been attempted in the United States. They offered to buy bonds that would not be part of the general obligation of the city itself, but would be paid out of the revenues of the water system alone.

These would be the first revenue bonds ever issued.

As practically everybody predicted, the Superior Court Judge in Spokane County threw the city out on its ear ... but there were some stubborn folks there who took it to the State Supreme Court.

And on a Sunday, August 25, 1895 an item appeared in the Spokane paper which noted that the Superior Court Judge had been over-ruled.

Revenue bonds were suddenly legal.

When this news got into R. H. Thomson's hands, he treated it like he was one of the conspirators in a South American revolution. He held a secret meeting of the Councilmen he could trust and ex-plained to them what it meant.

In Spokane it meant they could float a $100,000 bond issue.

The same principle applied to Seattle, meant we could float a $1,250,000 bond issue.

Well, the Council went through a lot of fol-de-rol like holding a se-cret meeting of the Lower House and another one in the Upper House so they could slip through an ordinance authorizing the bond issue without letting on to the Ammidown forces whose power in high places might have tipped over the apple cart if normal, time-consuming processes were observed.

The conspirators had a notion that the Mayor, who was a pro-Am-midown man, would veto the ordinance—just like Moran had done some years before. And they were correct. Mayor Byron Phelps slipped in a delaying action by vetoing the ordinance on the grounds it should be submitted to a vote of the people. The Council immedi-ately re-wrote the ordinance on October 29 and called for $1,250,000 revenue bond issue to be voted on by the people on December 10, 1895. The ordinance provided for a city-owned gravity flow water system from Cedar River.

The blow that nearly slew dad

The odds that the voters would approve an expenditure of $1,250,000 were generally considered to have about as much a chance of passing as that of a camel getting through the eye of a nee-dle.

In the past few years other cities had voted for their own water sys-tems and scandals of inefficiency had made headline news. Usually, some city official couldn't resist helping himself to the new revenues and blowing town. The memory of Seattle's own light-fingered City Treasurer—who couldn't vote at this election because he still was in the penitentiary—also was vivid.

In the most publicized cases, the bankers then had taken over the city's defunct systems and the water rates had gone higher than ever. Besides, the public was a lot more interested in bicycle paths than it was in an election which was too complicated for them to figure out in the first place.

So even with an election coming up, the Ammidown folks' prospects were still pretty good. Ammidown bettered them by offering to change the controversial clause in his proposed contract to read that the city would automatically own the ground in the watershed and along the pipeline. Ammidown's company would be paid for its investment in putting in the system over a period of half a century and then the whole thing would belong to the city free and clear.

Naturally, the moneyed people in town were interested in killing the bond issue. The newspapers were against it, along with the bankers, and the leading businessmen—let's just say that the Sons of the Profits and the Establishment spent money like water to defeat the proposed water revenue bonds. The Chamber of Commerce, of course, came out 50 to 8 against the ordinance.

But the very worst blow the proposed public water system took came from J. J. McGilvra. He was the only one who took the trouble to write a letter to the City Clerk, which he did 10 days after the ordinance calling for an election was passed. He thus became the only person on either side to make his feelings an official part of the city records. McGilvra was the dean of the Seattle Bar Association. He still was the hero of the fight against big corporations from the day some fifteen years before when he took five million acres of land from the Northern Pacific Railroad. Of even greater importance, he had to that date been an outspoken critic of Ammidown.

Suddenly, he was for him. In his letter to the City Clerk, he made the point that no matter which way you sliced it, a debt was a debt. And the city was in no position to go further into debt, no matter how fancy the deal might sound. He pointed out that the city just recently had gone ahead and fixed up the new streets in Pioneer Square and had fixed the sewage system on the premise that the landholders in the area would pay their assessments.

Well, they hadn't.

On the other hand, he pointed out that the Ammidown Corporation was offering pure, clean city water now on a contract that could be paid off in 50 years. If the ordinance was passed, the city would be forced into a debt far beyond its resources. If it was not passed, it could get clean water anyway on a fair proposal. It was his point that the Ammidown people needed the water primarily to produce power. After that it would be given to the city at very low rates. He concluded:

> "As a voter and a taxpayer, I protest the scheme of this ordinance. The city should not and will not act the part of a dog in the manger by attempting to prevent individuals and corporations from appropriating (only) the surplus water of Cedar River . . ."

The defection of J. J. McGilvra

R. H. Thomson who was as realistic as the Russian High Command, realized that McGilvra's statement was that last straw. McGilvra had been an outspoken critic of Ammidown personally, and if he came out for Ammidown's proposition in spite of his personal antagonism to the man, he must have felt strongly on the subject.

Thomson was enough of a politician to have coined the phrase "never underestimate the stupidity of the American voter." He knew that the philosophy of a revenue bond was far too advanced to be understood by the average citizen in town.

Average citizen?

It was even too deep for the reporters who consistently pointed out in their stories that we already had exceeded the city's legal debt limitation and passage of more bonds simply wouldn't hold up in court.

Thomson, the crafty old curmudgeon, decided to gamble everything on his ability to get McGilvra to change his mind. The papers had played the McGilvra story big. If McGilvra did a switcheroo, it would provide the bomb needed to put the ordinance through. Thomson says in his book:

> I therefore asked leave to have a conference with him. This was gladly granted, and one conference was extended to . . . a number . . . of conferences. Finally, the Judge called for a brief showing the city's side of the case, saying he would sit down and provide a brief opposing the city's side . . . I agreeing that until he finished his brief I would make no public addresses on the matter . . .

Thomson confesses that he really sweated that one out. The old man took his own sweet time making up his mind what he was going to do. Thomson had to play this one on a strictly hands-off basis. Any attempt on his part to push McGilvra would land an adverse decision. Meanwhile the anti-ordinance forces really went to town. Public opinion was swinging against passage of the ordinance.

The date of the election loomed closer. Three weeks went by and finally, McGilvra's letter appeared in the *Times.*

He had reversed his position.

No longer was the city the "dog in the manger" frustrating private enterprise . . . private enterprise, in his letter was referred to as "a cold, bloodless, soulless creature of the law called a corporation . . . domiciled at the very source of this necessity of life, claiming title and seeking to levy tribute . . . etc."

McGilvra's defection had the impact of a gunshot in a sleepy school room. It woke everybody up to the fact that an election was coming. The folks opposed to passage of the ordinance immediately turned to and attacked McGilvra.

When somebody from the other side accused him of swinging like a weathervane in a whirlwind, he replied: "When it comes to the matter of security to property and the necessities of life, I will take the liberty to think twice. Yes, sir, I will think twice . . ."

He also added a further thought at that time which I get a kick out of since he knew not that his friend Thomson was sneaking boulevards into the city's street system under the guise of building bicycle paths . . . or that Thomson would name one of the boulevards after McGilvra in honor of the stand the latter took on the matter of Cedar River Water. "I have always opposed, and shall continue to oppose contracting debts for municipal luxuries such as the . . . schemes for parks and *boulevards* and other wild and vicious speculations . . ."

Prior to McGilvra's entry into the fray, the city's forces were standing with their hands tied behind their backs. The newspapers were against them. A campaign kitty had been raised by the Ammidown people to provide speakers for public meetings, posters, literature— all of the sort of thing usually used to win an election. Thomson and Company didn't have a thin dime to spend. After McGilvra had made his statement—about three weeks before the election—Thomson called to thank him and McGilvra asked him what money there was for the campaign. "Not a dollar," Thomson replied.

With McGilvra footing the bill, the pro-public water people put on a full fledged campaign for the final three weeks . . . public speakers, bands, banners and newspaper advertising. The vote came out 2,656 for and 1,665 against . . .

The next day, Arthur Denny met J. J. on the street and although McGilvra had been Denny's attorney for about thirty years, the latter refused to speak to him.

Poor Mr. Ammidown!

And what of poor Mr. Ammidown?

What happened to the luckless man who failed on cornering either wool or water?

Well, he sold out his electric power firm for a nice chunk of money to the Seattle-Tacoma Power Company and obtained some stock in an outfit that we know today as the Puget Sound Power Company.

And what about his homestead . . . his little gray home in the west?

He changed his address to 816 Prospect Street, which was one of the high-rent residential districts in Seattle at the time . . . and he lived there in happiness and comfort ever after—or at least until 1909 when he went on to his great reward.

He could afford to.

He sold his little old $200 homestead claim to the great big city of Seattle . . .

For $63,000.

X

The Hostess With the Mostest

She was born Dorothea Georgine Emile Ohben sometime in 1860 in Germany and very likely would have died in obscurity but for a spirit of adventure, not possessed by the other members of her family, that brought her to the Pacific Coast of the United States. Her genial personality and shrewd business judgment made her the most important woman in the first fifty years of Seattle's history.

Her stage name was Lou Graham . . . she was one of the Sons of the Profits . . . and she was in the entertainment business.

Lou arrived in Seattle in the late 1880's with a small amount of capital, a burning ambition to become rich, and the necessary training in her field to do it. She amassed a fortune by providing the city with an ingredient that was necessary at that point in its evolution. She built a mansion that was the equal of that occupied by any of the other important Sons like Arthur Denny, or C. C. Terry, or Jacob Furth—well, maybe not as good as John Leary's, but his was really awfully fancy. The records don't show whether or not she was a member of the Chamber of Commerce, but they do show she contributed liberally to projects sponsored by that body.

And the record clearly shows that she made a greater cash contribution to the education of our children than all the others put together.

Call me madam

Lou stood about five feet, two inches . . . and at chest height, she was about three feet thick. She went for plumed hats and smart carriages. She was a fancy dresser and always was clad in the finest of raiment and the most ostentatious of jewels. She had jet black hair and blue eyes . . . strong teutonic features, with a prominent nose and a wide mouth. She could be regal as she swept into a room, or tell the latest off-color joke with a bonafide twinkle in her eyes.

There wasn't a man-about-town in town who didn't call her "Lou."

There wasn't a man on the Pacific Coast who hadn't heard of her.

And there wasn't a woman in the area—whether she lived on the humps or the hollows—who didn't despise every breath she took. Lou couldn't have cared less.

A lot of important things happened in Seattle in the 1880's. The decade started with our biggest snow-storm and ended with our biggest fire. We were the center of the biggest hop-producing country in America. We had our first telephone system and our best hangings . . . our first city hall and courthouse . . . first electric lights . . . first gas lighting . . . first street railway and ice house . . . first opera house and brick company . . . first city charter . . . first postal telegraph and free postal delivery. The Chamber of Commerce was born . . . and John L. Sullivan fought here.

But the most important event was the advent of Lou Graham . . . our first first-class madam.

Lou was the symbol of economic progress. She was the darling of the Sons of the Profits and the Establishment. Do you think we would have gotten the railroads here . . . or the headquarters of the Mosquito Fleet . . . or the world shipping without the assistance of Lou and some of her lesser counterparts? Lou stood for integrity in her field . . . and a kind of class that couldn't be matched outside of the other major cities of the world like San Francisco, New York, London, Paris. She was a first-rate businesswoman and there wasn't a man in town who didn't admire her business acumen. She ended up as one of the big landholders in the Pacific Northwest. She had the largest collection of costly jewelry anywhere around and invested heavily and profitably in the stock market.

Her economic impact on the city is illustrated by the contribution to the General Fund made by Lou and the people in allied industries such as liquor and gambling. They provided 87 per cent, via fines and licenses, until a new charter forced the businessmen in less colorful occupations to pay their fair share.

During her evolution, Seattle has been many cities, not just one. For instance, in today's complex world, our "think" people . . . the Ph.D.'s . . . are the city's most important economic resource.

In this respect, the Ph.D. of today has replaced the prostitute of Lou's day.

The ladies from Hades

When Lou arrived on the premises, women in general had about 2¾ strikes against them—regardless of whether they were running expensive residences for their husbands on the view property or cheap "houses" on the Skid Road.

It all began more than four years before, on November 23, 1883 to be exact, when the Territorial Legislature had unleashed the most destructive force that had been experienced in the city's first fifty years . . . and even on Lou's arrival the men in the business community were still in the process of encircling and killing it.

The Legislature had lost its mind and conferred the right of suffrage upon women.

Now I don't want to be in the position of saying that all of the women participated in this blight that had been cast upon the land. I can count thirteen prominent women in Seattle of that time who stuck to women's work like the Ladies' Relief Society . . . the Library Association . . . the Women's Home Society . . . the Home of the Good Shepherd . . . the Orphans' Home . . . and the Refuge Home for Fallen Women. But they were in the minority.

And for nearly half a decade, the city had suffered with suffrage.

Right after they got it, aided and abetted by J. R. Lewis and David Denny, the women had plunged headfirst into politics. I can understand Lewis. He was so hot for law and order he would have appealed to the Devil himself for help. And David's wife, of course, wore the pants in that family.

Anyway, the devastation began, I think rather portentously, on Friday the 13th of June, 1884—seven months after the Legislature handed the ladies the whip—with the convening of what was to be known as the "Apple Orchard Convention" because it was held in an apple orchard at Fifth Avenue and Marion Street. There were 400 people on hand, all of them hellbent for reform. They described themselves as those: "who favor the enforcement of existing laws and ordinances and the administration of municipal affairs by sober, honest and efficient men . . ."

They even took a running swing at the Establishment for its laxity in city affairs. They said they didn't mind the fact that John Leary was president of the Spring Hill Water System, but that if he was elected mayor (which he was, in spite of their attack) he would be in the position of signing the city's contract with that system—which they did mind.

It was unrealistic things like that which finally got 'em.

Well, Mrs. Charles K. Jenner was elected chairman and Mrs. Laura D. Hall, secretary. They formed an Apple Orchard Ticket and placed a full set of nominees in the field for the city election which was coming up in another month. Some naive young men formed groups with such spontaneous and unusual names as the Law and Order League . . . Young Men's Political Club . . . The Young Men's Independent Club . . . the Businessmen's Club, and the Protective Association.

The regular politicians threw up their hands and said, "Oh, No!"

The reformers flailed away. The women licked envelopes and went door-belling. They put out literature and provided baby sitting service. They stood at the polls and handed out hunks of propaganda. They brought old folks to the polls in carriages and had torchlight parades like there had never been an election before. There were 759 registered women voters. They all voted, and they actually elected their reform ticket—all except John Leary who made it as mayor, and he didn't have a thumb big enough to plug the hole in *that* dike!

The folks they elected were sober, honest and efficient—and what was even worse, they enforced all the laws and ordinances. Gambling joints were closed. Liquor licenses were revoked. Prostitutes were run out of town. The police department arrested people for spitting tobacco juice into passing carriages. The lights were turned off at nine o'clock and the sidewalks rolled up so they'd be nice and fresh in the morning.

Miners, loggers, sailors started going to Tacoma on Saturday nights. The purchase of supplies for lumber camps and ships shifted up the Sound about thirty miles and within a few months you could have shot off a cannon at First Avenue and Yesler and not hit anybody.

The fines and licenses on liquor, gambling and prostitution that had been the major source of income for the operation of the city dwindled to almost nothing. The bottom dropped out of the city budget.

Do you think the ladies noticed any of these details?

Don't be silly!

The following year, chirruping cheerfully, the ladies got together to re-elect their people to office. Only this time they weren't satisfied with an old apple orchard. They were in the big time now. They were the powerful interest. They didn't connive in any smoke-filled rooms, however, because they didn't smoke. They held their meeting in the Frye Opera House, which was the finest building in town. They selected their slate. They licked envelopes . . . went door-belling . . . put out literature and provided baby sitting service . . . handed out propaganda at the polls . . . brought old folks to the polls in carriages . . . had torchlight parades . . .

And failed to elect one single candidate.

After that, they quit fielding candidates . . . but managed to stir up a fuss, anyway. They backed the Knights of Labor who rioted against the Chinese . . . and a guy got killed. One of the ladies' more important successes involved Arthur Denny, the Father of our city. In 1886, he ran for mayor. They went out en masse against him and defeated him by 44 votes.

If they had taken no part at all, he would have been elected.

It was just an honorary position anyway, and he was 64 years old. I don't think he ever spoke to another woman for the rest of his life.

But, that defeat tore it as far as the Establishment was concerned.

They figured: "We gotta get these women outa here!"

In 1887, the question of suffrage was taken to court and the judge held that the Legislature had erred when it assumed that women were "citizens." He threw out woman suffrage. His decision was upheld in the Territorial Superme Court and the screaming females demanded that the case be taken to the United States Supreme Court.

Again, I defer to Bagley who was there at the time and, like the Greeks, had a word for it:

> The ill-advised action (Ed. note: in reference to the Chinese riots) of many women of Seattle . . . had aroused general indignation among the active supporters of law and order here; and men whose personal efforts had been liberally supported by their purses in carrying on the public campaign to secure woman suffrage in the Territory refused aid to the movement to carry the law to a higher court for adjudication . . .

The gals took it to the Supreme Court anyway and on August 15, 1888—half a year after Lou took up residence here—this is what the *P.-I.* had to say about *that:*

> Woman suffrage has proven a practical failure in Washington Territory. It has accomplished nothing in the way of public or private good. There have been no moral, social or political reforms as a consequence of it. On the other hand, it has made dissension and trouble everywhere.

The U.S. Supreme Court upheld the lower courts.

The right of equal suffrage was not proclaimed until August 26, 1920. How does that tickle your funny bone? Because Arthur A. Denny lost an election for mayor by 44 votes in 1886, the cause of woman suffrage was set back nationally 32 years!

The lady whose name was Lou

That was the attitude of the Establishment toward women in 1888 when Lou Graham came to its members with her proposition. Only

a woman of her deep character, business acumen and persuasive talents could have broken down the solid wall that the business leaders
of Seattle had built against any woman who might once more attempt to participate in directing the destiny of their city.

A lesser woman would have failed.

But not Lou!

Who in Seattle had the training and capabilities of operating an establishment of the kind she proposed? Who had the know-how to
build a profit-making business on the foundation which she proposed?

Nobody!

Lou pointed out that, like John Pinnell, she had served a proper apprenticeship and was the master of her trade. Her proposition was
simplicity itself. Now that the interruption of the lady reformers was
over, Seattle had ample facilities for catering to the needs of the run-
of-the-mill soldier, sailor, logger, miner or common adventurer.

But where was the city of Seattle when it came to providing for the
top hat and black-tie set? Where could they send visiting dignitaries
for a little bit of quiet music and relaxation from their arduous
travels in the company of a lovely, intelligent and complaisant
woman?

Nowhere!

Historically, beginning with the Greeks and the Romans, man had
seen the necessity of proper rest and recreation for visiting poten-
tates. Here Seattle was attempting to get a transcontinental rail connection and become a great city. What did she have to offer in the
way of the plush facilities that railroad moguls had come to expect
in a city like San Francisco?

Nothing!

Lou would conduct an enterprise the like of which Seattle had never
seen—not even in John Pinnell's heyday. She would provide a collection of the most gorgeous, the most talented, the most understanding hostesses from every corner of the globe . . . women who

could discuss the opera, or politics, or economics, or world conditions on an intelligent level with the leaders of America.

No crass, elemental undertaking, hers. She proposed a multi-storied building. A fine parlor would be located on the first floor for those who sought no more than a quiet drink and pleasant companionship against a background of fine music. For those who felt the need of deeper therapy, commodious quarters would be provided in the upper floors.

Lou would "fair trade" her prices for the basic commodity and publish price lists for her liquid refreshments. In the upper floors where complete anonymity would be preserved the price would be a straight $2 across the board regardless of a man's wealth, and $5 for those who wished to spend the night—a sum that compared favorably with the best hotels in town. The money and other valuables that the men carried would be as safe as if they were in Jacob Furth's bank. She also offered a money-back guarantee: If for any reason a man had to seek the services of a physician as a result of a visit to her establishment, she would pay the fee.

I don't know whether Lou used a velvet cloth for her presentation, but I do know she impressed the Establishment. She showed exactly what her profit margin would be and how her standardized prices would keep her from becoming a charge of the city.

She asked one thing of the Establishment, however . . . it must back her play.

This included, of course, notifying the necessary authorities that her enterprise was making as much of a contribution to the economic growth of the city as Henry Yesler's mill—or even the railroads. While she was quite willing to pay her fair share toward supporting city government, she proposed that she would send it in. She didn't want the police poking their noses in her business affairs any more than any other Son of the Profits wanted the Police Department breaking and entering his place of business any time of the day or night.

That was a wise precaution that was asked for, and it was accepted by the Establishment.

The Establishment was ecstatic.

The professional and business women in the tenderloin had been giving the city fathers as much trouble as the ladies from the view property. There were no fixed prices—they just charged what the traffic would bear. And there were many other practices that gave the city a bad name. If Lou could provide the most hospitable place in town at the prices she proposed, the police could enforce them in the places with a less pretentious atmosphere. Here was a woman who could give Seattle favorable publicity throughout the length and breadth of the land.

In spite of, and not because of, her fellow-women, Lou was admitted to the economic inner sanctum of the city. A member of the Sons of the Profits, she definitely was . . . and on some occasions her wise judgment was sought even in the meetings of the Establishment.

In the same year that suffrage was denied women by the Supreme Court of the United States, Lou Graham began the practice of her trade . . . and became a bright new star on Seattle's horizon.

Money on the line

Lou's property, which was part of Maynard's Donation Claim, was at the southwest corner of Third Avenue South and Washington Street. It cost her $3,000, and I must say she was far more business-like about it than old Doc, who originally sold it for considerably less but made up the difference by selling it to two different people. Lou bought it once and kept it for the rest of her life.

She put her money on the line on February 2, 1888.

"The Line" was Washington Street.

The Line ran for three blocks from First to Third Avenues South. At one end was the Dexter Horton Bank (predecessor of Seattle First National) and at the other end were Lou Graham's place and the largest Roman Catholic church in town, Our Lady Of Good Help. (During the depression of 1893 the latter were referred to as the two most financially solvent institutions in town).

In Lou's days, when prostitutes were booked at the city jail, they listed their occupation as "seamstress" . . . and there were more seamstresses on The Line between those two great financial institutions, Lou Graham's place and Dexter Horton's bank, than anywhere else in town. Billy the Mug's saloon, also famous historically, was located along The Line at Second Avenue South. Seattle's first City Hall (now occupied by the Salvation Army) was half a block above The Line on Second Avenue between Yesler Way and Washington Street—showing how wisely Lou had chosen her location.

It was her policy that private booths and whatever libation suited the occasion always were available at no cost to representatives of Seattle's city government—any time of the day or night.

More city business was transacted at Lou's than at City Hall.

South of Lou's and out toward the tideflats, which at that time came as far east as the railroad depots, was the city's tenderloin—known varyingly as the "white chapel" or "black chapel" district. Respectability went down First Avenue South on both sides of the street for about three blocks. There was a big mill on piling over the tideflats almost as far as Dearborn Street. But the area in between was a place where a man went at his own risk.

In his admirable and accurate little book, *This City Of Ours*, J. Willis Sayre said that the Sons of the Profits sold their land to the Chinese along The Line, which forced the city to grow north, because the Chinese were unpopular in town during the 1880's. I'm sure that Sayre knew better, but he was writing his book under the sponsorship of Seattle Public School District Number One, which undoubtedly would not permit a dissertation on prostitution and gambling, however economically important they were to Seattle's evolution.

Sayre was correct in that the city did grow north. But I hate to see the Chinese get the blame. It went north because certain businesses did not prefer to function next door to the seamstresses or Billy the Mug's, which really was a pretty wild place.

Despite the northward movement, Seattle's tenderloin was the greatest economic resource that the city had during the period of Lou's participation. Prostitutes were required to pay $10 per month. Gamblers paid $50 per month per gambling table. These funds operated the city . . . and had they not been there to pay there might not have been any city later on.

Like all of the other Sons of the Profits, Lou had set money aside and was able to rebuild immediately after The Fire . . . and she adhered to the new code which stipulated that only brick and stone buildings could be constructed in the burned area, which included Lou's establishment and all of the rest of the city's tenderloin. Lou bought additional land and erected a new brick building that was about eight times more pretentious than her original establishment. Some idea of the kind of wealth she had acquired during the eighteen months she had been in business before the fire wiped her out shows on the records. She paid $3,000 for her corner lot in the first place. When she took on additional land after the fire, she paid $25,000 for it.

In the ensuing years, the Dexter Horton Bank has been moved to a fine new location across the street from the Seattle Public Library . . . the Great Northern bought the Catholic church property when it built its tunnel under the city. Only Lou's house (not home) remains as a great historical landmark in the area.

It presently is occupied by the Union Gospel Mission.

Ah, women . . . Amen

The fire clearly indicates what I mean by the fact that Lou was a Son of the Profits. There were lots of women engaged in the same profession as Lou. But they were improvident. They didn't own their property. And when the fire burned them out, that was that. They couldn't rebuild on their former locations because they didn't own the ground . . . and they didn't have the capital to build again. As a net result they were forced to resume operations wherever they could find housing. That meant they became scattered throughout the city.

This created a crisis in city finances.

It also created a lot of squawks from the citizenry in the residential neighborhoods. They complained that men were calling at such-and-such an address at all hours of the night and disturbing the neighborhood.

Fines weren't being paid on time—and at that period the city's operation depended on those fines. Policemen were all over town trying to pacify neighbors and at the same time collect the fines.

Finally, some of the business leaders of the community . . . the men who owned the property down in the tenderloin . . . agreed to undertake a solution to the problem. They would build housing for the professional and business women back in the burned area where they belonged. These businessmen pointed out—rather logically, I thought—that their tenants were more or less transients and they couldn't conform to the standards set down about building only brick structures in the burned area . . . so would the city waive that restriction in this instance?

The city, with its back against the wall financially, had no other choice but to acquiesce.

They agreed it would be temporary housing. It was something like war housing of later years. They built small structures called "cribs" because they were about big enough to hold a baby crib. They were about ten feet square and were constructed in long lines—especially along Jackson Street, which at that time was on pilings.

They weren't beautiful, but they were functional.

Anyway, the girls were rounded up after the fire and stuck in this corral. But their resentment against the ceiling prices set by Lou Graham flared up, and they began to augment their income with other devices. On October 9, 1890, the *Seattle Telegraph* reported that hundreds of cribs had been built in the White Chapel District and that crime in the area had reached astronomical proportions. By the following year, the same paper reported the following information: "Scores of women are known to police as thieves and pickpockets. Robberies occur in broad daylight. Men have been known to go into alleys with hundreds of dollars and walk out half an hour later penniless . . ."

The situation was clearly out of hand. The newspapers, the good folks on the hills were yelling their heads off about it and even the Establishment was concerned. So the police adopted a new policy. If the professional and business women wouldn't conform to their code of ethics within the corral, then the police wouldn't let any custom-

ers in. Officers were stationed at "each street, alley and byway" leading into the district, the police chief reported. Even Lou was cut off.
The action was that drastic.

Lou could afford to close down while the heat was on, but the other
women in the tenderloin scattered to the four winds. The papers reported items like this: "The women are not particularly annoyed at
the quarantine. Last night many picked up bag and baggage and left
for other parts of the city." On October 12, the *Telegraph* announced that a notorious woman by the name of Mattie Arnold,
"also known as 'big-foot Matt', has been running houses in different
resident portions of the city by hanging out signs reading 'real estate
for sale' or 'fashionable dressmaking.' Big Foot Matt was arrested in
front of one of her houses at First Avenue and Pike Street and fined
$25 when she annoyed the police by bragging about her 'triumphs
over the law'."

Well, they finally reached a compromise and got the girls back
where they belonged—only to find that the police department was
in even deeper trouble than it had been before. And the "good"
women of town did it . . . thanks to the good intentions that the road
to Hell is paved with.

For goodness sake!

One of the problems that goes with being a good woman is that she
has to have something good to do. Nowadays, all the goodness is
being done by the federal government and the welfare agencies . . .
and all the good women in town tend to become alcoholics because
they have nothing good to do.

In the early days, however, there were many good things the ladies
could do. There was the picnic they prepared for launching the
Seattle and Walla Walla Railroad. And right after the fire things
were simply marvelous. They did the cooking and found sleeping
accommodations for the workers and the people who had lost their
homes. They worked harder than ever for the Women's Christian
Temperance Union, which had come to Seattle in 1887 and by 1891
had six units in the city. They organized a children's day nursery
and an orphan's home. To raise money for the support of these insti-

tutions, they managed baseball games, gave suppers and luncheons. They even sold drinking water to thirsty men from a booth in Pioneer Square—under police protection.

But the "goodest" thing of all was their concern for the city's fallen women.

Early in 1890, the ladies organized something called the Christian Committee. It would ferret out and save all the fallen women in the city of Seattle. What, somebody asked their leader, a Mrs. Ryther, is a fallen woman? Mrs. Ryther's reply was printed in the Seattle *Press-Times:* "My definition of a fallen woman is one who receives a valuable consideration as the price of her shame . . ."

I don't recall seeing the names of the members of the committee elsewhere in the history books. They were only cited in one or two issues of the newspapers at the time the fallen women were proving so troublesome to the Chief of Police. But I feel that Seattle's history would not be complete if the names were not incorporated as a part of it. Unfortunately the membership list is not entirely complete and we will have to be satisfied that the group included, besides Mrs. Ryther, Mrs. T. W. McConnell, Mrs. J. Farmers, Mrs. Ames, Mrs. Ceis and Mrs. Winnie Thomas.

For the next two years, they faithfully tromped the streets addressing their fellow females in kindly tones and saying, pardon me, but are you a fallen woman?

Well, I tell you, they found themselves working at this job seven days a week. It was a monumental effort. And they found fallen women by the thousands!

Or, at least that's what Mrs. Ryther said. She said, "We found 2,500." Mrs. McConnell said she'd had to quit for a while because her feet hurt, but she thought there were only about 2,000. The Chief of Police blew his cork and said there were only 250.

"Only 250?" Mrs. Ryther sniffed for the benefit of the *Press-Times,* "the Chief and the *Telegraph* seek to delude the public with the statement that there are but 250 fallen women in the city, and if this were generally believed, the Christian Women here would conclude that further work on the matter would not be necessary . . ."

Illustration from *West Shore Magazine* in the 1890's shows attitude of the public of that day toward police.

The papers had a splendid time with that one . . . and by interviewing one side and then the other, they kept the Chief publicly at war with the Christian Committee for weeks. Personally, I think the ladies were doing their counting just a little bit high and the Chief was going a "little" bit low. When the city actually got into it, the professional and business women and the related industries were only paying $100,000 a year based on the $10 per month per woman and the $50 per month per gambling table and the liquor licenses. For comparison's sake, if that program had been going on for a while on the same percentage basis today, it would make a difference of $5,800,000 per year in Seattle's budget.

To me the great historic point to be made concerns the deep philosophic approach to life on the part of Seattle's prostitutes who generously took time from their busy days to entertain the Christian ladies. Can you imagine a present day prostitute suffering a lady from one of the churches popping in on her for a pot of tea? And imagine the consternation of the unexpected customer!

How would he know which lady he had come to do business with?

Behold the halls of ivy!

Well, Lou wasn't bothered by the Christian ladies. They hollered their heads off in the papers that she wouldn't let 'em inside her front door, but she was not about to let them interrupt her busy day, which included a lot more business than handling her four-story brick establishment. When she wanted a peaceful cup of tea, she took it at her home at 2106 East Madison Street—a landmark that went the way of the bulldozer in 1966. She had her stocks and bonds to take care of . . . and there is the legend which I don't think is at all incompatible with her personality, that during the depressing days of 1893 when Jacob Furth couldn't find the money to loan a worthy prospect, he gave the man a note to Lou who was good for $500 if Jacob Furth endorsed the man. Lou is supposed to have saved the fortunes of many of our first families today with similar loans.

As a sort of favor to the Establishment, Lou also attended to the post graduate studies of some of our young men in the early days. Her educational facilities provided the young bucks of wealthy families with a brand of finishing school their mothers never learned about.

No young businessman was really considered a man about town until he could discuss with ease the interior decorations of Lou's establishment . . . and some of the finer points of the distinguished young ladies who were their mentors in that particular phase of their education.

One young man, whom I fear shall have to remain nameless, had it over his friends on that front. In those days, all of the best young men were members of the various volunteer hose companies of the Fire Department, and the insurance companies offered prizes to the hose company that had the first man on the scene of a fire. At one point Lou Graham's house had a small fire on the first floor. The young man in question was the first volunteer fireman to show up on the scene . . .

He simply slid down the drain pipe from Lou's top floor.

Lou's principal method of advertising took the form of carriage rides up and down the main streets on a Sunday afternoon. Dressed in their best finery, the young ladies of her establishment were regularly put on display . . . and no man of distinction in Seattle had any difficulty in pointing out the fact when there was a new girl added to Lou's ensemble. Lou accompanied the girls on these trips, waving grandly here and there to the leading citizens who were her personal friends.

Lou kept valuables belonging to her customers in her safe while they were in town . . . and on her death, Jacob Furth, the administrator of her estate, saw to it that the men who had diamonds, watches and money entrusted to Lou got their treasures with no embarrassing questions asked. Among the notes in her safe was a pledge of $100 toward subsidizing the construction of the Battleship "Nebraska." It was paid posthumously and became part of the 40 per cent of the pledges made that were actually paid in. Her greatest financial contribution, however, was approximately a quarter of a million dollars which went to the Common Schools in King County after her death.

Meanwhile, although Lou remained aloof from it all, the gals in the tenderloin were beginning to realize what a large segment of the city budget came from their earnings. They found that when they

kicked up their heels a little, nobody did anything about it as long
as they kept up their installment payments to the City Treasurer. So
they really went after the money. Many of their cribs were located
on pilings above the tidelands and many an unwary man found himself broke and chilly in the middle of an incoming tide as he recovered there from the knockout drops that had been administered
at some time the night before. The coroner also found himself doing
a lot of business in those muddy tideflats on cold winter mornings.

So the City Council passed an ordinance forbidding trap doors in
the Skid Road. After reports on the number of cracked heads that
appeared to have been obtained accidentally, by men who woke up
in the street with their wallets gone, the Council passed another
ordinance prohibiting flower pots in windows above the first floor.

A girl with a good aim could pick up more money with flower pots
than in bed.

The crackdown

Life may have been dull among the folks on the property that had
fine views of Mt. Rainier or the Olympics, but it certainly wasn't
down on the Skid Road . . . and the fellows running the newspapers
found that their circulation skyrocketed when they played up sin.

In the early 90's, despite the income that the city's tenderloin meant
to the business community, things got so bad that the Establishment
realized that it and all of the other Sons of the Profits might have to
start paying real estate taxes and support the city themselves. There
was too much of the philosophy in the tenderloin that if it was going
to pay the piper, it would call the tune. The Establishment first decided they would try and appease the growing rumbles from the
Blue Nose side of Seattle's split personality with a few token police
raids and temporarily putting the lid on the vice in the community.

So, in 1890, a luckless fellow by the name of Harry White was asked
to be mayor and see if he couldn't control things a little better. He
set the Police Department about the business of neatening up the
Skid Road . . . and the Police Chief decided on a general round-up
below The Line.

On Valentine's Day, 1891, 38 years and 364 days after Arthur Denny and the other fellows drove their stakes and founded the town, a rookie cop lit the match that blew the powder keg and started what has been unofficially dubbed the Pubic War.

Without even knowing who she was—he arrested Lou Graham.

Boom!

Trial and error

I'll just take a running guess and say that there were five or six hundred other women in the same field of endeavor as Lou who could have been arrested, and nobody would have been any the worse. But that dumb cop had to pick the one and only one that had the blessing of the Establishment. They had to stand behind her, no matter what the cost. Everybody in town except, perhaps, Mrs. Arthur Denny, knew it. The rest of the professional and business women hated Lou's insides for setting prices that the Establishment generally was able to enforce. The people in the view property knew about her through dinner table conversations at social affairs. And certainly every business man who knew anything at all was aware that she was operating under an arrangement with the Establishment. Most of them had taken advantage of her facilities for some of their out-of-town customers—or perhaps even for themselves.

Lou was the one madam in town that had to be protected if the Establishment wished to remain in power.

Now she had been hooked by the machinery of the law . . . and not even the Establishment could stop the normal processes of that phase of our government.

The newspapers, realizing all of this, gave her arrest their joyous headlines like the following: "Lou Graham Arrested! Notorious Madame Nailed! 'Madame' Lou Graham has been brought to trial! The proprietress of the most notorious house of ill-repute . . . the most gorgeous and sumptuously-furnished Palace of Sin in the city is in custody . . . It is a palatial three-story brick building, erected, at large cost, from the wages of sin . . ."

Was the fat ever in the fire!

On February fifteenth, 39 years after the town was founded, Lou's attorneys asked for postponement of the case until Saturday, the 21st. They needed time to plan . . . and here's what happened on the 21st.

The streets were lined with onlookers, from Lou's establishment to the police court which was housed in an old building some two blocks from Lou's. And Lou, arriving in her carriage with some of her girls, was dressed to the hilt. The papers said she was clad "in the richest of raiment . . . and jewels . . . adorned with a fashionable seal-skin sacque and bedazzled with diamonds and other jewels . . ." Lou waved gaily to her friends like Caesar returning from a triumphant war.

Long before court convened, businessmen assigned to be on hand had jammed the courtroom to what the newspapers said was "the point of suffocation." The judge had been operating with a panel of 18 veniremen, but the crowd in the courtroom was so dense and the courtroom attendants so hard of hearing that only two of the men on the panel were able to get into the courtroom. The judge selected those two and because the others were missing, he had to make up the balance of the jury from the men in the room.

The Establishment's people had appeared there en masse just in case something like this might happen.

Then Lou paraded in followed by some of her beauties and flanked by the two attorneys who would represent her in this historic occasion.

Her attorneys, thanks to the Establishment, were two of the most prominent men in town.

One of them was J. T. Ronald, who would head a reform ticket in the mayoralty campaign the following year . . . and serve as a Superior Court Judge in King County for the final fifty years of his life. Ronald had just completed a term as Prosecuting Attorney for the County. He was about six feet three inches tall and was noted for his ability to beller like a bull in court. Lou came about up to his belt buckle.

Her other attorney in this police court case was Samuel Piles, who had been assistant district attorney under Ronald and would one day be a United States Senator from the State of Washington. Piles was the best-dressed man in town and I defer to C. T. Conover's description of him in his book *Mirrors of Seattle:* "He had all of the best of it to a person of discriminating taste and invariably appeared in a dignified frock coat, light trousers and silk hat, all in the latest mode, with raven black tresses and a mustache . . ."

The Establishment didn't do things by halves.

Ronald, a great showman, handled the proceedings with an occasional whispered conference between himself and Piles. Ronald went right after the first juror to be examined by the counsel for the defense . . . and here's how it went:

Ronald: The *Press-Times* says here (Ronald held up the paper) that no jury can be secured to convict and no decent citizen would acquit these women. Now, are you decent or are you not?

Answer: I try to be.

Ronald: The *Press-Times* tonight charges Lou Graham with being the notorious keeper of the most expensive house of prostitution in the city. Do you believe that?

Answer: I can't believe all I read in the papers.

Ronald: You're dead right!

Ronald accepted this man as a juror and "challenged for cause" the second man who said he believed Lou was guilty until proven innocent.

At this point, the bailiff informed the judge that the building was swaying in a manner that indicated it might come down on top of everybody. He asked that the courtroom be cleared.

The judge ordered the courtroom cleared, but the crowd kept coming back in. The judge ordered the crowd out again after the jury was chosen. They began moving in a bunch and the building began to tremble. The judge cautioned the crowd to move slowly, pointing out that the building was extremely unsafe with so many people in it.

"Let 'em stay if you want," Ronald bellered, according to a press report of the day, "I will live or die with you!"

The judge, who was somewhat more conservative than Ronald, had the folks moved out and the trial went ahead. The arresting officer said he'd seen Lou on the corner . . . and he'd been ordered to arrest any woman he saw in the area, so he'd arrested her. He didn't know what her occupation was. A second officer testified he was not aware of the general reputation of Lou's house. A captain of police testified he had never heard of anyone in the neighborhood giving the building the reputation of being a house of ill fame and did not know who lived in the building. A police lieutenant testified he'd seen Lou Graham's name on the door and another officer testified he hadn't seen Lou Graham's name on the door.

It is clearly evident that Lou's good judgment in remaining aloof from the other people in the neighborhood was wise. The newspapers seemed to know all about her . . . but the witnesses didn't know nothin' . . . and hadn't seen nothin'.

With this overwhelming testimony in their hands, the jury retired to the jury room to deliberate the matter.

The deliberations took three minutes—by the clock. The verdict: Not Proven.

The Establishment had stuck by its own . . . and won.

This was the only time Lou ever appeared in court. She was released from custody and returned to her palatial commercial establishment where she practiced her profession in peace and paid her fair share in civic enterprises until she died twelve years later.

That was the end of trouble for Lou . . .

But not for Mayor White. He was considered expendable. A few months later, his resignation on the grounds of ill health, written on *P.-I.* stationery, was accepted by the City Council.

Although it may have been an underling who made the mistake, the Mayor was the boss and had to take the blame for the unfortunate arrest of Lou Graham.

So they fired the mayor.

XI

This Little Piggy Stayed Home

Then there was this gold rush.

The Mayor went. The Fire Department went . . . and the Police Department.

But not the Sons of the Profits.

Oh, no.

They stayed home and mined the miners. And they were very fair. In the decade that followed the arrival of the steamer "Portland" on July 17, 1897 with a whole bunch of gold on board from the Klondike, about $200,000,000 worth of gold came back through Seattle . . .

And the Sons of the Profits only kept half.

She's mine, all mine!

Seattle bought Alaska on October 18, 1867, just thirty years before the arrival of the "Portland," because the Russians wouldn't let our fishermen use the toilet facilities at Sitka.

I'd say it was the biggest real estate development in Seattle's early history—even bigger than Ballard. Of course, we had to work through the federal government because not even Henry Yesler could spring the $7,200,000 payment. But it was big, real big—here was a hunk of property twice the size of the state of Texas and one-fifth the size of the whole country.

We were pretty pleased at that purchase and became the only city in the United States with its own private Territory. Of course, the negotiations took quite some time. It all happened because the Russians were downright dirty about even letting us catch fish around Sitka, much less permitting us to refresh ourselves in Sitka. So one day one of our fishermen told the Russians we'd sic the United States Navy on them and that would teach them.

In January of 1866, we got a memorial through the Territorial Legislature asking President Andrew Johnson either to say "sic 'em" or buy the place—with the emphasis on the latter. President Johnson sent our statement on to a fellow named William Seward who became our real estate agent in the venture.

Although some people thought he had lost his mind—he got it for a nice price because the Russians figured that if Seattle bought Alaska, Great Britain wouldn't get it.

In our enthusiasm we put a statue of Seward in Volunteer Park . . . and it's probably still there unless somebody moved it over to make a parking lot.

And, except for the fracas in 1897 when a lot of towns made a college try at taking her away from us, Alaska had been a wholly-owned subsidiary of Seattle ever since.

Six (count 'em—6!) gold rushes

Seattle was a town that liked the rolling sound of the word "gold". Charlie Terry made a pile on the Fraser River rush in the spring of 1858 . . . we got our share of travellers from San Francisco to the Boise, Idaho rush in 1864, and in the strikes in the Upper Columbia and Coeur d'Alene mountains a year later. In 1878 the discovery of gold on the Sultan River north of this city brought the miners through here in droves, and in 1880 a rush to the Skagit River did the same thing.

Long before the Klondike rush we learned it cost the average man about $500 to grubstake himself for a prospecting expedition— whether or not he struck it rich.

The real dough was made by the guys who outfitted the miners on the way out and gave the lucky ones some place to spend their money on the way back.

By the time the big strike came along in 1897 we had the business of mining the miners honed to a fine edge. We learned what the miners needed on the way out and developed big outfits like Schwabacher and Seattle Hardware to provide them with it. And we knew what the rich ones wanted on the way back and Lou Graham and John Considine and the folks in the tenderloin were experts in providing them with that.

We got the miners coming and going.

We even developed a few privately owned assay offices to refine the gold dust and nuggets and all . . . and our banks worked out a system whereby they would advance money to the miners while they were waiting to find out from the assay offices how much their poke was worth . . . and we stored the gold for them in our bank vaults pending its purchase by the U.S. Government.

Prelude to "Our Song"

In the late seventies, there was a pretty big gold deposit discovered in what is known today as Juneau, but nobody felt like crossing the mountains into the Yukon Territory because the Indians up there had developed the nasty practice of killing anybody who did.

The City Council and the Seattle Chamber of Commerce felt that was no way to run "Our Territory" and we finally got our rich uncle, Sam, to negotiate a treaty with the Indians that stopped this barbaric practice.

The newspaper in Sitka thought that was nice of us and late that year printed a little editorial comment:

> When Seattle shall become, as it must, the true terminus of the Northern Pacific Railroad and the city that its natural water advantages will make it, unquestionably its proximity and accessibility to Alaska will make it the lap into which our gathered treasures will be emptied. God speed Seattle's growth and Alaska's development.

I don't like to be suspicious, but this has the ring of a Seattle Chamber of Commerce publicity handout. The folks in Alaska don't like us *that* well even now. On the other hand, perhaps it's a good thing the Establishment did let the Chamber fool around making friends in Alaska where nobody figured it could do any harm. The Establishment was too busy with railroads, anyway.

We kept hacking away at trade with Alaska all during the seventies and the eighties . . . and by the end of the seventies, San Francisco had given up the ghost. In the early eighties, thanks to the Pacific Coast Steamship Company, Portland was big in the Alaska shipping business. But when John Leary yanked the mail contract away from that city and brought it to Puget Sound, Pacific Coast practically abandoned its Portland-Alaska trips. By the late eighties, Pacific Coast, which easily was the giant of shipping companies on the coast, abandoned service between Alaska and Portland altogether.

Seattle just plain had the right geographic location . . . we were closer to Alaska than Portland.

By 1888, our relations with "Our Territory" were looking pretty good. Some $7,000,000 worth of canned salmon was coming out of the Territory through Seattle to the waiting world . . . along with a lot of furs. And there were literally dozens of gold mines in the Territory dribbling two or three million dollars worth of gold through Seattle. According to one of the Seattle papers there were reports of new gold finds every day that year.

And in 1888 the Chamber of Commerce sent its first goodwill mission to Alaska. Happily, it was a more successful mission than the one that took place a decade later and little by little our trade relations with Alaska were cemented.

In 1895, the biggest shipment of gold out of the Territory to date took place, and a combination of circumstances sent miners to Alaska in droves. On March 3, 1895, Charles E. Peabody and a couple of other guys includng Walter Oakes, the son of the Northern Pacific's Thomas Oakes, formed the Alaska Steamship Company with one boat—the "Willapa."

On its departure from Schwabacher's wharf, the "Willapa" carried seventy-nine passengers and was offered more freight than it could haul. Several mining outfits and some twenty horses were headed for

Skagway and Dyea. The lure of gold and the low prices for getting at it were a combination that filled the northbound ships during that summer.

By March of 1896 hundreds of miners had been outfitted in Seattle and were awaiting the departure of the northbound ships. Among those who stepped on board were Mr. and Mrs. Thomas S. Lippy. He was a secretary for the Seattle Y.M.C.A.—

Than which nobody on earth could be poorer.

There were no artificial computers in those days, but the sweet sound of miners' dollars tinkling in the till as the summer of 1896 rolled along set that certain something clinking in the minds of our merchants . . . and they upped their orders for mining supplies from the wholesale houses around the country.

Oh, kiss me Kate!

On August 16, 1896, Kate Carmack, the Indian bride of argonaut John Carmack (we called all of the miners argonauts in memory of Mr. Jason and his golden fleece and the Forty Niners) was giving her face a bath in a pool in Rabbit Creek up along the Yukon.

She saw some pretty yellow rocks at the bottom of the pool and thought wouldn't they make a nice necklace for her pretty brown neck. At least, that's how the story goes. It's just a personal opinion, but if Kate had been following John all over the Yukon Territory looking for gold, I'll lay a bet she knew what she had when she approached husband John with her find.

John got the favorite family pie tin out of the cupboard and washed out some sand in the creek. When the sand was gone, he looked at the yellow stuff in the bottom of the pan and, I would presume, let out a whoop. With one swipe at the sand in Rabbit Creek, he had come up with five bucks worth of gold. Then he got one nugget worth twelve dollars.

John and Kate staked out a claim five hundred feet wide and running from ridge to ridge on either side of the creek. Within a month, John and Kate were rich beyond their wildest dreams. The name of the creek was changed from Rabbit to Bonanza. And before the end of the year there were a hundred and fifty mining claims being worked in the area.

Tom Lippy and his wife were among those who were working claims in the district . . . and the word trickled back to Seattle that Tom had improved his cash position considerably over what it had been in his days as a Y.M.C.A. secretary.

Later, Carmack would shower dollars from the top of the Occidental Hotel upon the outstretched hands of the grateful populace below . . . and Kate, who always was confused by civilization, would blaze her way back to her hotel room on the ornate interior woodwork of the hotel.

In the meantime, Seattle merchants whose mental antennae were acutely attuned to the sound of gold, ordered an ever-increasing supply of materials that were near and dear to the hearts of the argonauts. And in January, the Chamber memorialized Congress on behalf of "Our Territory." We pointed out that in 1894, $2,000,000 in gold had come through Seattle out of Alaska . . . in 1895 that amount had increased to $3,000,000, and in 1896 it had gone up to $4,000,000.

Alaska, we observed, needs a Delegate to Congress.

Get off your bloomin' Assay Office

By March more than a dozen Alaska mining companies had their headquarters in Seattle . . . some 250 miners had reported back with $60,000 worth of gold.

When the miners assembled their little nest eggs, there was always someone willing to relieve them of their heavy burden. While the Royal Canadian Mounted Police protected them in the Northwest Territory and the express companies protected them while their gold was in transit, they felt they could get cheated out of their eye teeth at the counting house.

Nobody knew for sure just exactly how much gold existed in any given supply of gold dust or nuggets and how much was silver or copper or other metal until the stuff had been melted down into bars. Seattle's bankers were quite willing to take the stuff off the miners' hands in its raw state, but the banks were what you might call conservative in their evaluation of the real net worth of the raw material.

Inasmuch as the net worth could run from 20 to 50 per cent off of the actual weight the miner had in his poke, he wanted an official government appraisal of his net . . . not one by some banker who might weigh in his thumb and forearm on the scale when the count was being made.

So the Seattle Chamber of Commerce, which was betting that Carmack & Co. had hit on something big, realized before any other Chamber in the country that if we were to get the miners coming as well as going, we jolly well better have a Federal Government Assay Office in Seattle.

And on April 21, 1897 at 3:30 in the afternoon, the Board of Trustees of the Chamber, which was chaired by one of our prominent attorneys, General J. B. Metcalfe, and attended by I. A. Nadeau, general manager of the Northern Pacific in Seattle (we were friends now), Thomas Prosch and J. J. McGilvra, made the first move to get a Government Assay Office.

In another memorial to Congress, we pointed out that Seattle was the principal and natural distribution point for Alaska . . . that hundreds of miners had purchased their supplies in Seattle before going north and then had been forced to go to San Francisco, which had the nearest Government Assay Office, when most of their debts were in Seattle. We told Congress that we were the railroad and steamboat center of Puget Sound and that more ships than ever before had left the city laden with miners headed north and that we could expect a greater influx of gold than ever before. We told Congress the need was urgent . . . we couldn't wait for its next session in December . . . would it please get off its assay office right now.

Congress told us to try jumping into the lake.

The hoary story

Now we get into the myth about the "Ton of Gold."

I don't know at what point this story was concocted, but for at least half a century it has been a popular myth among Seattle historians that Seattle became the key city in the gold rushes to the Klondike and then to Nome because somebody was bright enough to inform the world that a ton of gold arrived in Seattle aboard the steamer "Portland" on July 17, 1897.

The psychology underlying the ton of gold story was that in Seattle they don't measure gold by ounces or by pounds—but by tons. In other words our unit of measure was something over $660,000, not the usual $20.67 an ounce.

It was a magic wand that we waved once and presto—instant riches.

Well, that isn't the way it happened . . . any more than you can get the barnacles off the bottom of a boat by putting it in fresh water . . . or pull a tooth by wishing it was out.

We weren't the bright boys that figured out the ton of gold gimmick . . . and for that matter, we didn't even try to use it in attracting miners to this city for their outfitting.

It was San Francisco that tried to milk the ton of gold story—and it didn't work.

The "Portland," which previously had been impounded a number of times for smuggling Chinese and opium in the United States, arrived in Seattle on the 17th. On the 16th, the Associated Press in San Francisco had placed a story on the wire reading in part, "The ton of gold which was turned into the Selby Smelting Company office on Wednesday (July 14) is only a slight indication of what is to follow in the near future . . ."

The AP dispatch was referring to the something more than a million dollars worth of gold that had arrived in San Francisco aboard the steamer "Excelsior" earlier in the week. Among those on board the "Excelsior" was the poor but proud Tom Lippy, the young man from the Seattle Y.M.C.A. Mr. Lippy was still proud—but no longer poor. He had brought down the first of many shipments that would come from his mining claim.

It consisted of 1,500 pounds of gold . . . about $500,000!

Of course there are some grounds for the myth about the ton of gold. The people in Seattle were well aware that something big in the way of gold was aboard the "Portland" and the *P.-I.* dispatched a reporter to meet the vessel off of Port Townsend and interview the argonauts on board. And, although it didn't hit the wire service, the story which appeared in the *P.-I.* the morning of the 17th did say a ton of gold was coming in.

But the *P.-I.* and the *Seattle Times* were not the bosom buddies then that they are today, and Alden J. Blethen, the pugnacious publisher of the *Times,* found in that news story something for which he could once more take the *P.-I.* to task.

The *Times* informed its readers there was only a *half* a ton of gold on board.

The scrambled yeggs

By 1897, when the word trickled out to the world that the Klondike gold rush was the beginning of something big, Seattle had been wooing Alaska for thirty years. Everybody else had consigned it to the "Seward's Folly" file and forgot about it.

But, oh boy, did they get interested when they got wind of all that loot!

San Francisco, Portland, Tacoma, Vancouver, Victoria and Juneau all suddenly discovered that each of them was the logical outfitting point for the gold prospectors and started thinking of reasons why everybody should commence his career as a millionaire by departing from their city.

They all agreed on one thing: Seattle was the worst place anybody could depart from.

San Francisco pointed out it knew all about outfitting gold miners because nearly half a century before it had outfitted them for the '49 rush. It pointed out it had good hotels and restaurants and a nice climate . . . and put on an exposition dedicated to showing miners how to mine. It said that argonauts in search of the golden fleece would first get themselves "fleeced" if they bought their outfits in Seattle.

Portland pointed out that miners could get an outfit for $46.05 less in that city than in Seattle . . . and because all steamers left for Alaska from Portland—just making a way stop out of Seattle (a nasty lie) —miners who wanted berths should start in Portland.

The Oregonian, however, printed a prophetic editorial when the business community down there was raising a campaign kitty to get and miners' trade. It was estimated that 50,000 miners would attend the gold rush—outfitting at an average of $500 each for a prize of $25,000,000. *The Oregonian* said: "Portland never does things by halves. We will be satisfied with no ordinary contributions. If you do not subscribe more liberally than you ever did before, you'll see Seattle go ahead with a bound..."

The Oregonian was right, Seattle went ahead with a bound—and has stayed ahead ever since.

Tacoma sent phoney stories out under the guise of news about prominent barons and dukes from Europe who said they planned to go to Tacoma to outfit rather than Seattle because they would get cheated in Seattle. Tacoma also made the pitch that all ships leaving for the north left from Tacoma—with Seattle as a way stop—causing Alden J. Blethen to pull the telephone off the wall in his office ... which was a habit of his when he got mad. In a note to the Chamber of Commerce, Blethen commented as follows:

> Let me not only have the names of the steamboats that are owned and operated and have their principal offices and starting points at Seattle, but also the names of the steamers which operate from Tacoma, if any, and all of the sailings for the Yukon Territory, whether they go to Skagway, Dyea or St. Michaels, and I will give it to Mr. Cowles (Paul Cowles, AP Chief in San Francisco) and we will pound the life out of those whelps in Tacoma.

Tacoma shortly changed its tactics and came up with the remarkable propaganda line that all great cities were at the heads of bodies of water ... Tacoma was at the head of Puget Sound and therefore was a great city.

Anyway, as Blethen later put it, we "settled this hash on Puget Sound in short order and to the advantage of Seattle ..."

Vancouver and Victoria pitched that the Klondike was in Canadian territory and men who outfitted there didn't have to pay a duty. The

Canadian Pacific Railroad cut the price of a transcontinental ticket to $25, which was about one-fourth of the going rate in the United States. They kept representatives in Seattle who button-holed prospectors and gave them a free trip to Canada to get them to outfit there. The Canadians also made problems for Americans crossing the border.

But we had a neat answer for this kind of stuff.

We pointed out that Canadian bacon was wheat-fed and would not stand up under the moisture in the gold fields.

That did it.

I liked Juneau's propaganda line the best . . . it was so homespun. Juneau pointed out that outfits in Seattle were stowed at the bottom of the ships' holds, while horses and mules were stowed just above them—and pee'd all over them for the three weeks' trip to Alaska.

In which we break our pick

If you don't note from the preceding that the other cities on the coast had a mutual enmity for Seattle in common, then I simply haven't been telling the story right. The combined adverse publicity performed the service requested by the unknown politician who said, "I don't care what you call me as long as you spell my name right . . ."

But, while the other cities were trying to get the miners to outfit with them on the way up, we were already trying for the higher stakes—getting them when they returned with the money.

On June 21, four days after the "Portland" arrived in town, the Chamber of Commerce fired off another memorial to Congress on the vital question of a Government Assay Office.

This memorial informed that august body of the "startling events of the last few days" during which "two steamships have arrived from Alaska during the past week, bringing with them a hundred miners and $1,208,000 in gold dust and nuggets. Two of the men had over $100,000 each and six others had over $40,000 . . . nor did the gold brought down by any means represent all of their earnings, for large amounts were left in claims and other investments in the mining company..."

To put the amounts in perspective, multiply them by three to get them in today's dollars . . . and then add on whatever you like for the income tax that would be charged today.

We further pointed out that there were single shovelfuls of earth containing $100 in gold . . . single nuggets worth $200 . . . and single pans worth $800 . . . that a day laborer earned $15 per day as opposed to the $1.25 he earned in the states. The memorial also said:

> By the energy and enterprise of our citizens, and by the lines of transportation and trade they have developed, this unprecedentedly rich country has been made tributary to our own . . .

> Now that the wealth of the far north country is known, efforts of every kind are being made to wrest from us its trade, to divert it to near-by foreign ports, to open new lines of communication by routes wholly without our domain, and to induce the marketing of this gold in centers in which our countrymen have no interest (Canada). To prevent this diversion is our aim and endeavor . . .

We pointed out that there were three Assay Offices on the Atlantic Coast and only one on the Pacific Coast, yet more gold had been mined in a single year on the Pacific Coast than in a century on the Atlantic Coast. We then got to the meat of the cocoanut by pointing out that the miners had brought the gold some 6,000 miles to deliver it in Seattle and it was not right to force them into a journey of another thousand miles to "get upon it the only satisfactory statement of value—the certificate of the United States assayer."

Thomas Prosch wrote the memorial, which stated flatly that if we didn't get an Assay Office in Seattle, the gold would go to Great Britain.

Congress told us to try another lake.

The right man again

Although it drove some of our individual citizens absolutely wild, the city didn't get its propaganda campaign underway for ten weeks after firing the Assay Office memorial off to Congress. All of the other cities competing with us for the argonauts' trade went at it hammer and tongs. Tacoma and Portland had sales representatives on every train headed to the Pacific Northwest. Our competitors lobbed literature into the travel offices of the nation.

And we sat.

Finally, at 8 o'clock in the evening on September 29, a hundred and fifty fellas got hijacked into a meeting of the Seattle Chamber of Commerce . . . and I'm really quite fond of the understatement with which it was played in the *Chamber of Commerce Minutes:* "Judge Burke addressed the meeting forceably upon the necessity of fostering the Alaska Trade . . . Upon the termination of Judge Burke's address . . . subscription lists were opened and the meeting subscribed $990 a month for five months . . ."

Schwabacher Brothers headed the list with $75 per month. The $50 per month subscribers were Cooper & Levy, Moran brothers, Seattle Hardware, MacDougall & Southwick and Fischer Brothers. Burke, himself, tossed in $20 a month.

We were going after $100,000,000 worth of trade with less than five thousand bucks. (The subscription later rose to $10,000.)

No wonder Seattle is the top dog!

Well, once more we lucked out with the right man at the right time in one Erastus Brainerd.

Mr. Brainerd was the first publicist to function on a major scale in the Pacific Northwest. He was a patron of the Arts. He considered himself a "statesman of the press" who advanced only admirable projects. He was a journalist who had served his apprenticeship on New York, Philadelphia and Atlanta newspapers before coming on stage as the directing genius of Seattle's little gold rush project at the age of forty-two years. He was enough of an egoist that he presented the Library of Congress with a fourteen volume scrapbook of his accomplishments. It included invitations to important social parties and the complete record of what he did to promote Seattle during the Klondike gold rush.

He was the editor of the *Post-Intelligencer* for a number of years, the consul for Paraguay with jurisdiction covering Alaska, Washington, Oregon and Idaho. He died in a state mental hospital at Steilacoom on Christmas Day, 1922 at the age of 67 years, leaving an estate of $2,000.

He was not a Son of the Profits.

But the Sons exhibited a remarkable degree of intelligence when they hired him to publicize Seattle as the city that was the key to Alaska.

Brainerd totally disregarded the ton of gold story which many historians credit him with creating. The heart of his campaign consisted of asking people all over the world if they or any of their neighbors had contracted the "Klondike Fever", and providing them with information that outfitting in Seattle for the gold rush was the only sure cure for the disease.

The psychology was simple.

San Francisco had caught the imagination of the world with its ton of gold story. Seattle would capitalize on this by thundering along with information on what interested people could do about participating in this magical event.

In addition, single-handedly Brainerd made our friendly neighbor to the north a "Foreign Power" and declared war, personally, on Great Britain . . . not because he hated those people, but because it was the best way he could think of to get Congress to come through with a Government Assay Office in the City of Seattle . . .

And it was pretty good.

The time and the technique

Just four years before Brainerd came on the scene, newspapers throughout the country had been permitted into the elite corps of the Associated Press, which was organized originally by six New York newspapers in 1848, and had been used exclusively by them. The newly-blessed newspapers thought it was the greatest thing since the invention of ice cream.

Associated Press dispatches came in by the yard and were printed in the smallest type the newspapers could buy. The front pages of the papers were filled with AP dispatches . . . and advertising. And nobody read them.

The local news, on the other hand was printed in larger type on pages 4 and 5—and everybody read that.

Well, Tacoma wasn't the only town that wooed its Associated Press correspondent with what it considered would be mortal blows to Seattle. All of the competing cities blissfully fed misinformation about Seattle into the maw of that wire service.

And Brainerd subscribed to a clipping service.

Most of the editors around the country neglected reading the massive influx of Associated Press news, and it was to their great astonishment that they began to get personal letters out of Seattle stating that their papers had printed such and such misinformation about Seattle and we demanded a correction.

We always got it.

We always got it on the well-read pages of local news.

We always slipped in a load of propaganda favoring Seattle as the jumping off spot for the Klondike gold rush.

By this route alone, we got five times as much space—in a better-read section of the country's papers—than our competitors.

Brainerd, who was an excellent writer, then would take his newspaper clippings from around the country and quote them in magazine articles about Seattle and the Klondike Fever. He then would write more newspaper articles from the magazine articles and more magazine articles from the newspaper articles, etc. . . . etc.

Brainerd initiated another device that has been used by publicists ever since for "making" local news. On a systematic basis Seattle's businessmen were asked to have their employees write letters about Seattle back to the old home town paper. The Chamber furnished the letters and the postage. The employees just addressed the letters and signed their names.

We hit it big on that basis, too.

For the Christmas season in 1897, Brainerd sent sets of beautiful pictures of Seattle to all government officials, members of Congress, governors and heads of foreign countries. He got lots of thank-you notes from important people—all of which were included in the scrapbooks given to the Library of Congress.

But he really hit the news jackpot in the set he sent to the Emperor of Germany.

The latter thought it was a bomb and had it destroyed—much to the delight of the world press.

Distance . . . dangers . . . expense

His cutest gimmick, though, and the one that brought the greatest discernible economic results to the merchants who were paying his salary, was the one that involved using State of Washington stationery.

Brainerd concocted the idea that his stuff would have greater impact if it looked like it was a legitimate part of the machinery of government. He tried to suck the Governor into signing a letter to mayors and other governors throughout the country, but had to be satisfied with getting the signature of William D. Jenkins, the Secretary of State . . . which really wasn't bad because he did have the official stationery he needed.

The idea was this: The State of Washington had taken cognizance of the fact that Seattle was outfitting so many miners from around the country who had contracted the Klondike Fever, that the time had come to offer some profound governmental advice that would be a service to the Fever victims yet to come.

The document delivered to the public officials involved carried the heading: "Distance, Dangers and Probable Expense." It discussed the problems and logistics of the trip to the gold fields. It asked such questions as, "Do your people have sufficient money to go north . . . where do they expect to outfit . . . how can they be contacted with proper information before they leave . . . and are any women planning to go?"

It was diffidently suggested that for effective coverage, the mayor or governor might hold a press conference and release the helpful message from Washington State with any appropriate comment he might wish to make.

Everybody was happy. The public officials had a new angle for getting their names in the papers. The papers themselves appreciated this aspect of the releases because the news was timely, official and of local interest. People who planned to go north told their local papers about their plans. Brainerd got the papers and Seattle got a whole slew of names and addresses of potential customers which were slipped on the q.t. to the merchants supporting the Brainerd program financially.

The individual letters from mayors came in by the hundreds and the smaller the town the sincerer the response. Sumner T. Bisby, Mayor of Keokuk, Iowa, and several other mayors confessed that they, themselves had contracted the Klondike Fever and planned to be arriving in Seattle soon.

Some of the comments were priceless.

The Mayor of Plymouth, Connecticut informed us that: "The fever had but one victim as far as we could learn. The young man, having married since, has recovered since and we think there is no danger from this point . . ."

W. R. Thomas, the Mayor of Oakland, California, opined there were between five hundred and a thousand people who had contracted the fever and that about 50 per cent of them were fully prepared for the trip. On the question of whether or not any women were going, Thomas said, "A few of the women of the "new stripe" may go, but they can take care of themselves . . ."

My very favorite of them all, however, was sent to us on October 18, 1897—about three weeks after Brainerd officially took over his job. This, by the way, gives us some idea of the speed and skill with which Brainerd worked. They hadn't even raised any money until September 29 and he was getting this kind of a reply on October 18 from James L. Robeson, secretary to the mayor of Detroit:

> The city of Detroit comprises about 375,000 inhabitants and the State of Michigan several million. It is absolutely impossi-

ble for us to give you even an approximate idea of how many people there are in this city or state who are affected by the Klondike Fever.

I respectfully submit it is a matter probably only known to Providence, himself, and I doubt that if you could communicate with Providence he could give you any reliable data.

Busy, busy, busy!

While Brainerd was building his big hook to bring 'em in, the rest of the town was busier than a whorehouse during a half-price sale. The Mayor of the city was in San Francisco when the big news broke. He promptly wired his resignation and headed north for the gold fields. Dog rustling became a major enterprise because the argonauts had heard of dog sleds in Alaska and would buy almost anything with hair and four feet at about twenty bucks apiece.

The *P.-I.* got a wild hair about spelling the word "Clondycke" . . . meeting with only mediocre success in getting its advertisers to go along with the gag, so that while the editorial columns were spelling it Clondycke the advertisers clung to the traditional Klondike spelling. Finally, on September 1, 1897, John L. Wilson of Spokane, who had been appointed to an unexpired term in the United States Senate and aspired to continue in that position, bought out the *P.-I.* and got the spelling right, in time for a big special "Klondike" edition of that paper in October.

Brainerd, who aspired to be editor of the *P.-I.* one of these days, bought nearly 100,000 copies which were sent to every postmaster, library, and mayor he could find, as well as the offices of the Great Northern and Northern Pacific . . . and the telephone repairman made another call on Blethen.

About eight hundred argonauts from Seattle had already rushed to the Klondike—including most of the policemen in town. They were tired of hauling drunken miners out of Skid Road dives and up the hill to the police station in the wheelbarrows that were provided for that purpose. And three quarters of the men in the Fire Department made it out of town headed north in the first two weeks after the "Portland" arrived.

Let 'er rip!

The en masse departure of city employees suffering the Klondike Fever was a portent of change.

It had been five long years since J. T. Ronald had been elected as a Reform Mayor. Lou Graham had been plying her trade quietly, and the city's tenderloin, partly due to pressure from the moralists in town and partly to the depressing effects of the 1893 panic, had settled down to a dull roar. The trees that had been planted in the streets in 1893 by the ladies were beginning to make an impression of the model city center that had emerged from the fire. The buildings erected in the burned area had been developed with a more or less homogeneous unity . . . and the window boxes were planted and ivy had begun to grow up the sides of the brick and stone structures. Streets and sidewalks were regularly washed and swept. The Pioneer Building, referred to as the finest business structure west of Chicago, even had beautiful Italian marble in its hallways.

It was that era when we looked as slick as Fifth Avenue in New York. The "archytecks," moralists and esthetes all joined hands and clapped.

Then—the Sons of the Profits saw money coming!

Overnight all that monkey business about iron and brick and stone structures being required in the burned-out area went down the drain. Wooden structures ranging from cribs for the ladies of easy virtue to gaudy saloons and dance halls blossomed anew, ever closer to the center of the city's beauty and culture.

The merchants sold $325,000 worth of supplies to miners heading north during the month following the arrival of the "Portland." There wasn't enough room in the stores for the merchandise. Down went the decorative trees in the sidewalks. Up came stacks of merchandise as high as a man's head—and on both sides of the streets.

Second-hand stores, cheap clothing stores, questionable rooming houses sprang up overnight. One hundred Alaska mining companies with offices in Seattle were listed in the 1898 city directory. The hordes poured in—rough and tumble loggers, farm-hands, merchant

seamen . . . and the kind of business they were interested in trans-
acting didn't require Italian marble or shaded streets.

Seattle's cultural atmosphere had never been more than a block
wide, about two blocks long—and skin deep.

It was easy for her to revert to the pre-fire status, and let 'er rip!

The miners were demanding, but we were inventive and the advertising columns of the newspapers listed such important items as the
Clark Improved Air Tight Camp Stove . . . Palmer's Portable
Houses which allegedly stood up better than a tent or an old miner's
shack . . . the Holloway-Duncan Harness Company sold pack sad-
dles, straps, horse blankets and "everything required for man, horse,
dog or ox in Alaska." The Lilly-Bogardus Company sold Hydraulic
Compressed Hay for horses and Alaska Dog Feed fresh from the
Chicago stock yards, packed dry, sweet and clean in fifty and one
hundred pound packages . . .

One enterprising outfit pointed out that "Your nose . . . cuts no ice
when covered with Reed's Blizzard Defier Face Protector". There
were gold saving machines "within the price of all. . . . Your money
back in Nome if found other than represented" . . . J. F. Yoho's
Scientific Gold Trap and Swain's Amalgameter for small mining
plants. New businesses cropped up in town for evaporating soups,
onions, peaches, apples, potatoes and currants.

Probably as significant a contribution as there was to come out of
the gold rushes in the Yukon and at Nome was the creation of what
today is known as the Carnation Milk Products Company. E. A.
Stuart, who came to the Pacific Northwest at the age of 43 years during the gold epidemic supplied some 3,000 cans of evaporated milk
per day from his little plant in Kent. Stuart who went on to become
a member of the Seattle Establishment, has the Stuart Building
named after him, and was president of probably the biggest milk
products company in the world.

The Argus for January 8, 1898 caught the spirit of the times with an
item stating that the Klondikers had taken over the town so that old
residents had difficulty sorting one another out . . . that the miners
filled the hotels and streets and theaters . . . and that:

They glory in their rough mountain costume, wearing it on the streets in order to get accustomed to it and, incidentally, to attract attention by being pointed out as Klondikers. The goods designed for their use have crowded out almost everything else in the store windows and almost every sign has some reference to the Klondike or Alaska. Dog teams drawing sleds are a familiar sight on the streets, as an advertisement, and dogs have become so valuable that a dog-thief will soon become a byword in Seattle as a horse-thief in other sections of the country.

The Sons of the Profits got their mining in before the argonauts ever left town.

. . . and Davy Jones' locker

I am indebted to the H. W. McCurdy *Marine History of the Pacific Northwest* for most of the spectacular marine history about transporting the argonauts from the States to Alaska in that massive invasion of the northland, and some of the stories—well. . .

The Pacific Coast Steamship Company's crack liner, "Mexico," was the fourth ship to head north after the "Portland" arrived in town with all that gold . . . but it only got as far as Dixon's Entrance when it hit a rock.

It was the first of the thirty-six ships that were wrecked in 1897 and 1898 either going to or coming from the golden north . . . and that one was lucky. No lives were lost.

Not so the "Clara Nevada," which apparently caught fire in a hurricane on the return from her first voyage to Skagway and Dyea. She went down with an estimated 100 persons on board and the body of the purser was the only one recovered.

Altogether a total of 164 persons lost their lives at sea during those first two years . . . not to mention the wreck of the "Islander" just south of Juneau on a return trip from Skagway in 1901 with a loss of seventy lives and $3,000,000 in gold.

I suppose if you consider the number of ships that were involved in transporting the army of gold seekers, the thirty-six wrecks don't seem like much.

On the other hand, try thirty-six wrecks between here and Alaska today and see how many newspaper headlines you get.

The best count I can make of it, there were more than 150 steamers brought into service out of Puget Sound from all over the world.

We built seventy-four ships in Seattle alone during the first six months of 1898 . . . in addition to bringing out of the boneyard every boat that could float or people thought could float. They packed on men and animals with such indiscrimination that one man observed the only difference between First Class and Second Class was that the people with First Class tickets slept with the horses . . . and the Second Class passengers had to sleep with the mules.

Robert Moran, who had retired from public office in order to make money some years before, was king of the shipbuilders in the city. Within ten days of the "Portland's" arrival he had put over 400 men to work in his shipyard. He was typical. All businesses in Seattle started running two and three shifts after the arrival of the Portland.

One of Moran's great feats consisted of patching up that venerable, forty-year-old sidewheeler, the "Eliza Anderson," well enough so that she could be pointed north. Historian Gordon Newell points out that she travelled slower and made more money for her owners than any other ship in the Mosquito Fleet.

And she went out with one of the great tales of the sea.

She ran out of coal in the middle of a storm off Kodiak Island and all seemed to be lost when a ghostly figure of a man—presumed to be the ghost of one of her former skippers, Tom Wright—appeared in the pilothouse in the fog and steered her to a safe harbor. The ghostly pilot then disappeared as mysteriously as he had arrived.

The explanation of the story came many years later in an article, "A Stranger Came Aboard" by Thomas Weidemann, Sr., in a collection of stories called Blood on The Arctic Snow. It seemed there was a stowaway aboard who knew the coast line. He had remained hidden until he realized the ship would be wrecked if he didn't take charge. In the confusion of reaching safety, nobody noticed that his brother had come out from shore in a skiff and removed him.

The patched up "Anderson" got as far as Unalaska where her passengers joined a sealing boat for the remainder of the trip to the Yukon . . . and the venerable old ship fell apart where she had stopped.

In January of 1898, Moran started constructing twelve flat bottomed boats for the Yukon River trade . . . by June the ships were launched and on June 28, they left Roche Harbor in the San Juans . . . as a fleet with Moran as the admiral.

He found himself with a mutiny on his hands as he prepared to leave the sheltered waters of southeastern Alaska. He promptly beached two recalcitrant captains who feared making the hazardous trip across the Gulf of Alaska . . . and by August—eight months after the keels were laid—eleven of the twelve ships went into service.

The twelfth was one of the thirty-six ships that lost their lives in the business of putting men where the gold was.

Even before the gold rush, Moran was operating an extremely healthy shipyard. He came out of that period of frenzied activity with one of the biggest yards in the United States.

He was another Son who stayed home, and was the prize example of what the gold rush did for the shipbuilding industry in Seattle . . . an industry that has been one of our most important ever since.

Another gold star for the gold rush.

Baby, it's cold outside

I've committed myself to telling about the Sons of the Profits who stayed home and mined the miners, but a gold rush attracts such unique figures that I can't help placing in these annals of history two of the more colorful "Sons" who went north to extract their gold. . . . Not from the mines—from the miners.

A Greek fella by the name of Alexander Pantages came wandering through Seattle in 1898 enroute for the gold fields. He could neither read nor write the English language, and even his mastery of the spoken word was what you might term extremely limited.

It wasn't so limited that he couldn't lose his last thousand dollars to the professional gamblers who worked the northbound boats, but it was too limited for him to read the most profitable purchase he ever made in his life.

That purchase was a copy of the *P.-I.* which he bought to wrap around his mukluks when he was getting himself outfitted here for the gold rush. That paper was three weeks old when he got to Skagway with two bits in his pocket—and little else.

The first miner Pantages met on the pier offered him five dollars for the newspaper . . . and the man immediately behind him upped the offer to ten dollars. Now Pantages may not have been very good at poker . . . but he was a man with acquisitive instincts and a little birdie in his head told him that he had something of value in that newspaper he couldn't even read.

So he hired a guy who could read . . . and he hired a hall . . . and he sold tickets at a buck apiece to three hundred and fifty miners who wanted to hear the news read to them aloud—even if it was three weeks old.

And that was the start of the Pantages enterprise—which was operated out of Seattle and in time became the biggest vaudeville circuit in the world.

And then, of course, there was Charlie Ross.

I never knew Charlie, but I know his widow, Cene, and she's the one who passed this story along . . . a story that shows the type of ingenuity that crops up in this city and more than any other single attribute consistently gives her a leg up on her competitors.

Charlie was attracted to Seattle and became one of our capitalists, and I can only say we can thank our lucky stars that we had a few like him around. He sort of makes up for the stuffed shirts.

Anyway, Charlie arrived in Nome on a day when an icy wind would have been breaking through the trees if there had been any trees, and his bright mind detected a business opportunity that the thousands of miners who were buzzing around the beach had overlooked. Having a little investment capital, he invested it wisely in some boards and brought into being a series of little structures at regularly spaced intervals along the sand that proved to be a matter of great convenience and necessity to the miners and enormous profit for Charlie.

They were operated sort of like slot-machines . . . but there was a pay-off every time, because the door opened when the miner dropped a quarter in the slot.

To me, the crowning glory of the entire operation consisted of the ingenious judgment that Charlie used in making his fortune on the golden beaches at Nome.

His little buildings were so located that the tide—not Charlie—came in twice a day and cleaned them out.

The Case of the toted totem

I don't know whether it was the *P.-I.* or the Chamber of Commerce —or both—but somebody cooked up this bright idea of sending a goodwill mission headed by a committee to "make a thorough canvass of the needs of Alaska and to better relations with Alaska businessmen . . ." in the summer of 1899.

I think it was a *P.-I.* promotion because otherwise the two opposition papers wouldn't have kicked up such a fuss later on . . . and it was the *P.-I.* that actually chartered the sumptuous liner the "City of Seattle," and it was the *P.-I.* that whomped up the attendance through its editorial pages.

Anyway, they got a pretty good bunch of leading citizens on board in August, and with flags flagging and bunting blowing, they took off for the north land to see where all that gold was coming from and to drop a line over the side and catch a case of canned salmon.

Jacob Furth was the leading citizen on the committee. By that time, he not only was the head man in the Establishment, he was the complete boss of Seattle. J. W. Clise, lawyer and president of the Chamber of Commerce was another on the committee, along with James D. Hoge, Jr., who was president of the First National Bank.

There also was Jacob Frauenthal . . . venerable, early day merchant prince, member of the Board of Trade, and building owner . . .

J. P. D. Llowyd, rector of St. Mark's Episcopal Church . . .
Thomas Prosch, secretary of the Chamber of Commerce . . .
N. H. Latimer, manager of the Dexter Horton Bank . . . George
William Fischer, president of the Fischer Brothers Grocery . . .
George Higbee, general manager of the Empire Transportation Com-
pany . . . E. F. Blaine, attorney-at-law and member of the Denny-
Blaine Land Company, and E. B. Piper, publisher of the *P.-I.*

I'm sure there were other people on board. They needed that additional bulk to pay for the charter. But their names didn't make the
papers. Besides, who needs more names than those of the blue
bloods above?

There's a whole hatful of explanations of what made the goodwill
expedition un-good. But it all boils down to the fact that some of
the members of the expedition went ashore on Tongass Island about
four o'clock in the morning when the ship was anchored near
Ketchikan and swiped a great big fat totem pole from an Indian
graveyard.

The pole was over fifty feet long and they cut it in half so they could
handle it. Two guys got on each half and paddled the beast out to
the ship where a cargo winch loaded it on board.

And when the rest of the folks woke up, there sat that dirty old
piece of wood on the deck. On sober thought they couldn't find anybody who wanted a fifty-foot totem pole a yard in diameter at the
base, in his front yard.

So they concocted the bright idea of giving it to the City of Seattle
which they knew would take anything it could get for free . . . and
they took up a collection among the passengers to buy some garish
paint. On October 18, 1899, with the band playing and the politicians speaking, they unveiled it in Pioneer Square.

Then the United States Marshal came down from Alaska and
pinched a whole bunch of them for stealing government property. A
federal Grand Jury in Juneau had indicted the Reverend Mr. Llowyd,
E. B. Piper, Thomas Prosch, N. H. Latimer, George Fischer,
J. W. Clise, George Higbee and E. F. Blaine.

The Times and *The Star,* which had not participated in the venture, had a field day. And some of their headlines must be preserved for posterity:

MORE PLUNDER IS DISCOVERED . . . P.I. EXCURSIONISTS TOOK PLENTY
WHILE IN ALASKA . . .

WHO SWIPED THE TOTEM POLE?

INDICTMENTS AGAINST P.-I. EXCURSIONISTS RETURNED . . .

SENATOR TURNER NOW ARGUING THE CASE IN WASHINTON, D.C.

TOTEM POLE LIES ARE NAILED

Well, the opposition papers had fun with it for a while. Then Senator Turner was able to persuade the rest of the Senate that government property had not been stolen. A new judge, headed for Alaska, was waylaid as he passed through Seattle. He was wined and dined at the Rainier Club and as *Northwest Magazine* pointed out a couple years later: "There in a merry speech the Totem Pole Incident was explained and soon after he took the bench, the indictments were quashed with the approval of the Alaskan people."

The Indians, who originally wanted $20,000 for the desecration of their graveyard, finally settled for five hundred bucks.

Blethen, with unsuppressed glee, informed the public that the *P.-I.* ended up paying most of the bill.

The gold in the golden west

Let's face it, the period of the two gold rushes in Yukon Territory and Nome—were the wildest years in Seattle's history. More crazy things happened in that short period than in any other time either before or since.

But like most of the things that have happened to this city, the timing was right. We were in the right place. We had the right collection of people.

It is of primary importance that the Establishment was well established by the time the "rushes" came along. The members of the Establishment were calling the signals and if people didn't like it, they got knocked in the economic head. There was a lot of bleating around the edges by the "Christers" who felt we were indeed a very naughty town. And they were allowed to do all the bleating they wanted as long as they stayed on the sidelines while the game was in progress.

It was during this period of unbelievable wealth that the Establishment finally came to the realization that a heavy industry like steel was not essential to our financial stability. We realized that the city's future was that of a jobbing center . . . that our wealth lay in distributing goods to Alaska and getting its fantastic natural wealth in return and even being a marketing center for the Orient.

By this time, we were no longer the northwest corner of no place . . . we were the hub of a huge gold rush.

And we had found that outfitting the miners going north was peanuts alongside of inducing them to return to the United States via Seattle, either to stay here or at least drop a large part of their wealth here. So one of the major chores was that of getting the Government Assay Office here.

We had tried for the Assay Office in the winter and again in the summer of 1897—with absolutely no success. We then sent Ernest Ling, secretary of the Chamber of Commerce to see what he could do—to no avail. So we put a hammerlock on the head of Senator John L. Wilson who had been appointed to the U.S. Senate from Spokane to do the job.

Wilson reported that the director of the United States Mint had told him that under no circumstances could Seattle ever have the Assay Office. We were suspicious of Wilson. We figured that he was more interested in the health and welfare of Spokane than of Seattle.

But there was one guy who had already delivered for us . . . a man who knew his way around in the intricacies of newspapers and politics: Erastus Brainerd. In the spring of 1898, the Establishment provided him with an unlimited expense account, and said to him: "Go get the Assay Office!"

Brainerd at first tried to work with Senator Wilson . . . and in the beginning the correspondence between them was terribly jolly. But

Brainerd was interested in only one thing, and when he didn't seem to be getting help from Wilson he went either through or around him.

Wilson complained:

> It is to be regretted that the citizens of Seattle do not find their own Congressional Delegation competent to attend to the business of the state and find it necessary to call upon outsiders to do work that already has been done for them . . . I am not and never have been "rather neutral" . . . this is not the first instance of such reports having been circulated concerning my attitude relating to our state and I think I can pretty accurately locate the original source . . . (Ed. note: He sure could. It was Brainerd.)

It's kind of a thoughtful note that Wilson got over his mad later on and was so impressed with Brainerd's capabilities he hired him to handle his next campaign.

Brainerd got the same answer as the others from the Director of the Mint. Absolutely not. Seattle would *never* get the Assay Office. Brainerd then added the Director of the Mint to his list of people to either go around or through . . . and he did both to that gentleman.

One of the first little things he learned was that Congress had set aside $15,000 for an assay office in Deadwood, South Dakota—but that the money had never been spent. So he had the answer to the first question Congress would ask when it was approached: "Where will we get the money?"

Poor Deadwood!

But there were a lot of other people who suddenly had discovered Alaska, and Congress was faced with six hundred bills relating to that Territory. Brainerd's chore was to keep his bill from being lost in the crush. He needed somebody in a high place who had a particular interest in Seattle. He found him in Congressman Charles W. Stone, of Pennsylvania. Stone not only was a senior member of the Committee on Coins, Weights and Measures in the House, Stone had a brother who was in business in Seattle. The latter was an enthusiastic Son of the Profits who was quite willing to apply any and all of the necessary family pressure to provide his Congressman brother with an enlightened attitude about the importance of our city.

About that time, both Portland and Juneau got the bright idea it would be nice to have an assay office in their towns. But they learned what a disadvantage it was to try getting that prize from that distance. They didn't have anyone but their congressional representatives in Washington, D.C.

Stone's committee asked the Director of the Mint what he thought about an assay office in Seattle. He filed an official report that hedged a lot, like those bureaucratic reports do, but wound around to an intricate and complicated conclusion that we could get all the gold we wanted in the United States without the help of an assay office in Seattle.

The committee disregarded this report.

When the matter got to the floor of Congress, Stone said that he was sort of an amicus curiae, not having any special interest in Seattle. On the other hand, he pointed out that the materials ordered by merchants in Seattle were made in Pennsylvania and a whole bunch of other eastern states . . . that the poor miners worked hard for their gold . . . that everybody and his brother tried to steal it from them. He declared it had been the policy of the government to provide convenient assay offices for miners because theirs was an unusual product and they had no guarantee they would be given fair value for their gold any place except in an assay office.

Stone's speech would have been approved by Brainerd—after all, Brainerd wrote it. And on May 16, 1898, Brainerd had the pleasure of sitting in the House Gallery and, after a forty-minute debate, seeing the House approve his bill by a vote of 128 to 17. It already had been slipped through the Senate with no debate . . . and shortly thereafter became law.

Ooh, Mr. Adams!

Well, there we were with our nice big Assay Office going for us up there on top of the hill . . . like a shrine visible to all miners either going or coming. It was on Ninth Avenue near Cherry Street where the German Club is today, and betokened a sense of sound security to all from 1898 to 1908.

One George Edward Adams came with the new structure.

He was a clerk, with an annual salary of $1,500, but Mr. Adams was a would-be Son of the Profits. He lived rather high on the hog for a man making a lousy $1,500 a year and was generous to a fault. On July 5, 1900 when a couple of men presented what they said was 233.9 ounces of pure gold and got back cash money for only 133.9 ounces, the people employed in the Assay Office took up a contribution to make up the difference of $1,663.68. Mr. Adams tossed $115.50 of his own personal funds in the pot, and when the others opined this was pretty generous on his part—considering his total salary—he replied that he had a rich uncle in Washington, D.C. and easily could afford it.

Mr. Adams rose to a prominent role in the social end of the community—although he never made the exclusive Rainier Club. He sported one of the first cars in town—valued at $4,500.

He wooed and won the hand of Emily Clary, the lovely young daughter of the socially prominent Charles Clary who had been the United States Bank Examiner in the area for years . . . and after their marriage on October 16, 1904, the happy couple moved into millionaire's row in a mansion at 525 Harvard Avenue—the view side of the street—and settled down with every intention of living happily ever after.

But about this time, the United States Secret Service developed a morbid curiosity about one of Mr. Adams' hobbies.

He was a collector of sand. . . .

And an extremely discriminating collector at that. He bought his sand in both Neah Bay and in Gray's Harbor. It had to be black. It had to be fine. And to the suspicious minds of the men in the Secret Service, it strongly resembled the kind of sand that existed on the ocean shores around Nome.

One day, when Mr. Adams was out to lunch, these government men took a peek in his desk and found that during the past five years Mr.

Adams had bought some 750 pounds of the stuff. They also found in
his drawer an extremely accurate gold scales which was not the
property of the United States government.

This caused them to get a search warrant and conduct an explora-
tion of Mr. Adams' socially-prominent basement where they found
some $7,000 worth of pure gold dust and nuggets in his socially
prominent coal bin. In his desk drawer they found correspondence
indicating Mr. Adams had been selling gold in San Francisco and
New York in rather substantial quantities.

Then they had a little off-the-record chat with Mr. Adams. They
learned he had been substituting sand for the gold in the miners' envelopes for about five years, and deduced that if all of the sand he
had bought had been exchanged for gold, he had been augmenting
his annual salary of $1,500 to the tune of $35,000 yearly for a gross
of $175,000.

He had added his own fillip to the business of mining the miners,
but the folks frowned on that sort of thing.

Mr. Adams told the Secret Service he would be a lot more coopera-
tive if the government men would wait until his wife, who was in a
delicate condition had delivered his first born. So they all spent the
next few months figuring out from whom Mr. Adams had extracted
his gold.

On November 19, 1905 when Mrs. Adams delivered a son—the Secret
Service put the bracelets on the father's wrists.

The rich relative that Mr. Adams had mentioned lived in Washington, D.C. . . . his name was Uncle Sam.

Jackpot!

I wonder what would have happened to the site where the city of
Seattle is today if Arthur Denny had just tossed in the sponge while
he was down there in Portland and stayed in that city for the rest of
his life? It would have been an easier life . . . and with his instincts,
he probably would have made a lot of money there. After all, Portland was a big city when he and his party arrived there . . . and during his lifetime, it grew as fast if not faster than Seattle.

But he had that little extra drive that pushed him on.

And from the start, Seattle attracted that kind of man.

I'm sure that some shallow intellect will come up with the suggestion that there were other men than the Sons of the Profits who had something to do with the building of Seattle. There is no question but that this is true. There also were other madams besides Lou Graham, but, unlike Lou, they were not Sons of the Profits. There were other businessmen in the town, but they followed the leaders mentioned in this book. Engineer R. H. Thomson had a great deal to do with what the city looks like today—but he did it with the money provided by the Sons.

Seattle's Sons were a stubborn lot who insisted on staying in town and making the money come to them. It was not in character for them to race off to some cold place like Alaska and trust to luck they could bring back a fortune. They weren't that kind of gamblers. They stayed with the town—no matter who else came or went.

Over the years they built a city on the only basis which can be considered a permanent contribution . . . by making money for themselves and their firms, which in turn paid the taxes and hired the folks who lived here and made the city grow. I don't think the Sons really care whether you choose to emulate them—which a lot of people don't. But those people don't build a city, either.

The Sons' formula was to cast a little bread upon the waters and see what they could get to come back. They gave Henry Yesler his land and the first steam sawmill on the Sound. They gave fifty bucks worth of land for a University and got an immediate return of something over $30,000 . . . and a long range return of hundreds of millions. They subsidized a telegraph station and became the communications center of the Pacific Northwest. They coughed up a few bucks for a railroad of their own that went just as far as Newcastle about twenty miles away and millions of dollars worth of coal came thundering back. They stood on their own two square feet against the Northern Pacific and finally ended up with three transcontinental railroads.

But the Gold Rush was the jackpot of their first fifty years.

We cast $10,000 worth of Erastus Brainerd's time on the water. He came back with a Government Assay Office worth $15,000—at the expense of Deadwood, South Dakota . . . and, as we had figured, the Assay Office brought us considerably more than that.

When the glamor of the little fellow with his pick and shovel and his strong back died down, the big companies with their heavy machinery started moving through Seattle and spending their money here for equipment and supplies. The city celebrated its Golden Anniversary with real gold. In the decade following its appearance here, the Assay Office handled $200,000,000 worth of gold . . .

About $100,000,000 of that stayed in Seattle.

And how does that all add up?

Well, we had wiped out the other cities on Puget Sound rather handily before the turn of the century. However, by the census of 1900 Portland was still the top dog with a population of some 90,000 to our 80,000.

But that gold kept rolling to us for ten long years.

Come 1910, Portland had a population of 207,000. Seattle was the top dog for the whole Pacific Northwest with 237,000 . . .

And she's been the big city ever since.

ACKNOWLEDGMENTS, SOURCES, BIBLIOGRAPHY

Generous assistance on the part of more people than I can count, have made it possible to dig up the little-known facts of Seattle's history that are the essence of this book. However, there are some who have gone above and beyond the normal call of duty, and they are the people whom I especially wish to acknowledge.

My wife, Shirley, has provided a pleasant, relaxed home atmosphere in spite of the storms that were kicked up during the four years it took to research and write this book. Jeanette Rathfelder has done a monumental job of research, editing, counselling and consistently forcing me to distill the welter of information unearthed into the best presentation of which I am capable. Louise Dewey, as chief editor, gathered up all the loose ends and created a unified entity from the material developed. Jo Addison diligently went through endless detail to research in depth many of the more obscure informational "leads," and turned up several of the best stories in the book.

Thanks to the generosity of the Washington Title Division of the Pioneer National Title Insurance Company, Leo Boyajian of that company ferreted out who owned what land when, providing a basic foundation for the book. Hervey Ballou of the City of Seattle Engineering Department devoted countless hours and his engineering know-how to finding out about the sixty or more regrades which have given the city its present shape.

Robert D. Monroe, chief of the Special Collections Division, University of Washington Libraries; Miss Phoebe Harris, head of the History Department of the Seattle Public Library, and Bernice Kulesza, acting head of the same department for a year, have all struggled with the keys to ancient and rusty locks, opening the way to priceless information.

Henry Broderick and Joshua Green, who knew many of the men who shaped Seattle's first fifty years, helped give viability and color to the history of the period.

The docents at Seattle's Museum of History and Industry undertook more than a dozen individual research projects. The Historical Museums of Madison County, New York and Massillon, Ohio and the Public Library of Colusa, California helped fill gaps, as well as the Bancroft Memorial Library in Berkeley, California.

Others who deserve special mention for providing otherwise unobtainable details are: Howard F. Grant and his unpublished manuscript, "Skid Road"; Jim Stevens, father of the Paul Bunyan stories; Mrs. Arthur P. Nute, grand-daughter of Charlie Terry; George Bundy, who supplied us with an invaluable, authentic Seattle Fire map and other information, and Raymond C. Beauchamp of the King County Engineers office, who provided rare detailed downtown maps of old Seattle.

My thanks, too, to the late Professor Charles M. Gates for his encouragement in writing this book; to Bennye Price, for her work researching and typing, to Dorothy Ferguson, who assembled and filed our research, and to Eileen Ruppeck and Robert McCarthy, for assistance in the design and production of this book.

BOOKS

AVERY, MARY W., *History and Government of the State of Washington;* BAGLEY, CLARENCE B., *History of Seattle from the Earliest Settlement to the Present Time,* 1916, *History of King County,* 1929; BARTO, H. E. and BULLARD, CATHARINE, *History of the State of Washington;* BASS, MRS. SOPHIE (FRYE), *Pig-Tail Days in Old Seattle, When Seattle Was a Village,* 1947; BEATON, WELFORD, *The City That Made Itself,* 1914; BECKER, ETHEL A., *Klondike '98,* 1958; BERELSON, BERNARD and GRANT, H. F., *The Pioneer Theater in Washington,* 1937; BRODERICK, HENRY, *Early Seattle Profiles,* 1959, *First Person Singular,* 1943, *The Gravy Train of 1906,* 1960, *#1717 39th,* 1950; CALHOUN, ANNE H., *A Seattle Heritage, 1942;* COCHRAN, THOMAS C., *Railroad Leaders 1845-1890,* 1953; DENNY, ARTHUR ARMSTRONG, *Pioneer Days on Puget Sound,* 1965 Ye Galleon Press—Reproduction; DENNY, EMILY INEZ, *Blazing the Way,* 1909; *Encyclopedia Americana; Encyclopedia Britannica;* ESCOBOSA, HECTOR, *Seattle Story,* 1948; Federal Writers' Project, Washington: *A Guide to the Evergreen State;* GATES, CHARLES, *The First Century at the University of Washington,* 1961, *Readings in Pacific Northwest History;* HANFORD, C. H., *Seattle and Environs,* 1924; HARNEY, THOMAS PORTER, *Charles Barstow Wright 1822-1898,* 1956; HUNT, HERBERT, *Tacoma, Its History and Its Builders,* 1916; JONES, NARD, *Northwest Narratives;* LAWING, NELLIE NEAL, *Alaska Nellie,* 1940; McNEAL, VIOLET, *Four White Horses and a Brass Band,* 1947; McWILLIAMS, MARY, *Seattle Water Department History, 1854-1954;* MEANY, EDMOND STEPHEN, *History of the State of Washington;* MEEKER, EZRA, *Ox Team Days on the Oregon Trail, Pioneer Reminiscences of Puget Sound, Seventy Years of Progress in Washington Territory West of the Cascades;* MORGAN, MURRAY CROMWELL, *Skid Road,* 1960; *National Cyclopedia of American Biography;* NESBIT, ROBERT, *He Built Seattle,* 1961; NEWELL, GORDON R., *H. W. McCurdy Marine History of Pacific Northwest;* NEWELL, GORDON R. and SHERWOOD, DON, *Totem Tales of Old Seattle,* 1956; PIGOTT, H. C., *History and Progress of King County,* 1916; POLLARD, LANCASTER, *From Frontier Village to World Metropolis, Seattle,* 1939; POTTS, RALPH BUSHNELL, *Seattle Heritage,* 1955; PROSCH, THOMAS WICKHAM, *David S. Maynard and Catherine T. Maynard,* 1906; *A Chronological History of Seattle from 1850-1897,* 1900; PROSSER, W. F., *History of the Puget Sound Country;* SAYRE, J. WILLIS, *The Romance of Second Avenue,* 1933, *This City of Ours,* 1936; SNOWDEN, CLINTON A., *History of Washington;* WATT, MRS. ROBERTA (FRYE), *The Story of Seattle,* 1931, *Four Wagons West,* 1931; WINSLOW, KATHRYN, *Big Pan-Out,* 1951; WOOLEN, WILLIAM WATSON, *The Inside Passage to Alaska, 1792-1920,* 1924; WRIGHT, E. W., *Lewis and Dryden's Marine History of the Pacific Northwest,* 1895.

GENERAL

ELLIOTT, EUGENE CLINTON, *History of Variety-Vaudeville in Seattle,* 1914; FITZGERALD, WILLIAM, interview (former Seattle Fire Chief); FRANCISCO, MARJORIE J., *Raising of Streets in Sacramento Business District: 1864-1870.* Thesis, 1959; GREAT NORTHERN RAILWAY PROPERTY DEPARTMENT, PUBLIC RELATIONS DEPARTMENT, *Seattle and the Great Northern Railway;* GUY, G. O., PhD, *The Klondike Doctor,* about 1897; LAMB, JOHN, Report written for L. B. YOUNGS, Superintendent, Seattle Water Department, 1914; LAKEVIEW CEMETERY, RECORDS; LEHMAN, S. P., MD, MPH and RAVENHOLT, REIMERT T., MD, MPH, "History, Epidemiology and Control of Typhoid Fever in Seattle", *Medical Times,* 1964; McDONALD, R. T., *Collection of Seattle Mayors;* MILLER, CARRIE LOWRY, *The History of Education in Seattle,* Thesis, 1929; MORAN, ROBERT, An address at the fiftieth jubilee meeting of the Pioneers' Association of the State of Washington in Seattle June 6, 1939; NATIONAL CYCLOPEDIA OF AMERICAN BIOGRAPHY, biography of Morton McCarver, Vol IV, pp. 548-549; PIONEER NATIONAL TITLE INSURANCE COMPANY, records; RAND McNALLY COSMOPOLITAN WORLD ATLAS, MCMLIX; Library scrapbooks: Erastus Brainerd, Gilbert Costello, Paul S. Dubuar, W. C. Fonda, Pacific Northwest (chiefly clippings from Seattle newspapers, 1904-1963); Seattle Bank Clearings (1895-1908); SEATTLE CHAMBER OF COMMERCE, History and Minutes, *Seattle Story* (historical episodes adapted for radio), 1948; SEATTLE DIRECTORIES, 1870-1900; BILL SPEIDEL'S UNDERGROUND TOURS, *Seattle Underground,* 1967; TACOMA CHAMBER OF

COMMERCE, *Tacoma Illustrated*, 1889, *The New Northwest and Tacoma, its Metropolis*, 1890; Union Pacific Railroad records; UNITED STATES COAST AND GEODETIC SURVEY, *Atlas for Alaska Boundary Tribunal*, 1903; University of Washington Libraries, School of Public Health; WICKERSHAM, JAMES, Tacoma Academy of Science proceedings, Feb. 8, 1893, "Is it Mt. Tacoma or Rainier?"; WIESE, L. K., "Pacific Northwest Telephone History", paper, 1962; WILEN, STEPHEN, "Architect E. H. Fisher", paper, 1967.

GOVERNMENT SOURCES

California State Health Department; Charter, Official Code and Ordinances Seattle 1896, as amended; Congressional Record; 1877, 1878, 1879 and 1898; Congressional Record Index; 1877, 1878, 1879 and 1898; Index of Street Ordinances—City of Seattle; King County Clerk's Office; Mayor's Annual Messages and Departmental Reports—City ot Seattle, 1885-1898; Organic Act, Washington Territory; Seattle City Clerk's Office; Seattle Comptroller's Office; Seattle Engineering Department; Seattle Health Department; Seattle Mayor's Office; Seattle Municipal Reference Library; Seattle Water Department; State Archives, Olympia; Street Profiles—City of Seattle; Washington State Health Department; Washington State Library, Olympia; Washington State Supreme Court Records; Washington Reports, 13-550; WILKES, CHARLES, *Exploratory Expedition and Hydrographic Survey*, 1841, CHART OF ELLIOTT BAY.

CONTEMPORARY NEWSPAPERS AND PERIODICALS

American City; American Mercury; Appleton's Journal; Argus, 1894-1900; Atlantic Monthly; Brooklyn Eagle; Century; Coast Magazine; Columbian, 1852-1854 (Pioneer Democrat) Olympia; *Dawson City News; Engineering Magazine; Engineering News Record; Forum; Frank Leslie's Illustrated Newspaper; Harper's Weekly; Harvard Business Review; Idaho Yesterdays; Lippincott's Magazine; National Magazine; New England Magazine; New York Herald; New York Times; Northwest Magazine; Oregon Historical Society Quarterly; Overland Monthly; Pacific Builder and Engineer; Pacific Monthly; Pacific Northwest Quarterly; Portland Oregonian; Puget Sound Dispatch 1871-1880.* (Merged with Seattle Weekly Intelligencer later Seattle Post Intelligencer); *Puget Sound Gazette, 1867-1881; Puget Sound Gazetteer; Review of Reviews; Scientific American; Seattle Chronicle, 1881-1886; Seattle Daily Call, 1885-1886; Seattle Daily Herald, 1882-1884; Seattle Daily Post, 1878-1881* (Merged with Daily Intelligencer to form Seattle Post Intelligencer); *Seattle Daily Times; Seattle Mail and Herald; Seattle Post-Intelligencer, 1867-1907* and 100th anniversary edition, 1963; *Seattle Press, 1886-1891; Seattle Press Times, 1895; Seattle Telegraph, 1890-1894; Seattle Weekly Intelligencer; Seattle Weekly Post-Intelligencer, 1888; Tacoma Herald, 1877-1880, 1891-1900; Tacoma Ledger; Tacoma News; Tacoma News Tribune; Tacoma Sun; Walla Walla Statesman; Walla Walla Union; Washington Historian; Washington Historical Quarterly; Washington Standard; Washington State Law Review; West Shore Magazine; World's Work.*

PAMPHLETS, PAPERS AND LETTERS

AUSTIN, C. W. and SCOTT, H. S., *The Great Seattle Fire*, 1889; BLAINE, DAVID EDWARD and BLAINE, MRS. C. P., *Letters and Papers of David E. and Catherine P. Blaine*, 1932; BRINGHURST, HARRY, map—Great Seattle Fire; COLANG, ARMAND R., *A Brief Glimpse into the Life of Charles Carroll Terry;* Deeds of Cavanaugh Land—Site of Boeing Field (Museum of History and Industry); GARFIELD, VIOLET E., *The Seattle Totem Pole;* GRAY, HENRY L., *The Metropolitan Tract Story,* 1964 (Museum of History and Industry); HATTEN, MARIE, *Arthur Denny's Dream,* 1953; HODGINS, THOMAS, *The Alaska Boundary Tribunal and International Law,* 1904; JACOBS, ORANGE, *Memoirs,* 1908; JOHNSON, FRED and USHER, PHIL, *Seattle's Underground; A Product of Regrading;* King County, Washington, County Road Engineer, *State Golden Jubilee;* comp. under the direction of H. H. Sisler by Harold Laufer, 1939; KINNEAR, GEORGE, *Anti-Chinese Riots,* 1911; PHELPS, THOMAS STOWELL, *Reminiscences of Seattle, Washington Territory, and the U.S. Sloop-of-War "Decatur" During the Indian War of 1855-56, 1908;* PROSCH, THOMAS WICKHAM, *David E. Blaine and Catherine P. Blaine,* written for the Seattle Historical Society, 1914, *McCarver and Tacoma,* 1906; RADE-

BAUGH, RANDOLPH FOSTER, *Tacoma the Pacific Metropolis; Where and Why;* Real Estate Owned by John Leary et al., March 1900 (Museum of History and Industry); RICH, JOHN M., *Chief Seatile's Unanswered Challenge,* 1947; SCURRY, JOHN G., Report on Streets Raised to Grade July 18, 1890 (Municipal Reference Library); SEATTLE FIRE DEPARTMENT, *News Letter,* June 4, 1965; *Seattle Police Journal,* "Before the Fire", 1926; SLAUSON, MORDA C., *Renton From Coal to Jets,* 1965; SPIKE, W. D. C. & CO., *Illustrated Description of the City of Tacoma,* 1891; TERRY, CHARLES C., notebook (University of Washington Libraries Special Collection); WHITWORTH, F. H., letter to Herbert Strandberg on City Datum Point (University of Washington Libraries Special Collections Division, 1927; WILKESON, SAMUEL, *Notes on Puget Sound,* 1869 (From Horace McCurdy Collection); YESLER, HENRY, "Washington Territory", MS 6 (University of Washington Manuscript Department).

A NOTE ON DESIGN

The text of this book is set in 11 point Linotype Baskerville and the headings in Linotype Caslon Old Style Italic and Caledonia Bold. The jacket and title pages are set in Bodoni and Ultra Bodoni. The text is printed on Bergstrom's Cooper Cream, substance 55 and the endsheets and jackets on Weyerhaeuser Kilmory text "1776", substance 70. It was printed on a Cameron Belt Press, perfect bound and cased in Bayside Linen binding cloth. Design and production by Robert McCarthy and William C. Speidel.

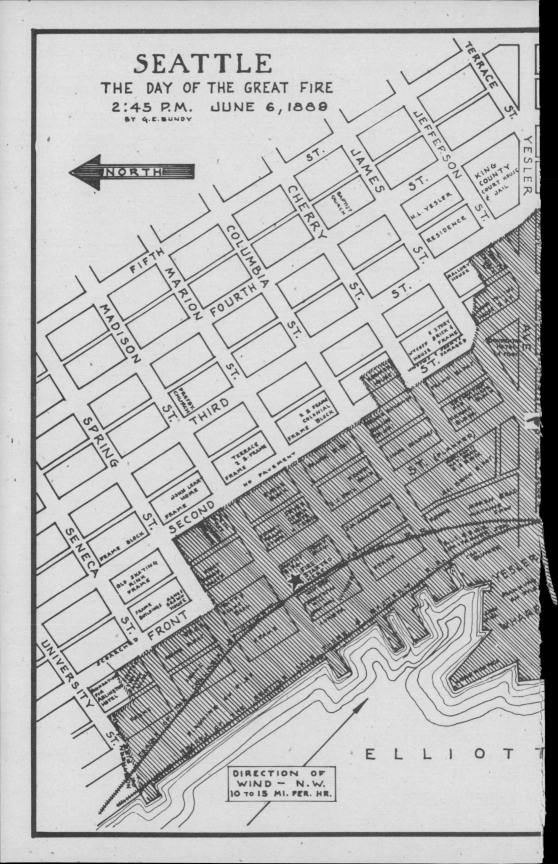